Caribbean Romances

# Caribbean Romances: The Politics of Regional Representation

*Belinda J. Edmondson, Editor*

*New World Studies*
A. James Arnold, editor

University Press of Virginia
*Charlottesville and London*

Acknowledgments for previously published information appear on p. vii.

The University Press of Virginia
© 1999 by the Rector and Visitors
of the University of Virginia
All rights reserved
Printed in the United States of America

*First published 1999*

⊗ The paper used in this publication meets the minimum requirements of the American National Standard for Information Sciences—Permanence of Paper for Printed Library Materials, ANSI Z39.48-1984.

Library of Congress Cataloging-in-Publication Data
Caribbean romances : the politics of regional representation / Belinda
    J. Edmondson, editor.
        p.    cm. — (New World studies)
    Includes bibliographical references and index.
    ISBN 0-8139-1821-9 (hardcover : alk. paper). — ISBN 0-8139-1822-7
(pbk. : alk. paper)
        1. Caribbean Area—Civilization. 2. Politics and culture—
Caribbean Area. 3. Popular culture—Caribbean Area. 4. Caribbean
fiction—History and criticism. 5. Literature and society—
Caribbean Area. I. Edmondson, Belinda. II. Series.
F2169.C368 1999
972.9—dc21                                                        98-26770
                                                                       CIP

# Contents

# Acknowledgments

I thank all those who have helped make this book possible: the Caribbean Studies Association, for allowing me to test the premise for this collection as a panel chair for "Caribbean Romances" at the CSA conference in Mérida, Mexico, in 1993; Cathie Brettschneider, my editor at the University Press of Virginia, for her assistance at all stages of publication; the departments of English and African/African-American Studies at Rutgers University for giving me the time to complete the project; the contributors, for their enthusiasm and scholarship; and last, Gene Lake, for putting up with my bad moods, nail biting, abrupt non sequiturs and all the other symptoms of an editor with a publication in process. Thank you all.

A portion of chapter 1 has been published as "Race, Rape, and Representation: Indo-Caribbean Women and Cultural Nationalism," *Cultural Critique* 36 (spring 1997). Chapter 7 was originally published as "Shadowboxing in the Mangrove," *Cultural Anthropology* 12, no. 1 (1997): 3–36; reprinted courtesy of the American Anthropological Association.

Caribbean Romances

# The Caribbean: Myths, Tropes, Discourses

*Belinda J. Edmondson*

The germ for *Caribbean Romances* was conceived in a series of apparently unconnected conversations I had with a fellow scholar of Caribbean literature, in which we pondered various aspects of Caribbean literature and culture. We both grew up in the Caribbean, and we would consistently point out to each other the considerable "lag" between the subjects that preoccupied contemporary Caribbean society and the general turn of Caribbean literary theory. It seemed that we—and Caribbeanists generally—were always using the same vocabulary in any discussion of the latter, perhaps because it seemed concerned mostly with an immutable core set of themes and issues, initially produced to articulate particular historical relationships within Caribbean society, that have now acquired an ahistorical status and come to define the region generally.

In our roles as scholars my colleague and I could quickly produce theoretical "sketches" of the ideas that have come to symbolize the Caribbean. It was almost as if key words and phrases could stand for an entire discourse: words like multiracialism, *mestizaje*, oppositionality, otherness, colonialism, neocolonialism, shipwreck, mimicry, metropole, migration. Yet in our role as Caribbean citizens we would have a whole new—and yet, it seemed, so ancient!—set of concerns, such as urban/rural divisions and inter-Caribbean rivalries, that did not necessarily involve the same axiomatic definitions of Caribbeanness evident in literary theory. What was the connection between our Caribbean origins and our "professional" selves?

The answer seems to lie in the discourse itself, which bridged the present and the past. The Caribbean that has developed in scholarly discourse over the past forty years or so sometimes seems to have a life of its own, at times bearing only a cursory relation to the events of today. Yet the words, ideas, and discourses of these archetypes of "Caribbeanness," if you will, have such power to shape the way the region now imagines itself that they have become mythic: to invoke these archetypes to explain particularities in Caribbean life is often enough. So my interest in this project became to discover the current uses of these "romance" tropes, as I have now termed these definitive ideas, within scholarly as well as popular discourse.

For the purposes of this book, the term "romance" is used to describe the idealized representations of Caribbean society, of "Caribbeanness," both in hegemonic European-American discourses and, perhaps more important, in *intra*-Caribbean discourses. I use the term "romance" both with quotation marks and without, to distinguish between its better-known literary-historical meanings—those references without quotation marks—and my own more idiosyncratic usage. As I have defined the term, the "romance" of particular tropes and paradigms identified with an essential Caribbeanness (such as carnival and cultural hybridity, to name two of the more striking examples) marks the process by which concrete ideological-political issues are mystified into regional symbols divorced from their ideological context.

Further, my use of the term "romances" to designate what are swiftly becoming the iconic—clichéd, if you will—tropes of Caribbean discourse, though understood as distinct from the term's more conventional uses as either allegorical heroic medieval narrative or more contemporary love story, nevertheless is meant quite deliberately, to implicate precisely those traditional meanings of the term. What appear to us now as contained and predictable plotting, formulaic heroes and villains in both the medieval and love story variety, have become the classic clichés that are staples of fictional narrative as we know it.

The definition of romance that I am using here intentionally draws on what Northrop Frye has called the "vulgar sense of the word"— that is, a sentimentalized or rose-colored view of reality—because the idealized is inevitably the sentimentalized ("Drunken," 11). Frye of course was invoking this sense of the word to connect it with his view that romantic poetry attempted to "defy external reality by creating a uniformity of time and mood," as he argues in his pivotal studies of the romantic period of European history and literature of the early nineteenth century (11).[1] Further, he states that romanticism is "historically and generically . . . akin to *romance,* with its effort to maintain a self-consistent idealized world without the intrusions of realism or irony" (11).

This book is in no way meant to comment on either the literary-historical period of romanticism *or* the classic romance genre—that is, narratives depicting marvelous heroic personages or events as exemplified by particular medieval fables that emphasize military engagement, or later narratives, such as Walter Scott's, that emphasize love and erotic desire. Nevertheless, Frye's observations on romanticism and the romance genre bear an interesting similarity to my use of the term "romanticism," by which I imply a uniformity and an ahistoricity in the way particular tropes of Caribbeanness are employed. If the romantic movement was an artistic-intellectual response to the French Revolution and a concomitant desire to find an ideal society, as Frye and other scholars of the period contend,[2] that would suggest a certain revolutionary engagement with political reality that seems in direct contrast to the term's implications of dissociation and fantasy. On the other hand, a relationship has been noted between the more extreme forms of romantic conservatism and the subversive revolutionary movements of fascism and Nazism (Frye, "Drunken," 13).

Out of this confusion between the various forms and meanings of the romance—the romance as romanticism, as historical romance, as romanticized history, as apolitical, as politically revolutionary—emerges a dynamic term whose contradictions and implications are particularly resonant to me as I attempt to articulate the contradictions of contemporary Caribbean thought. In *Foundational Fictions: The National Romances of Latin America,* Doris Sommer has done some very important work on the romance genre as it relates to nationalism in Latin America. Her particular interest is how the romance genre—romance in the sense of both erotic love story and allegory—managed to reconcile the contradictory desires of the Latin American elite so as to both modernize and retain the "practically feudal privilege" inherited from its colonial history (*Foundational,* 48). This ability to contain a contradiction through a genre that has been dissociated from political discourse is what Fredric Jameson also identifies as its most central political function in his discussion of the genre: it solves the dilemma of difference by "something like a semic evaporation" (*Political,* 118), "an imaginary resolution of a real contradiction" (*Political,* 77).

The identification of romance as a construct is central to the purpose of this collection. In this sense the "romance" is singular because it effects the resolution of real political conflict in the realm of the imaginary. Consequently, our project here is to uncover how dominant or contending groups—whether political, social, economic, or scholarly—reconcile ideological interests and conflicts by disguising them through such mystified tropes and discourses. The conflict between the desire for modernity—modernity in the sense of that phase of modernization associated with Western culture and "progress" in the region—and the paradoxical nostalgia for the old or "backward" cultures that modernity is meant to erase is where I would pinpoint the origins of what I am terming the contemporary "romances" of Caribbean discourse. This central conflict connects the essays' disparate discussions of various "romance" tropes, the romance genre, and the Harlequin-style romance novel.

As Sommer reveals, the classic examples of the romance novel in Latin America "are almost inevitably stories of star-crossed lovers who represent particular regions, races, parties, economic interests, and the like. Their passion for conjugal and sexual union spills over to a sentimental readership in a move that hopes to win partisan minds along with hearts" (*Foundational,* 5). It is this ability to mystify certain moral or ideological positions by presenting them in the form of stock characters that gives the romance genre its power. And it is precisely this quality, this petrification of ideology into stock characters, ideas, and phrases, that connects the romance genre to the themes of classic Caribbean discourse, defined by the key words and phrases I outlined at the start of this introduction. Since the Caribbean itself has historically functioned as the matrix of European eroticized romantic fantasies, it seems fitting that a critique of the clichés of Caribbean discourse should focus on this particular genre as well. Therefore the essays in this collection range in focus from interrogating "romance" tropes in Caribbean social discourse to uncovering the politics of a fairly new genre, the Caribbean romance novel.

At first I wanted to put together a collection of studies on the contemporary Caribbean from many different disciplines that would examine various definitive ideas on the region that had become transformed, refigured, or merely reheated in the contemporary Caribbean. Scholarly books in the humanities, for the most part, still confine themselves to presenting the Caribbean as a newly "discovered" field for the American and European academy. But in fact there is now a substantial body of Caribbeanist and non-Caribbeanist scholars who are familiar with the basic issues in Caribbean scholarship and need to start an interdisciplinary discussion that integrates the multiplicitous approaches to Caribbean studies.

However, I found that the issue always seemed to return to the *way* ideas are communicated: finally, it came back to language, to discourse, to literature in its broadest sense. Some of the essays here were first read as papers at a panel discussion, also titled "Caribbean Romances: The Politics of Regional Representation," for the Caribbean Studies Association conference in Mérida, Mexico, in May 1994. There was obvious tension in the room; from the ensuing heated discussion, it seemed the problem was that members of what was essentially a panel of literary theorists were theorizing on matters that some of the Caribbeanist social scientists deemed to be social science issues. Moreover, there were questions of territory and "authenticity": those Caribbeanists who were residents of the Caribbean made mention of North American academics who misunderstood local Caribbean customs and language. One panelist who critiqued a well-known Caribbean scholar's work was told to "go back and read the book." Part of the "romance" of Caribbean studies is the belief that attends so much work on so-called Third World societies: that is, that you must live it to theorize it. The question of what "living it" really means (Precisely *which* experience of Caribbean life "speaks" for that society? The immigrant from America who sends money back to the family at "home"? The family who receives money from the immigrant?) is never really settled. Again, these were issues that centered not simply on where the critic stood, but on the way discourse had encoded that critic's place and the parameters of where and when he or she ought to speak. So, again, we were back within the realm of language.

Consequently the contributions to this volume of interdisciplinary essays tend toward literature but fall under the more general rubric of "cultural studies." They focus on the various ways the "romance" trope is employed within contemporary Caribbean political-social-historical discourses to (re)present the "new," newly independent, postcolonial societies of the region in ways that merely reconfigure old imperial or colonial "romance" tropes. As I have already remarked, the Caribbean as romantic symbol in the erotic sense of the word has always played a heavy part in the objectification of Caribbean society and people in Western societies and discourses—the islands as a sensual paradise, abundant with exotic fruit and happy (if stupid) men and willing women. What I am arguing for here, however, is a vision of "romance" that is more complex and far more insidious, by which Caribbean political and social discourse itself becomes shaped by "romance" tropes that then become integral to the vision and language the society constructs for itself.

As such, how do the old romanticized images of the region, initially constructed in the imperial European or American imagination, reinvent themselves in discourses that apparently come from the newly independent, decolonized Caribbean subjects themselves? One of the central discursive issues in this book is the way "romance" tropes that Europe and America have employed within their own societies as well as in their imaging of the Caribbean have been resuscitated for the postcolonial Caribbean. For example, the common Renaissance images of the "New World" as noble, naked native peoples surrounded by fruits arguably reappear in the current discourses over nationalism and racial harmony.

Similarly, the rhetoric of United States–style democracy, embodied in the "E Pluribus Unum" inscription on its coins, is utilized in several Caribbean nations' discussions on class, race, and democratic rule, thereby reaffirming a New World mythology of racial harmony and consequent democratization. In "Canonized Hybridities, Resistant Hybridities: Chutney Soca, Carnival, and the Politics of Nationalism," Shalini Puri argues that this romance of hybridity as harmony in Caribbean societies serves to symbolically "whiten" these mostly nonwhite nations so that the nations can see themselves as modern. She critiques the contemporary theoretical celebrations of "hybridity" as a de facto resisting mechanism, assessing the hybrid cultural musical form, Indian or "chutney" soca, that has recently emerged out of Trinidad in the context of Trinidad's complex racial politics as well as in the larger discourses of hybridity as democracy that have arisen in other Caribbean–Latin American societies, such as the *jibarismo* movement in Puerto Rico and the concept of *mestizaje* that has come out of Mexico.

In my essay "Trinidad Romance: The Invention of Jamaican Carnival," however, while I similarly note a cooptation of the American "melting pot" national romance in Jamaica through the importation of a Trinidad-style carnival, I argue that it is not the "whitening" of the nation that is sought, but rather the "browning" of it. "Brownness" in Jamaica is considered a separate racial category, but it also signifies a desire to erase painful histories of white hegemony and black anger by blending them into a group that, in containing both, embodies neither. Carnival, in its apparent apoliticality, therefore becomes important precisely because of its political function.

Catherine Den Tandt also explores the political use of hybridity discourse in her essay "All That Is Black Melts into Air: *Negritud* and Nation in Puerto Rico." The Puerto Rican literary discourse of *negritud* of the 1970s and 1980s was radical for its emphasis on the fundamental Africanness-blackness of Puerto Rican culture; contemporary literary representations of Puerto Rican culture as "postnational" or "postmodern" simply continue the idea of Puerto Rican culture as "spectacularly indeterminate" first set out by negritudinist discourse by emphasizing hybrid cultural forms such as salsa, Nuyorican poetry, and Puerto Rican rap. Den Tandt questions the link between the apparent radicalism of the "new" negritudism and the continuing paralysis of Puerto Rican activism in the political realm, since Puerto Rico's ongoing colonial status renders it, in one scholarly phrase, "at once postnational and prenational" (Flores, Milagros López, and Natarajan, "Dossier," 94).

Caribbean music has always had a significant role in producing discursive symbols of the region. "Positive Vibration? Capitalist Textual Hegemony and Bob Marley," by Mike Alleyne, dissolves the "romance" of reggae as a "pure," unmediated form of expression of the Jamaican people by analyzing the ideologies of marketing reggae superstar Bob Marley, whose socially radical lyrics critiqued the neocolonial politics of the Caribbean. Alleyne explores how the inherently conservatizing process of commerce was wedded to the image of the political rebel of the Rasta via Bob Marley to produce a central symbol of the Caribbean that is at once revolutionary and reactionary, a symbol that can be found in left-centered political discourse as well as in American cereal commercials.

However, in "Soca and Social Formations: Avoiding the Romance of Culture in Trinidad," Stefano Harney argues that cultural theorists who rely solely on Caribbean cultural expression—such as salsa, soca, and reggae—to make political judgments risk a dangerously reductionist view of the Caribbean. Focusing on soca and how it reflects Trinidadian society, Harney makes the point that, in contradistinction to the academic view that calypso is the people's "newspaper," soca is in fact "particularly unreliable" as a reflection of social formations in that society.

The remaining essays in the collection also explore the inversion of First World romance tropes but are more specifically concerned with their literary representations in fictional Caribbean narratives. The "romance" of hybridity in the *créoliste* movement among novelists in the francophone Caribbean is critiqued by Richard and Sally Price in their essay "Shadowboxing in the Mangrove: The Politics of Identity in Postcolonial Martinique." Touted as the "new" voice of the modern Martinique and Guadeloupe, the *créolistes* nevertheless resurrect old conflicts in their revision of Caribbean history. For instance, the *créolistes* argue that "the real heroes of the historical narrative are the plantation slaves who, 'secure in their secret dignity, often laid the groundwork for what we are today, and did so more effectively than many a maroon.'" The Prices contend that by removing the maroon as an icon of Caribbean resistance movements to colonial domination and replacing him, in effect, with the house slave, the *créolistes* risk reinscribing "the old colonial grimace of the laughing nigger," to use Walcott's phrase, as the dominant archetype of West Indian subjectivity. (I use the pronoun "him" deliberately here, given the *créoliste* emphasis on black masculine subjectivity, according to the Prices' description.)

One of two essays that explores the romance as a literary genre, Faith Smith's "Beautiful Indians, Troublesome Negroes, and Nice White Men: Caribbean Romances and the Invention of Trinidad," explores the meaning of race, gender, and slavery in *Ti Marie,* a novel that is described on its jacket as "a Caribbean *Gone with the Wind.*" Concerning a romance novel that has spawned a line of Harlequin-style West Indian romance novels by Heinemann Publishing, its author proclaims that its subject—a love affair between a white aristocrat and a black slave—is a liberating image for black West Indian women. Yet this appropriation of the paradigms of the romance genre on behalf of an apparent black and feminist nationalism, Smith argues, is actually embedded in many of the old European presuppositions on race in the Caribbean that the narrative seeks to rewrite.

In contrast to Smith's treatment of the romance genre, and in opposition to the general thrust of this collection, Kevin Meehan sees revolutionary potential in the ways that "romance" tropes of the romance genre itself can create myths of national genesis. Like Doris Sommer, Meehan regards the use of the romance in Haitian fiction and political discourse as a way to resolve ideological conflict. He explores the "romantic patriotism" of Haitian leaders Jean-Bertrand Aristide and Touissant L'Ouverture as well as classic Haitian novelists in his essay, "'Titid ak pèp la se marasa': Jean-Bertrand Aristide and the New National Romance in Haiti." In particular, he is interested in former Haitian president Jean-Bertrand Aristide's transformatory use of the romance genre for political effect, with romantic plots culled from classic Haitian novels. Meehan argues that traditional Haitian revolutionary discourse uses romance plots in which traditional gender roles—where women are subordinate to the "real" revolutionaries—are emphasized as natural to the revolution. He claims that Aristide reverses this paradigm by drawing on these traditional romance plots in his speeches and writings and essentially rewriting them to highlight the importance of women in revolutionary struggle.

Also concerned with apparently liberating images of black Caribbean women within and without literature, Supriya Nair examines the meaning of home and homelands in immigrant literature. She argues that the gendering of the nation (usually the "motherland") breaks down in hostile confrontation with women's actual bodies-histories, specifically working migrant Caribbean women in the "First World" who refuse to sustain a romanticized discourse of return to the motherland. Nair views Caribbean immigrant nostalgia for "home" through the prism of Paule Marshall's oeuvre, revealing it as a trope that has mystified the gender politics of immigration by simultaneously eroticizing male desires for the motherland and critiquing female desires for material success in North America.

Finally, Tejumola Olaniyan's essay "Derek Walcott: Liminal Spaces/Substantive Histories" seeks to deconstruct Walcott's ideal of Caribbean art as a kind of militant creolization of history and fiction, European and African aesthetics. Walcott's radical aesthetics is based on the claim that the revolutionary impulse is a filial one and that, in this context, for Caribbean artists mimicry of European aesthetics with a difference is itself mastery and transformative in its effects. Olaniyan asserts that Walcott's romance of mimicry essentially recreates the colonialist enterprise in its stark imperative, "imitate or die." Walcott's militant vision is founded, he argues, on an ancient, profoundly imperial vision of the Caribbean as a global tabula rasa.

If these essays level consistent critiques of neocolonial "romanticism" at apparently progressive, modern, and postcolonial structures, they also imply, by the centrality of the critique, that the epistemological romances of the Caribbean are apparently inevitable to Caribbeanness itself, founded as it was in the confluence of radical mythic visions of the New World and ancient political traditions of occupation and conformity.

However, the central thesis of these essays is not, as one might then suppose, merely to point out the reinscription of the mystified social schemas that the postcolonial state–postcolonial theory is meant to dissolve. Rather, they seek to complicate the idea that radical change and radical structures bear only an antagonistic or inverse relation to the traditional paradigms they broke away from. If, as Julius Nyerere has asserted, nation building is an inherently conservatizing process, then the central aim of these essays is to discover in what ways the Caribbean region has managed to fuse competing revolutionary and reactionary paradigms in its discourses about itself. I certainly hope that we, the contributors, have taken the first steps toward that difficult task.

### Notes

1. See Northrop Frye, "The Drunken Boat: The Revolutionary Element in Romanticism," in *Romanticism Reconsidered,* ed. Northrop Frye (New York: Columbia Univ. Press, 1963); also see Northrop Frye, *The Secular Scripture: A Study of the Structure of Romance* (Cambridge: Harvard Univ. Press, 1976).

2. See, for example, M. H. Abrams, "English Romanticism," in Frye, *Romanticism Reconsidered,* which attributes the origins of romanticism to exhilaration over the French Revolution and then disillusionment with it (26).

### Works Cited

Abrams, M. H. "English Romanticism." In *Romanticism Reconsidered,* ed. Northrop Frye, 26–72. New York: Columbia Univ. Press, 1963.

Flores, Juan, María Milagros López, and Nalini Natarajan. "Dossier Puerto Rico." *Social Text* 38 (1994): 93–95.

Frye, Northrop. "The Drunken Boat: The Revolutionary Element in Romanticism." In *Romanticism Reconsidered,* ed. Northrop Frye, 1–25. New York: Columbia Univ. Press, 1963.

Frye, Northrop. *The Secular Scripture: A Study of the Structure of Romance.* Cambridge: Harvard Univ. Press, 1976.

Jameson, Fredric. *The Political Unconscious: Narrative as Socially Symbolic Act.* Ithaca: Cornell Univ. Press, 1981.

Sommer, Doris. *Foundational Fictions: The National Romances of Latin America.* Berkeley: Univ. of California Press, 1991.

# 1

## Canonized Hybridities, Resistant Hybridities: Chutney Soca, Carnival, and the Politics of Nationalism

*Shalini Puri*

Cultural hybridity has taken its place at the center of a range of discourses with otherwise divergent agendas. It occupies this privileged position for various reasons. In liberal multicultural discourse, "cultural hybridity" has long offered a way of advancing culturalist notions of difference as inclusion or nonconflictual diversity; it functions there as an assimilationist discourse at a time when *separate* ethnic identities and inequalities threaten to become unmanageable. In contemporary corporate discourse, the cultural hybridity symbolized by the "global village" provides an enabling discourse for the aggressive economic expansion of capital. With the rise of postmodernism in metropolitan academies, a third position has emerged: Discourses of cultural hybridity have been mobilized to critique Enlightenment epistemology, its historic political achievement the nation-state, and the modern conception of a stable, unitary subject. In the work of such cultural theorists as Gloria Anzaldúa, Homi Bhabha, James Clifford, and Antonio Benítez Rojo the tropes of hybridity exist in conjunction with the idea of the demise of the nation-state. In such constructions, hybridity is often treated primarily as a *formal* principle of interruption of pure origins and destabilization of centers: "The 'difference' of cultural knowledge that 'adds to' but does not 'add up' is the enemy of the *implicit* generalization of knowledge or the implicit homogenization of experience" (Bhabha, "Dissemi-Nation," 313); hybridity is now reframed as a "structure of undecidability" (312). It is in the context of this critique of Enlightenment that border crossing, nomadism, travel, homelessness, and nationlessness have emerged as important tropes for cultural liberation.

Yet this formal equivalence between discourses of hybridity cannot distinguish between the very different political histories and agendas that shape diverse kinds of cultural hybridity. As Ella Shohat points out in her essay "Notes on the 'Post-colonial,'"

> A celebration of syncretism and hybridity per se, if not articulated in conjunction with questions of hegemony and neo-colonial power relations, runs the risk of appearing to sanctify the fait accompli of colonial violence. . . . As a descriptive catch-all term, hybridity per se fails to discriminate between the diverse modalities of hybridity, for example, forced assimilation, internalized self-rejection, political cooptation, social conformism, cultural mimicry, and creative transcendence. (109–10)

The erasure of the distinctions Shohat points to can be understood as part of a larger academic retreat from Marxism. Yet while I agree with criticism of the economism of some strands of Marxism, it seems to me that the new culturalism or formalism is equally problematic. What those otherwise unlikely discursive partners—liberal multiculturalism, corporate capital, and sections of the academic Left—share is the displacement of the issue of equality, a displacement of the *politics* of hybridity by the *poetics* of hybridity.

I contend that interrogating this displacement might challenge the now almost formulaic association of cultural hybridity with the disruption of the nation-state. For if, on the one hand, as theorists such as Homi Bhabha have persuasively shown, cultural hybridity points to destabilizing and subversive contradictions in purist and homogenizing narratives of the nation, it is by no means clear that these contradictions necessarily *disable* the nation even at the level of rhetoric, far less at the level of political economy. It seems important to analyze how the discursive resistances cultural hybridity might offer can be either recontained or elaborated into a more properly *oppositional* discourse, as well as to analyze how they can be recontained.

Moreover, I would argue that the discursive displacement of issues of equality that so many discourses of cultural hybridity perform can provide a powerful means of *securing* rather than disrupting the status quo. In both nationalist discourse and antinationalist academic commentary on it, there often occurs a slippage between the critique of purism and the critique of inequality. In this slippage lies the means by which cultural hybridity may not disrupt, but may actually secure, the interests of a national ruling class. From this analytical perspective it becomes apparent that there is no necessary opposition between hybridity and the nation.

Nowhere are the complexities, contradictions, and multiplicities of cultural hybridity more pressing than in the Caribbean, which Derek Walcott has poignantly called a "shipwreck of fragments." The Caribbean offers an instance where imagining "the people" has been a project fraught with particular difficulty. And yet the ability to imagine "the people" and to distinguish between different constructions of "the people" is crucial for any emancipatory project of social transformation. The Caribbean has some of the world's most precarious nation-states, often marked by neocolonial dependency, global capital's assaults on sovereignty, cyclical and mass migrations of population, environmental and cultural ravages, and bitter ethnic tensions among the members of its disparate diasporas—European, Native American, African, Indian, Chinese, and Middle Eastern. If ever the term "global culture" had relevance, then, it is to the Caribbean. My objection, therefore, is not a purist refusal of cultural hybridity, nor a rejection of global culture; rather, I object to the terms of their dominant theorizations.

In Caribbean cultural studies, Antonio Benítez Rojo's *The Repeating Island: The Caribbean and the Postmodern Perspective* represents a provocative but problematic engagement with the issue of cultural hybridity. Benítez Rojo is centrally concerned with addressing the Caribbean's "supersyncretism" (12) and "extremely complex cultural spectrum" (269), but in a telling parenthetical elaboration on that complexity, he designates it a "soup of signs" (2, 269). That this formulation renders these signs opaque and equivalent Benítez Rojo recognizes when he defends his use of postmodern chaos theory and refuses a "Euclidean coherence" (12). He argues: "Chaos looks toward everything that repeats, produces, grows, decays, unfolds, flows, spins, vibrates, seethes; it is as interested in the evolution of the solar system as in the stock market's crashes, as involved in cardiac arrhythmia as in the novel or in myth" (3).

Elsewhere Benítez Rojo claims: "[The Caribbean] is, in the final analysis, a culture of the meta-archipelago: a chaos that returns, a detour without a purpose, a continual flow of paradoxes; it is a feedback machine with asymmetrical workings, like the sea, the wind, the clouds, the uncanny novel, the food chain, the music of Malaya, Gödel's theorem and fractal mathematics" (11).

These sentences are striking in the insistent epistemological leveling they undertake; clause after clause energetically inscribes a series of equivalences. Benítez Rojo's "soup of signs" functions rather like Bhabha's notion of hybridity as a "structure of undecidability." And yet while Benítez Rojo's strategy might successfully critique logocentrism and purism, in surrendering the ability to distinguish between different signs of cultural hybridity, it obscures the inequality among the signs and their imbrication in particular social interests and (in)-equalities.

In contrast, refuting abstract conceptions of difference deriving from Saussurian linguistics, Peter Stallybrass and Allon White point out:

> Whilst it is true that meaning does indeed slip away down a chain of substitutions because of the relational and differential nature of linguistic signs, the smooth metaphor of "chain" wrongly suggests a certain regularity and equality of the "links" which make up each different term. On the contrary, the most significant kinds of displacements are *across* diverse territories of semantic material and always appear to involve steep gradients, even precipitous leaps, between socially unequal discursive domains. (198)

Stallybrass and White's caution is useful in elaborating a materialist Caribbean cultural studies, and it informs this essay. For formalist celebrations of cultural hybridity in the Caribbean leave us ill equipped to distinguish between the cultural hybridities and border crossings metonymically represented by, say, the slave ships, United States warships, Haitian refugee rafts, and luxury cruise liners. These hybridities, it seems to me, must be read in relation to unequal histories of expansionism, oppression, and creative resistance. Furthermore, *refusing* some of these hybridities and border crossings may have less to do with a modernist nostalgia for secure origins than with a will to physical survival and a struggle for political self-determination. In the pages that follow, I attempt a materialist analysis of the tensions and the alliances between a range of Caribbean discourses of hybridity and the nation.

For colonialists such as James Anthony Froude, the cultural hybridity of the Caribbean served to delegitimize the West Indian colonies as potentially sovereign nation-states. His declaration in *The English in the West Indies* that the Caribbean had "no people in the true sense of the word" served to rationalize his advocacy of continued British rule over the West Indies. His insistence on the failure of an imagined community in the West Indies hinged in turn on an imperial fiction of a homogeneous and unified imperial Britain and an elision of the divisions and tensions between the constituents of the "United Kingdom."

Postcolonial Caribbean nationalisms have had to contend with the enduring legacy of Froude and have needed to continually provide legitimating narratives to link the diverse elements of the Caribbean.[1] Yet Froude's model of nationhood as an ethnically and culturally homogeneous entity clearly marks anticolonial and postcolonial nationalisms as well. Eric Williams, the first postindependence prime minister of Trinidad and Tobago, was quite explicit about the need for unity and singular allegiance:

> There can be no Mother India for those whose ancestors came from India. . . . There can be no Mother Africa for those of African origin, and the Trinidad and Tobago society is living a lie and heading for trouble if it seeks to create the impression or to allow others to act under the delusion that Trinidad and Tobago is an African society. There can be no Mother England and no dual loyalties; no person can be allowed to get the best of both worlds, and to enjoy the privileges of citizenship in Trinidad and Tobago whilst expecting to retain United Kingdom citizenship. There can be no Mother China, even if one could agree as to which China is the mother; and there can be no Mother Syria or Mother Lebanon. A nation, like an individual, can have only one mother. The only Mother we recognize is Trinidad and Tobago, and Mother cannot discriminate between her children. (*Forged*, 281)

Williams's admonitions clearly reveal the dangerous proximity of diversity and division. If he is to legitimize a Trinidadian nation, he must produce it as *both* hybrid *and* homogeneous. In this regard, he struggles to produce a nation in the rhetorical mold of Froude's unified

Britain. In fact Williams uses the divisions within China to secure a familial Trinidadian unity by mimicking the very strategies by which Froude dismissed Trinidad. In regard to China, then, Williams effectively repeats Froude's "no people there in the true sense of the word" even as he refuses Froude's applicability to Trinidad.

If "hybridity" offers Williams a vocabulary for unifying Trinidad by producing a hybrid identity that is different from the identities of the ancestral lands of its inhabitants, it is important to note that it is a cultural hybridity, or a selective racial hybridity, that Williams invokes. For if, on the one hand, Williams's passage demonstrates an attempt to stitch together what Bhabha calls the "scraps, patches and rags" of daily experience into a national Trinidadian unity, on the other hand Trinidadian nationalist (and regional) politics have resorted as much to tearing *apart* the fabric of "the people" along racial lines. In postcolonial Trinidad, race has provided the means of populist nonclass integration of the masses into politics, enabling the development of opposed bourgeois nationalist Afro-Creole and Indian political parties. The need to consolidate and elaborate racialized voting blocs required that Williams produce a culturally hybrid Trinidad yet at the same time maintain a racially distinguishable "us" and "them."[2]

Racial and nationalist discourses in the Caribbean thus offer contradictory instances of tearing apart and stitching together the people, and discourses of hybridity offer a crucial means of managing those contradictory tendencies. The Trinidadian metaphor of the callaloo, for example, rather like that of the American melting pot and the more recent language of "multiculturalism," attempts to manage difference by projecting an image of nonconflictual diversity. Jamaica's motto Out of Many, One People, Guyana's One People, One Nation, One Destiny, Trinidad's Together We Aspire, Together We Achieve, and Haiti's Unity Is Strength (Stewart, "Ethnic," 151–52), all bear out Bhabha's claims about the nation's anxious "double time," which must continually refer to an achieved unity in an attempt to produce it. Haunting all of these assertions is a recognition of the fragility of the "we" of the race- and class-divided nations. Also common to the slogans above is the fact that their rhetoric of hybridity displaces the issue of social equality between and within groups. Moreover, and particularly striking, this displacement is common both to hegemonic nationalist discourses in the Caribbean and to many oppositional discourses of hybridity. In this displacement of equality, then, lies an unexpected congruity between dominant and oppositional discourse. It may therefore be useful to note a few instances in the Caribbean where the rhetoric of cultural hybridity has been perfectly recuperable to conservative and antiegalitarian social arrangements. In the cases of Jamaica and Trinidad, for instance, the racial hybridization represented by mulattoes did not disrupt the racial stratification of society but was absorbed into that structure: mulattoes came to compose the middle class, situated between a white upper class and a largely black and Indian lower class. In the case of Mexico, as Doris Sommer points out, promoting a mestizo identity as the national identity sanctioned the mixing of Native American and Spaniard but repressed from the national imaginary the black population of the nation.[3] If Sommer draws attention to the persistence of racial inequality in the imagery of *mestizaje,* Benítez Rojo points out that *mestizaje* "involves a positivistic and logocentric argument, an argument that sees in the biological, economic, and cultural whitening of the Caribbean society a series of steps towards 'progress'" (26). In other words, the rhetoric of hybridity can be coopted to serve rather than disrupt a modernist-modernizing logic.[4]

In Puerto Rico, the symbol of the Jíbaro or poor rural, white or mestizo peasant served a function similar to that of *mestizaje* in Mexico, nationalizing a whitened Creole identity and symbolically erasing the troubled issues of slavery, black and white racial mixing, and the claims of blacks and mulattoes upon the nation.[5] While constructing a Creole identity was crucial to resisting Spanish colonialism, constructing a whitened or Creole identity entailed its own racism and vision of nationalist development. In all these examples, moreover,  sanctioning nonthreatening hybridities is accompanied by disallowing threatening hybridities. It may be significant that the Jíbaro went on to become the emblem of the Partido Popular Democrático (PPD), a party that, after initially advocating independence from the United States, went on to advocate "commonwealth" status for Puerto Rico. In the 1950s, as the pro-Commonwealth party, the PPD implemented "Operation Bootstrap" or "industrialization by invitation." In this instance, then, a Creole-hybrid poetics was appended to the antiegalitarian economic policies of dependent capitalism. That linkage was possible in part because of the ability of that symbol to gloss over or *stabilize* the contradictions in populist bourgeois nationalism.

These historical instances should serve as a warning against the belief that hybridity understood as contradiction or ambivalence disrupts the "linearity" of reason and is therefore necessarily subversive.

Contrary to an abstractly conceived hybridity that always threatens the center, the examples I have sketched show how particular constructions of hybridity may actually consolidate the center. At the very least, we need to be able to negotiate analytically between the *epistemic disruption* of the center by the margin, of which theorists such as Bhabha so eloquently speak, and the *economic consolidation* of the center by the margin, which the neocolonial economic dependency of most of the Caribbean makes so painfully clear.

It is not just official nationalist discourses in the Caribbean that only selectively address the political economy of cultural hybridity. Many oppositional Caribbean discourses betray a residual displacement of the problem of racial inequality, even as they seek to address it. The canonized Barbadian poet and cultural theorist Edward Brathwaite, for example, in his important book *Contradictory Omens: Cultural Diversity and Integration in the Caribbean,* offers an analysis of hybridity that both refuses dominant discourses and overlaps with them. Brathwaite places creolization at the center of the Caribbean experience. He traces the etymology of the word "creole" to the Spanish verb *criar* (to create, imagine, found, or settle) and *colon* (a colonist, a founder, a settler). *Criollo* refers to "a committed settler, one identified with the area of settlement, one native to the settlement though not ancestrally indigenous to it" (10). "Creolization," then, comes to mean the indigenization of the population of the Caribbean; it includes both "acculturation" and "interculturation:"

> Started as a result of slavery and therefore in the first instance involving black and white, European and African, in a fixed superiority/inferiority relationship, it tended first to the culturation of white and black to the new Caribbean environment; and, at the same time, because of the terms and conditions of slavery, to the acculturation of black to white norms. There was at the same time, however, significant interculturation going on between these two elements. (11)

What is so helpful about Brathwaite's analysis is its careful attention to the unequal terms of interculturation—an analysis that would be useful to apply to the postcolonial era as well. What is problematic about the work, however, and its continued application of creolization as a concept to grasp *contemporary* Caribbean cultural hybridity, is that a Creole hybridity encompasses only those parts of the Caribbean population that are black, white, or the mixed offspring of black and white; the term "Creole," even as it is used today in much of the English-speaking Caribbean, does not include people of Asian descent, groups that together constitute about 20 percent of the population of the West Indies and that in Guyana and Trinidad form the largest ethnic group. Using creolization as a figure for Caribbean hybridity thus has its own complex legacy of exclusion. Brathwaite's formulation allows us to glimpse this exclusion: he refers to "the arrival of East Indian and other immigrants" and to the fact that these "other elements had to adjust themselves to the existing creole synthesis and the new landscape." The arrival of these elements, he points out, effected a shift from a Creole to a plural society (11). But describing the East Indians who arrived in the Caribbean as "immigrants," rather than as indentured laborers who replaced slave labor after the abolition of slavery, blocks an understanding of *their* position of social subordination, from which they negotiated their Caribbeanization. Moreover, in his reference to East Indians, Brathwaite appears uninterested in making the useful distinction between acculturation and interculturation that he makes in regard to black-white creolization. In fact, implicit in his discussion of Indians in Trinidad are three contradictory or underspecified claims: that Indians are simply "assimilated" into the Creole society; that although they are creolized, they do not thereby become Creoles; and that with their advent the Caribbean became a "plural" society. It is important to read in Brathwaite's analysis both the strength of his insight, made in relation to Creoles, that Caribbean hybridity is the result of accommodation and transformation between *unequal* social elements and the analytic danger of losing sight of those inequalities, which his discussion of East Indians reveals.

If Brathwaite's casting of an anticolonial nationalist narrative reveals some exclusions, Derek Walcott's Nobel Prize acceptance address, titled "The Antilles: Fragments of Epic Memory," offers an alternative anti(neo)colonial narrative of the nation, one that resists a certain kind of border crossing. Yet Walcott's poetics of the nation-state in a global economy is not without its own exclusions and evasions.

The structuring opposition in Walcott's narrative is the opposition between the traveler and the native. He says: "A traveler cannot love, since love is stasis and travel is motion. If he returns to what he loved in a landscape and stays there, he is no longer a traveler but in stasis and concentration, a *lover* of that particular part of the earth, a *na-*

*tive*" (30; emphasis added). The figure of the traveler offers Walcott a means of critiquing the cultural and economic dependency of the Caribbean, marked in his address by colonial travel narratives and tourism. The image of the "native," on the other hand, is crucial for Walcott's validation of Caribbean nationalist projects. However, the opposition "traveler versus native" also glosses over Walcott's own position as a *traveling native,* It is precisely as a traveling native that Walcott takes up his position in a global economy, as the *interna*tionally canonized *national* writer from the Caribbean. His own address, made at his acceptance in Sweden of the Nobel Prize, therefore circulates in an international economy of exchange, where it exists in a tense relationship with the other texts to which he alludes: the tourist brochure, the colonialist-anthropological narrative, and the texts of other Caribbean writers. Moreover, the opposition between traveler and native is a particularly vexed one in the Caribbean context, for figures such as Fanon, Césaire, James, and Martí are all in some sense traveling natives who elaborated Caribbean nationalisms from a location in the heart of colonial metropolises. Finally, the terms of Walcott's opposition between traveler and native— indifference versus love, motion versus stasis—enable him to deal differently with international and "domestic" cultural hybridity. I will argue that while he addresses in terms of power and inequality the hybridity that occurs through the international economy of tourism, he displaces analysis of power and inequality when he addresses hybridity with*in* the nation-state.

Walcott's critique of the border crossing represented by tourists— "rootless" travelers, he calls them—takes the form of an attack on the pastiche of tourist aesthetics. He claims:

> In our tourist brochures the Caribbean is a blue pool into which the republic dangles the extended foot of Florida as inflated rubber islands bob and drinks with umbrellas float toward her on a raft. . . . this is the seasonal erosion of their [the islands'] identity, that high-pitched repetition of images of service that cannot distinguish one island from the other. . . . What is the earthly paradise for our visitors? Two weeks without rain and a mahogany tan, and at sunset local troubadours in straw hats and floral shirts singing "Yellow Bird" and "Banana Boat Song" to death. (32)

For Walcott, tourism entails a homogenizing hybridity that threatens Caribbean national identities. It is a neocolonial hybridity that draws the Caribbean islands into the economic and epistemological sphere of the neocolonizing United States, metonymically represented in his text by Florida's penetration into the Caribbean sea.

If Walcott rejects the pastiche of tourist aesthetics, he similarly rejects purist aesthetics, which he also locates with respect to power: Walcott might as well have been describing Froude when he wrote: "Purists look on such ceremonies [hybridized and fragmented Caribbean cultural practices] as grammarians look on a dialect, as cities look on provinces, and empires on their colonies. . . . In other words, the way the Caribbean is still looked at, illegitimate, rootless, mongrelized" (27). Refusing both Froude's colonial cultural purism and neocolonial hybridity, Walcott nonetheless celebrates hybridity as the basis for distinctively Caribbean national identities: "Poetry," he says, "is an island that breaks away from the main." In the light of his critique of tourism, and of the United States–satellite status of much of the Caribbean ("islands floating *towards* Florida"), Walcott's claim that "poetry is an island that *breaks away* from the main" appears to represent a project of linguistic and epistemological delinking from institutionalized or dominant language, as well as a project of economic delinking from the mainland.[6] Unlike Benítez Rojo's, Walcott's celebration of hybridity is accompanied by a nationalist refusal of subordinate incorporation into the global economy. His statement that Caribbean culture's "proportions are not to be measured by the traveler or the exile, but by its own citizenry and architecture" (30) is  animated by precisely such a nationalist refusal. Walcott's poetics of marginality, then, is inseparable from a global politics of political, economic, and cultural autonomy.

However, the national "citizenry" Walcott produces to oppose foreign cultural and political imperialism and the collectivity he marks when he speaks of "our history" achieve their stability only through a discursive displacement of issues of power and inequality in Walcott's dealing with hybridity with*in* the postcolonial Caribbean nation-states. In fact, the slippage between the word "citizen," with its connotation of democratic equality in a national context, and the word "native," which carries no such connotations, underwrites his selective attention to power. His highly poeticized construction of the native in terms of love, stasis, and rootedness in the earth sets the stage for his displacement of power. "Break a vase," he says, "and the *love* that reassembles the fragment is stronger than that *love* that took its symmetry for granted when it was whole. . . . It is such a *love* that reassembles our

African and our Asiatic fragments" (28; emphasis added). Within the nation-state, the language of political economy is replaced by the language of love, the vocabulary of material interests by that of sentiment. Walcott's narrative bears out Marxist warnings that a dependency school analysis of "foreign domination" may be consistent with bourgeois nationalism. What Walcott's treatment of hybridity within Caribbean nation-states achieves is an aesthetically accomplished reinscription of Caribbean national mottoes such as Jamaica's Out of Many, One People and Trinidad's All o' We Is One. Like those mottoes, the passage attempts to forge a unity without attending to the unequal terms of inclusion in the national imaginary or the unequal access to the resources of the state; it posits in advance a unity and equality that have yet to be achieved. Thus, Walcott asserts: "They [the remembered customs] survived the Middle Passage and the Fatel Rozack, the ship that carried the first indentured Indians from the port of Madras to the canefields of Felicity, that carried the chained Crom-wellian convict and the Sephardic Jew, the Chinese grocer and the Lebanese merchant selling cloth samples on his bicycle" (28). The syntactic equivalence of these different subnational groups that Walcott inscribes here sutures over their economic and cultural inequalities. Conspicuously absent from this list is the privileged French Creole elite, which represents not the small business to which Walcott pays homage in this passage, but the immensely powerful node between national and international capital. The point I am making is that Walcott's strategy for organizing difference within the nation amounts to a liberal multiculturalist project of inclusion, which leaves the relations of production and attendant ordering of class and gender within the nation essentially untouched. The peaceful syntactic coexistence of East Indian and African in Walcott's sentence belies Trinidad's postcolonial history of intense economic and cultural competition between the two groups.[7]

As the various texts I have touched on show, then, discourses of hybridity in the Caribbean perform several functions: They elaborate a syncretic New World identity distinct from that of its "mother cultures"; in doing so, they provide a basis for national and regional legitimacy. Second, they offer a way of balancing or displacing discourses of equality, which has led to their importance in many instances for securing bourgeois nationalist hegemony. Third, they have been implicated in managing racial politics—either by promoting cultural over racial hybridity or by sanctioning racial hybridities that do not threaten the status quo.

What, however, might a hybridity that threatens the domestic status quo look like? How might it redraw existing lines of class, race, and gender power? I will draw out one historical example by returning to a sticking point common to Williams's, Brathwaite's, and Walcott's constructions of cultural hybridity: the relationship of Afro-Caribbeans and Indo-Caribbeans.[8] I have shown how each of these Afro-Creole theorists offers a strategy of managing the tensions between these two groups: Williams resorts to racial distinctions and racialized voting to prop up a bourgeois-nationalist divide-and-rule politics even as he advocates cultural hybridity in the form of creolization. Brathwaite's endorsement of creolization, too, manages Afro-Caribbean/Indo-Caribbean tensions either by separating Indians out in the name of a "plural" society or by assimilating them to a Creole Caribbean norm; Walcott, celebratory of both racial and cultural hybridity, nonetheless glosses over the economic competition between these groups through recourse to the language of love. Each of these discourses is invested in a particular arrangement of class and race power that it attempts to conceal. Also common to all three discourses is the erasure of the problem of gender inequality that is characteristic of so much cultural nationalist discourse. Yet Williams's insistent references to "Mother Trinidad" should alert us to the politics of gender, sexuality, and family undergirding his cultural nationalist project.

One of the striking features of the antagonism between a racialized "us" and "them" in Trinidad is that it draws heavily on the terms of colonial racial discourse, which provides a resonant vocabulary through which Afro- and Indo-Trinidadians structure and express their relational antagonisms today. Thus we continue to hear the familiar series of oppositions that James Anthony Froude mobilized in 1888 when he declared that "the African and the Asiatic will not mix": the thriftless African/the thrifty Indian; the lazy African/the hardworking Indian; the childlike and promiscuous African unable to control his sexual appetites/the calculating and ascetic Indian.

The question I have asked elsewhere is, What happens when, contrary to Froude's declaration, Africans and Asiatics *do* mix? What happens when they give birth to a "dougla"?[9] In the context of racial competition, the anxieties around black/Indian racial ambiguity are often expressed as disavowals of the dougla—either through the discursive repression of the dougla or through explicit attack on the category. There is considerable evidence for my claim that the dougla constitutes what I will call a disallowed identity. Aisha Khan, Rhoda Reddock, Niels Sampath, and Daniel Segal have provided extensive current data showing that many douglas choose not to identify as such, and that Indo-Trinidadians commonly consider douglas to be "Creoles," attributing to them all the stereotypically undesirable characteristics of "creolized behavior," including vice, idleness, mental problems, and vagrancy. Bridget Brereton and Rhoda Reddock trace contemporary Indian disavowals of the dougla back to the highly skewed sex ratios within the Indian population during the period of indentureship, as well as to Hindu notions of caste endogamy. It is in this context that the pejorative term "dougla" or bastard was initially applied to people of mixed Indian and African descent. In the post-colonial context of racial competition, the dougla disrupts what Daniel Segal has called the system of "racial accounting." The erasure of the dougla in dominant discourses of race is tellingly glossed by the fact that the word "dougla" does not even appear in the *Dictionary of Common Trinidadian Hindi;* the erasure symptomatizes the dougla's vexed position with respect to various processes of Indian cultural reconstruction and affirmation of which the writing of the dictionary is a part. In the late 1980s, however, douglarization became the subject of open public debate. In 1990 the Sanatan Dharma Maha Sabha would take out an advertisement in the *Trinidad Guardian* explicitly attacking cultural douglarization as a conspiracy to assimilate Indians and wipe out Indian culture. In the arts, too, the issue of douglarization has been a fraught one, particularly in the field of music, where the emergence of chutney soca[10] created great controversy, particularly when performed by Indo-Trinidadian women. When the Indo-Trinidadian Drupatee Ramgoonai brought chutney soca to the calypso stage, she was condemned by many Indian cultural nationalists for her participation in carnival, for her sexually suggestive lyrics, and for throwing "her high upbringing and culture to mix with vulgar music, sex and alcohol in Carnival" (quoted in Constance, *Tassa,* 51). By the logic of conservative cultural nationalists, the demand must not be that carnival be Indianized or douglarized, but that a conservative construction of a monolithic Indian culture be given the *same* national status as carnival. In the cultural sphere the demand is to be "separate but equal."

Thus, many conservative Indo-Trinidadians celebrate chutney, which they see as an authentically and distinctively *Indo*-Trinidadian musical form, performed as it historically has been in all-women's gatherings during Hindu wedding festivities. In a carefully demarcated space—female, Indian, or female and Indian—even the ribald sexuality of chutney singing and chutney dancing is amenable to identitarian projects and is endorsed by Indian cultural nationalists. These same conservatives, however, fiercely resist the "crossover" from chutney to the further hybridized chutney soca, the "Africanized" and carnivalized form of chutney performed during carnival. For, first, in the context of carnival, chutney's distinctive Indo-Trinidadianness is potentially compromised or rendered invisible, and second, the sexuality of the Indo-Trinidadian woman is staged in a public, commodified, and racially mixed calypso tent, where it becomes the ground of a paternalistic cultural nationalist battle of protection and dominance. For the same reason, vigorous controversy has accompanied Indo-Trinidadian chutney dancers accompanying Afro-Trinidadian calypsonians. The "separate but equal" formula must therefore arrest the hybridization of chutney at the point of crossover from Hindu-Indian wedding tent to Creole calypso tent.[11]

Such are the racial and cultural nationalist politics that framed Drupatee Ramgoonai's success on the national calypso stage in 1988. However, I have argued that Drupatee's dougla poetics has enabled the discursive emergence of potentially contestatory and *disallowed* Indian identities. Drupatee's soca chutney song "Lick Down Me Nani" caused a particular furor. At the most obvious level, a description of the narrator's response to seeing her grandmother being knocked down by a maxi-taxi (privately run group taxis known for driving recklessly), the song turns around two central double entendres: the first is between two meanings of "nani": in Hindi it means maternal grandmother, and in Trinidad street slang it means vagina. The second double entendre is around "lick," that is, either licking with the tongue or beating. The maxi-taxi's knocking down the grandmother thus doubles as sexual violence. In contrast, if you attend only to the catchy chorus and exuberant beat, the narrative could be describing pleasurable oral sex. Thus, for example, the song goes:

*(Chorus)*
*(De man) lick down me nani*
*(De man) lick down me nani, oy*
Neighbour I ain't makin' sport

*Nani get bounce down*
I takin' the driver to court
*Nani get bounce down*
The doctor say she in coma
I don't know when she'll recover.
I miss she phulari, I miss she roti
And every day I grievin' for me nani.
*(Chorus)*
Neighbour don' hold me, I want to buss some lash on he.

Conservative Indo-Trinidadians have attacked the song on several scores: it is "disrespectful" toward the revered Indian grandmother; it is at best "frivolous," at worst "vulgar"; Drupatee is a "sellout," degrading Indian culture, symbolized by the revered grandmother, in order to gain admission to an Afro-Creole public space. Significant and troubling also, given the high incidence of violence against women in Trinidad, is that none of the cultural nationalist attacks on the song have addressed the narrative of *violence* in "Lick Down Me Nani." For while the sexual connotations of the song are unmistakable, so are the references to sexual violence—bouncing Nani down, breaking her bones, "driving too hard" because his "brakes cut away."

That the "degradation of the nani" in the song *can* be appropriated by racialist agendas is undeniable. If one reads the song in the satire-cum-boast tradition of calypso, then the pleasure of the narrative could indeed lie in the symbolic violence against the Indian woman, who is in turn a metonym for Indian culture. But the song's reversals and degradations occur along not just a racial axis but along several other axes—something conservative cultural nationalists consistently ignore. The nani not only is Indian but is also a symbol of female family authority and order that are quite compatible with patriarchal ideology. One could argue that it is this authority and idealization of the grandmother that are parodied or reversed by the hyperembodiment of the nani through the pun on grandmother-vagina—and through the image of her wanting to wine.[12] Furthermore, the idealization and de-sexualization of the grandmother are embedded in a logic of coerced chastity for Indian women (the terms of the outcry against Drupatee make this logic abundantly clear—Drupatee is cast as the whore, and the grandmother as the virgin–respectable woman.) At one level, therefore, *refusing* that idealization constitutes a utopian transgression. Given the erasure of the active sexuality of Indian women by conservative Indian discourse, producing and reveling in that sexual vocabulary, despite its obviously sexist genealogy, might thus still be transgressive. Furthermore, both the song's narrator and the neighbor in the song serve as *witnesses* to masculine violence against women, witnesses who demand revenge or justice, expressed in the song in terms of personal physical retaliation and recourse to the state ("I'm gonna buss some lash on he," "arrest him," take away his license, take him to court).

The song, then, yields several feminist interpretive possibilities: it could be read as a mischievous and playful affirmation of a woman's sexual assertiveness (the chorus's imperative "lick down me nani,"), a feminist critique of loss of control over her own sexuality (rape and coerced chastity), and a feminist attempt to reclaim control by punishing the offender. Finally, Drupatee's song nowhere suggests that the sexual violence is *inter*racial. A further threat to the status quo that Drupatee's song poses, then, is that, unlike conservative Indian discourse, it does not permit the question of violence against Indian women to be displaced onto African men. I am interested in the attacks on Drupatee's participation in carnival for another reason as well. Charges that Drupatee embraced the "gods of sex, wine, and easy money" construct Indian culture as the morally superior and sexually restrained *antithesis* of a licentious Afro-Creole culture of carnival. This construction, however, ignores the existence of carnivalesque traditions within *Indian* culture. Addressing the parallels between carnival and, say, the Hindu carnivalesque festival of Holi or Phagwa might offer a means of thinking differently about the relationship of Indo-Trinidadians to carnival (and therefore to the national imaginary).[13]

Although I clearly differ with the Indo-Trinidadian orthodoxy on the value and possibilities of the song, I share its view that "Lick Down Me Nani"—and more generally, chutney soca—participates in a dougla poetics. For, first, chutney soca's musical form and instruments hybridize Indo- and Afro-Trinidadian musical traditions. Second, it intervenes in the historically "African" calypso tent rather than in a separate "Indian" space. Third, if we think of the original sense of dougla as "bastard" or illegitimate, we can think of "Lick Down Me Nani" as indeed articulating a dougla—that is, delegitimized or disallowed—Indian or woman's identity.

These claims are strengthened, I believe, if one situates Drupatee's dougla poetics in relation to a minor history in which the figure of the dougla has served as a means to rethink cultural hybridity in relation to projects of political equality and critiques of the racialized national bourgeoisies. The Mighty Dougla's 1961 calypso "Split Me in Two" is one early example that ruefully recounts the position of douglas in a society marked by black/Indian political division. In both his stage name and his song, the Mighty Dougla resists both the characterization of "dougla" as raceless and the pressure to choose one race or the other:

If they serious about sending people back for true
They got to split me in two. . . .

When he say I have no race he ain't talkin' true
Instead of havin' one race you know I got two.

Nearly thirty years later, Delamo's "Soca Chutney" (1989) uses the figure of the dougla to refuse divide and rule politics:

Now who come to divide and rule
Eh go use we as no tool
Any time they comin' racial
I dougla, I staying neutral.

(Quoted in Constance, *Tassa*, 43)

Similarly, Bally's song "Dougla" fuses Afro- and Indo-Trinidadian musical vocabularies and explicitly refers to the dougla as a figure for the linked interests of most Afro- and Indo-Trinidadians:

Dougla—a mutual link, absolute bond, the symbol of unity
The hope for him, the hope for her, the hope for you and me.

Most recently, in the 1996 carnival, Brother Marvin's "Jahaji Bhai" (Brotherhood of the Boat) employs rhythms and instruments deriving from India and Africa to make a claim for Indian and African unity based on their shared conditions of entrance into Trinidad and the impossibility of separating out those two histories:

The indentureship and the slavery
Bind together two race in unity
. . . For those who playing ignorant
Talking 'bout true African descendant
If yuh want to know the truth
Take a trip back to yuh roots

And somewhere on that journey
You go see a man in a dhoti
Saying he prayers in front of a jhandi.[14]

The song ends with the refrain "Let us live under one sky / As Jahaji
Bhai." The Hindustani phrase "jahaji bhai," meaning brothers or
brotherhood of the boat, has historically referred to the human relationships built on the *Fatel Rozack* and later ships that brought
Indian indentured labor to Trinidad. Brother Marvin's song, however, deploys the phrase to inscribe a broader brotherhood, one that
is forged in history rather than assured by blood. I would argue that
the song is also a rewriting of Black Stalin's controversial 1979 calypso "Caribbean Unity," a call for unity based on a black nationalist vision of the Caribbean as the inheritance of the descendants of
slaves:

Dem is one race—De Caribbean Man
From de same place—De Caribbean Man
That make the same trip—De Caribbean Man
On the same ship—De Caribbean Man.[15]

If Black Stalin's Caribbean unity was achieved through an implicit
exclusion of Indians, then "Jahaji Bhai," in its conjoining of Indian
journeys across the kala pani and African journeys across the middle
passage, refutes Black Stalin's purist history with a dougla history.

Based on these various examples, what general claims might one
make for the political possibilities of a dougla poetics? I am emphatically not suggesting a dougla poetics as somehow paradigmatic of
postcolonial, West Indian, or even Trinidadian aesthetics; indeed, the
example of a dougla poetics does not necessarily offer a way of thinking about the place of minority groups such as the Chinese, Syrians, or
Lebanese in the national imaginary and in an unequal society. Rather,
I am making a conjunctural—and conjuncturally circumscribed—
claim about the possibilities of a dougla poetics in Trinidad today; to
claim more would be to repeat the essentializing and overgeneralized
claims for cultural hybridity I have critiqued and to forget that any
identity or aesthetics can be coopted.

I think it is also likely that a dougla poetics offers different options
and faces different challenges in the fields of literature and music; certainly dougla poetics has generated much less controversy in litera-

ture. For this there are probably several reasons: literature in Trinidad has a relatively small audience compared with music; its popular impact is therefore significantly narrower. But perhaps more important, in the context of an ethnic politics that has entailed the "objectification" and "commodification of ethnicity" (Yelvington, "Introduction," 11), music is often seen as part of the cultural capital of particular ethnic groups; blurring the ethnic boundaries of the music therefore risks both a loss of cultural capital and its appropriation by the culturally dominant group. In contrast, in the field of literature, although particular authors might be seen as ethnic cultural capital, the literary genres of the novel, short story, and poetry are not so clearly marked as African or Indian and may therefore escape some of the controversies surrounding hybrid music. In literature, one might begin with C. L. R. James's *Minty Alley*, the first novel I know of in which the dougla ethnicity of one of the characters is understood as causally relevant to the action. Other literary attempts to negotiate dominant constructions of race and gender in a way that fits with the kind of project I have outlined include the fiction of Earl Lovelace, Sam Selvon, Ismith Khan, and Ramabai Espinet.[16]

I have tried to outline the political reasons for the popular and academic erasure of what we might call dougla histories. To further specify, elaborate, and delimit the possibilities of a dougla poetics, more scholarship is needed. Besides music and literature, other areas of inquiry might include the multiethnic celebration of Indian cultural practices such as Hosay; comparative analyses of the overlapping histories of regulation and resistance revealed by colonial legislation on Hosay and Creole carnival, especially canboulay; social scientific studies, such as those of Khan and Reddock on the experience of douglas, including attitudes toward them and their relation to Indo-Trinidadian and Creole culture; and various attempts at labor organizing across racial lines by James, Rienzi, Butler, Hosein, and the oil and sugar unions.

What I have been suggesting is that the very anxiety surrounding the figure of the dougla may well be a measure of the radical possibilities of the latter. If creolization as a figure for hybridity has exhausted its radicalism in contemporary Trinidad and now serves status quoist class agendas, and if, as Aisha Khan's work suggests, the fluid hybridity designated "Spanish" is nonthreatening in part because it functions as a euphemism for more conflictual identities, then a dougla hybridity might offer some alternatives. For if "the Indian" and "the African"

*sedimentation des significations*

are discursively held apart by a series of stereotypical oppositions, then the figure of the dougla becomes a potential site for the collision of classifications, for negotiations over the dougla's racial "value" and place in a racially hierarchized society, and for the disruption of notions of racial purity upon which racial stereotypes depend. Based on several examples from Trinidadian musical and literary traditions, I suggest that the figure of the dougla and a dougla poetics could provide a vocabulary for disallowed racial identities; furthermore, they could offer ways—and have offered ways—of reframing questions of black-Indian party politics and of race and gender relations.

It is undeniable, however, that "dougla" carries many sedimented meanings, not all of them politically suggestive or progressive. If interracial sex is frowned on by some, it is often invoked equally problematically, if more playfully, as the solution to racial division and inequality. The figure of the dougla often functions in both African and Indian purist discourses, as well as in some pro-PNM discourses, as a code word for assimilation and racial "dilution."[17] But in a cultural context of marginalization of Indians, I think it is important to make visible *as Indian* the Indian elements of a dougla poetics such as chutney soca's—in other words, to *contest* rather than acquiesce in such assimilationist deployments. This contestation is doubly important because pejorative readings of *cultural* douglarization all too often name "biological" douglas pejoratively as well; behind antiassimilationist disavowals of cultural douglarization sometimes lurks a more insidious set of practices of exclusion and delegitimizing directed against "biological" douglas. Cultural antidouglarization, then, can both deploy and mask an underlying racism.

Keeping in mind, then, that the original meaning of the word "dougla" was "bastard" or "illegitimate," I suggest that one might think of a dougla poetics as a means for articulating potentially progressive cultural identities delegitimized by both the Afro-Creole dominant culture and the Indian "mother culture." For, first, as against purist racial discourse, the figure of the dougla draws attention to the reality of interracial contact; it *names* a contact that already exists. Second, a dougla poetics could provide a rich symbolic resource for interracial unity, as it does in Bally's soca chutney melody "Dougla" and in Brother Marvin's "Jahaji Bhai." To break the stranglehold racial politics of the PNM and the UNC, any egalitarian politics clearly needs to emphasize the shared histories of oppression of Afro- and Indo-

Trinidadians, just as it needs to articulate their economic advancement in nonexclusive racial terms. What distinguishes a dougla hybridity at this conjuncture from liberal multiculturalist tropes of hybridity such as callaloo, "Spanish," and, arguably, Creole, is the ability of a dougla identity to think cultural hybridity in relation to equality and the potential of a dougla poetics to unmask power and symbolically redraw its lines. A dougla poetics thus offers a vocabulary for a *political* identity, not a primarily biological one.

Moreover, in its confusion of stereotypes, a dougla poetics could elaborate alternative discourses of femininity, as it does in Drupatee's "Lick Down Me Nani." On one hand, it seems important to caution that we have no reason to think a dougla identity would *necessarily* be any less masculinist than existing racial identities; but on the other hand, because constructions of race are gendered in very particular ways, the dougla's potential disruption of dominant racial stereotypes could provide an opportunity for specifically *feminist* contestations of dominant gender and race imagery. Whether such discursive resistances translate into a specifically *oppositional* politics cannot be predicted. Elaborating a dougla poetics offers no guarantees, then, but it does offer a symbolic *resource* in the reconfiguration of racial and gender identities. The unstable and diverse functions of different mobilizations of a dougla hybridity caution against making inflationary generalizations and point instead to the need for more careful contextual and conjunctural claims for cultural hybridity. My purpose in this essay, then, is not to set up a dougla identity or a dougla poetics as some kind of "ideal" hybridity; rather, I have tried to shift the emphases of the kinds of questions we ask about cultural hybridity and to historicize our answers. I offer my exploration of a dougla poetics, therefore, as but one of many possible elaborations whose goal is to analyze the poetics and politics of cultural hybridity and to interrogate the articulations and disarticulations between them.

### Notes

For many helpful clarifications, criticisms, and conversations, I thank Carlos Cañuelas, Catherine Den Tandt, and Biodun Jeyifo.

1. See, for example, the Cuban revolutionary intellectual Roberto Fernández Retamar's famous essay "Caliban," which is an extended affirmative response to the skeptical question of a European journalist: "Does a Latin-American culture exist?" For reasons of space, I cannot address here the

important question of the relation between Caribbean and pan-Caribbean identities, nationalist and regionalist ideologies; for the purposes of this essay, I treat them analogically.

2. The "us" versus "them" logic has led to the domination through most of Trinidad's postcolonial history of competing "black" and "Indian" parties, the People's National Movement (PNM) and the United National Congress (UNC) and its predecessors, respectively. The PNM has been in power consistently, with three exceptions: 1986, when the multiracial coalition, the National Alliance for Reconstruction, won the elections; 1990, during the short-lived Muslimeen coup; and 1995, which saw the historic election of the first Indo-Trinidadian prime minister, Basdeo Panday. The impact of this most recent election on Trinidadian politics remains to be seen. The significance of racial voting is such that the 1990 census, in which the Indian population overtook the African population by a fraction of a point, was greeted with jubilation by many Indians and with anxiety by many Africans.

Throughout this piece, following Trinidadian usage, I use the terms "African," "black," "Afro-Creole," and "Afro-Trinidadian" synonymously; I also use the terms "East Indian," "Indian," and "Indo-Trinidadian" synonymously.

3. As Sommer argues with respect to Latin America, and as we glean from Eric Williams's "Mother Trinidad," inclusion in the national "family" by no means ensures inclusion as equal.

4. Where I disagree with Benítez Rojo is in his claim that an appropriate counterpoint to the modernizing logic of *mestizaje* is the resolution of Caribbean differences into "insoluble differential equations, which repeat their unknowns."

The rhetoric of *mestizaje* in postrevolutionary Cuba is more complex still, clearly functioning within a modernizing logic but linked nonetheless to social policies of racial equality and redistribution of wealth.

5. For discussions of the symbolism of the Jíbaro, see Márquez, "Nationalism," and Den Tandt, "Tracing."

6. Here I allude, of course, to Samir Amin's concept of "delinking," outlined in a book of that name.

7. Walcott's celebratory references in his Nobel acceptance address to the Indo-Trinidadian Ramleela, or performance of versions of the Hindu epic *Ramayana,* are an important gesture at including Indo-Trinidadian cultural practices in a national imaginary often thought of as exclusively Creole. However, he performs this inclusion by celebrating the Ramleela as sheer "exuberance," a "celebration of a real presence," "faith," and ritual renewal through sacrifice; the Ramleela becomes the sign of a naturalized and spontaneous Indo-Trinidadian culture, and Indo-Trinidadians become sentimentalized natives rather than struggling citizens implicated in political contestations. Cul-

tural production itself is thus wrenched out of the realm of politics. His strategy for "including" Indo-Trinidadians in the national imaginary, then, ignores the fact that performances and funding of the Ramleela are embedded in a politics of intercultural *competition*. For the Ramleela is not a site of timeless and spontaneous celebration, or even of inevitable cultural hybridity, but of cultural struggle. I suggest that Indo-Caribbean cultural production may be better understood not only in relation to a politics of cultural hybridity, but also as an assertion of ethnic identity, which may sometimes participate in a politics of racial purism and separatism. Moreover, if we think of Walcott's discursive displacement of class and race differences as symptomatic of a deep anxiety about those differences, it becomes striking that the profound *gender* inequalities in the Caribbean provoke no such anxiety or accompanying fantasy of equality. I will return to this point later.

8. It is one of the great ironies of decolonization in Trinidad that racial tensions have taken the form of horizontal competition between blacks and Indians (the two largest ethnic groups) rather than vertical competition of blacks and Indians together against the small and economically privileged French Creole elite. Despite an oppositional tradition that has attempted to unite Africans and Indians along class lines since the 1930s, hegemonic political discourses have consistently posed the economic advancement of Africans and Indians in mutually exclusive terms. In particular, according to mainstream Afro-Trinidadian discourse, Indians dominate the private sector and threaten to "take over" the economy. Mainstream Indian discourse, on the other hand, charges that Africans have historically been favored in the public sector and that Indians have been culturally marginalized. Crucial to my analysis is the claim that PNM and the UNC, the "black" and "Indian" parties, have historically shared an interest in maintaining these racial demarcations and oppositions. For evidence of the collusion between the leadership of the "black" and "Indian" parties to crush the Black Power struggles of 1970, when it appeared that the mostly Indian sugar workers would join the Black Power demonstrators, see Raffique Shah. For evidence that reports of income disparities between Africans and Indians are greatly overstated, see Yelvington's *Producing*, 66–68, and Ryan and Barclay's *Sharks*, 144.

9. "Dougla" is the only word that specifically designates a person of mixed African and Indian descent; it derives from a Hindi word for bastard. For an extended discussion of the cultural politics Trinidadian discourses of race and the dougla, see Puri, "Race."

10. Chutney soca is the recent musical form that hybridizes two already hybrid forms: chutney, which is generally thought of as predominantly Indo-Trinidadian, and soca, which hybridizes soul and calypso and is generally thought of as predominantly Afro-Trinidadian. In each case, however, "Trinidadian" marks a variety of musical influences.

11. For a fuller statement of this cultural nationalist position, see Parmasad, "Wedding." For feminist analyses of the chutney dancing phenomenon, see the archives of the Caribbean Association for Feminist Research and Action and works by Tejaswini Niranjana and Rosanne Kanhai. The following pages offer a very abbreviated version of my reading of Drupatee's song "Lick Down Me Nani" and the debate the song triggered; the complete version appears in Puri, "Race, Rape, and Representation."

12. "Wining," or "winding the waist," is a dance movement in which the waist, hips, and pelvis gyrate. It is often seen during carnival in response to calypso or soca. From an Indian cultural nationalist point of view, therefore, it would be considered Afro-Caribbean. For an excellent account of wining and carnivalesque sexuality, see Miller, "Absolute Freedom."

13. Holi provides a space within Hindu culture in which intoxication, drunkenness, and public expressions of sensuality, caste, class, and gender boundaries are much less rigidly policed. Moreover, just as in carnival, instances of a ritual reversal of power occur in association with Holi, as for example, in the North Indian town of Mathura, when the women ritually beat the men of the town.

14. "Dhoti" refers to the loose-fitting draped clothing worn by Indian men; "jhandi" refers to Hindu prayer flags. Both are commonly used markers of Indian difference. In Brother Marvin's song, however, they are used to mark the inseparability of self and other.

15. For an account of the controversy surrounding this calypso, see Constance, *Tassa*, 46–48, and Warner, "Ethnicity," 282–90.

16. In "Race, Rape, and Representation," I read Espinet's short story "Barred: Trinidad 1987" as elaborating a dougla poetics. A similar claim might be made for her recent play "Indian Robber Talk."

17. The dougla poetics of Chris Garcia's 1996 "Chutney Bacchanal," for example, is only marginally different from any number of "all o' we is one" or "wine and jam" tunes. That being said, however, lest the "frivolity" of "Chutney Bacchanal" be chalked up to the corrupting influence of Creole carnival, I note that the video of the song, with its construction of a coyly titillating femininity, probably derives more from the song-and-dance sequences of commercial Bombay cinema than from Creole carnival.

## Works Cited

Amin, Samir. *Delinking: Towards a Polycentric World.* London: Zed Books, 1990.

Benítez Rojo, Antonio. *The Repeating Island: The Caribbean and the Postmodern Perspective.* Trans. James Maraniss. Durham: Duke Univ. Press, 1992.

Bhabha, Homi. "DissemiNation: Time, Narrative, and the Margins of the

Modern Nation." In *Nation and Narration,* ed. Homi Bhabha, 291–322. London: Routledge, 1990.

Brathwaite, Edward Kamau. *Contradictory Omens: Cultural Diversity and Integration in the Caribbean.* Mona, Jamaica: Savacou, 1974.

Brereton, Bridget. *Race Relations in Colonial Trinidad: 1870–1900.* Cambridge: Cambridge Univ. Press, 1979.

Constance, Zeno Obi. *Tassa, Chutney and Soca: The East Indian Contribution to the Calypso.* San Fernando, Trinidad: Privately published (Jordan's Printing Service), 1991.

Den Tandt, Catherine. "Tracing Nation and Gender: Ana Lydia Vega." *Revista de Estudios Hisp nicos* 28 (1994): 3–24.

Espinet, Ramabai. "Barred: Trinidad 1987." In *Green Cane and Juicy Flotsam: Short Stories by Caribbean Women,* ed. Carmen C. Estévez and Lizabeth Paravisini-Gebert, 80–85. New Brunswick: Rutgers Univ. Press, 1991.

Fernández Retamar, Roberto. "Caliban: Notes towards a Discussion of Culture in Our America." In *Caliban and Other Essays,* trans. Edward Baker. Minneapolis: Univ. of Minnesota Press, 1989.

Froude, James Anthony. *The English in the West Indies, or The Bow of Ulysses.* London: Longmans, Green, 1888.

James, C. L. R. *Minty Alley.* London: New Beacon, 1971.

Kanhai, Rosanne. "The Masala Stone Sings: Indo-Caribbean Women Coming into Voice." Paper presented at conference Challenge and Change: The Indian Diaspora in Its Historical and Contemporary Contexts, University of the West Indies, Trinidad, 11–18 August 1995.

Khan, Aisha. "What Is a 'Spanish'? Ambiguity and 'Mixed' Ethnicity in Trinidad." In *Trinidad Ethnicity,* ed. Kevin A. Yelvington, 180–207. Knoxville: Univ. of Tennessee Press, 1993.

Mahabir, Kumar, and Mahabir, Sita. *A Dictionary of Common Trinidad Hindi.* El Dorado, Trinidad: Chakra, 1990.

Maharaj, Satnarayan. "Mahasabha Answers Back. Debate: Douglarisation or Pluralism." *Trinidad Guardian,* 7 October 1993, 25.

Márquez, Roberto. "Nationalism, Nation, and Ideology: Trends in the Emergence of a Caribbean Literature." In *The Modern Caribbean,* ed. Franklin W. Knight and Colin Palmer, 293–340. Chapel Hill: Univ. of North Carolina Press, 1989.

Miller, Daniel. "Absolute Freedom in Trinidad." *Man* 26 (1991): 323–41.

Niranjana, Tejaswini. "'The Indian in Me': Gender, Identity and Cultural Politics in Trinidad." Paper presented at conference Challenge and Change: The Indian Diaspora in Its Historical and Contemporary Contexts, University of the West Indies, Trinidad, 11–18 August 1995.

Parmasad, Kenneth. "The Wedding Tent and the Public Space: Towards an Understanding of Indian Cultural Practices in Trinidad." Paper presented at Conference, Challenge and Change: The Indian Diaspora in its Historical and Contemporary Contexts, University of the West Indies, Trinidad, 11–18 August 1995.

Puri, Shalini. "Race, Rape, and Representation: Indo-Caribbean Women and Cultural Nationalism." *Cultural Critique* 36 (May 1997): 119–63.

Reddock, Rhoda. "'Douglarisation' and the Politics of Gender Relations in Contemporary Trinidad and Tobago: A Preliminary Exploration." *Contemporary Sociology* 1, no. 1 (1994): 98–127.

Ryan, Selwyn, and Lou Anne Barclay. *Sharks and Sardines: Blacks in Business in Trinidad and Tobago*. St. Augustine, Trinidad: Institute of Social and Economic Research, University of the West Indies, 1992.

Sampath, Niels M. "An Evaluation of the 'Creolisation' of Trinidad East Indian Adolescent Masculinity." In *Trinidad Ethnicity*, ed. Kevin A. Yelvington, 235–53. Knoxville: Univ. of Tennessee Press, 1993.

Segal, Daniel. "'Race' and 'Colour' in Pre-Independence Trinidad and Tobago." In *Trinidad Ethnicity*, ed. Kevin A. Yelvington, 81–115. Knoxville: Univ. of Tennessee Press, 1993.

Shah, Raffique. *Race Relations in Trinidad: Some Aspects*. San Fernando, Trinidad: Classline Publications for the Committee for Labour Solidarity, 1988.

Shohat, Ella. "Notes on the 'Post-colonial.'" *Social Text* 10, nos. 2–3 (1992): 99–113.

Sommer, Doris. *Foundational Fictions: The National Romances of Latin America*. Berkeley: Univ. of California Press, 1991.

Stallybrass, Peter, and Allon White. *The Politics and Poetics of Transgression*. Ithaca: Cornell Univ. Press, 1986.

Stewart, John. "Ethnic Image and Ideology in Rural Trinidad." In *Social and Occupational Stratification in Contemporary Trinidad and Tobago*, ed. Selwyn Ryan, 149–65. St. Augustine, Trinidad: Institute of Social and Economic Research, University of the West Indies, 1991.

Walcott, Derek. *The Antilles: Fragments of Epic Memory*. New York: Farrar, Straus and Giroux, 1993.

Warner, Keith Q. "Ethnicity and the Contemporary Calypso." In *Occupational Stratification in Contemporary Trinidad and Tobago*, ed. Selwyn Ryan, 275–91. St. Augustine, Trinidad: Institute of Social and Economic Research, University of the West Indies, 1991.

Williams, Eric. *Forged from the Love of Liberty: Selected Speeches of Dr. Eric Williams*. Ed. Paul Sutton. Port-of-Spain: Longman Caribbean, 1981.

Yelvington, Kevin A. "Introduction." In *Trinidad Ethnicity*, ed. Kevin A. Yelvington, 1–32. Knoxville: Univ. of Tennessee Press, 1993.

———. *Producing Power: Ethnicity, Gender, and Class in a Caribbean Workplace*. Philadelphia: Temple Univ. Press, 1995.

## 2

# Soca and Social Formations: Avoiding the Romance of Culture in Trinidad

*Stefano Harney*

The expressive cultural forms of the English-speaking Caribbean are receiving increased scrutiny. The growth of postcolonial theory has meant new attention not only to traditional literary forms (however renewed) but also to other forms of expression such as dancehall, dub poetry, calypsos, and chutneys, both in the Caribbean and in the diaspora. In this sense the growth of postcolonial studies in the Caribbean differs from the earlier attention of what is sometimes called the West Indian literary renaissance (Ramchand, *West Indian*). New attention to other forms should be welcomed, not least because it might finally help bring commercial success in the new "world music" marketing category to numerous struggling artists in the Caribbean or make local production easier. As someone who studies the Caribbean, I am happy to see the new attention and to see new critical voices rising from the Caribbean itself and its diaspora.

But in our enthusiasm to bring to light the practices and inventions of Caribbean musics and of Caribbean carnivals, to name two important expressive forms, there are dangers too. At the risk of downplaying some of the potential liberatory and transformative aspects of these cultural forms in the Caribbean, I will focus instead on some of the dangers of reading too much into these forms. By extension, I mean to comment on the attendant danger of relying too heavily on readings of cultural ideology in any interpretation of Caribbean nation-states. I suggest instead that any analysis of ideology in cultural practices should to be articulated with other kinds of analysis, with other measurements and interpretations. These might include a range of interdisciplinary concerns including state formation, class formation, institutional practices, social mobilizations, and larger conditions of political economy. In fact, my argument is that without this kind of articulation, we risk a cultural reductionism as harmful in its own way as the economic reductionisms that have often plagued the study of the Third World. Put another way, if we want to understand Trinidad, we should not suppose a priori that Black Stalin's "Burn Dem"—a calypso famous for its incisive social commentary on racism—is a more fruitful site of analysis than *Platt's Oilgram Price Report,* a petroleum industry newsletter that reports on the social and political investment climate in oil-producing Third World nations (Renwick, "Government," 32).

To argue that these dangers are real, I will focus here on one musical form, the calypso, also called soca music. I hope to show that an isolated interpretation of calypsos could very easily lead to a social description of Trinidad plagued with inaccuracy and deficiencies. At a time when some theorists in disciplines like performance studies, cultural studies, and postcolonial studies are in fact using readings of cultural forms to interpret nation-states and their conditions, I think such a cautionary note is vital.[1] Such studies do not disengage expressive forms from the socius but rather use them as the primary evidence in arguing a description of that socius. But as primary evidence, expressive culture in Trinidad, for instance, can be unreliable. I aim to show, in fact, that soca is particularly unreliable as a reflection of social formations in Trinidad.

## Calypso and Society

What does even the casual visitor to a calypso tent in Trinidad encounter? First a social space of great energy. Creativity, certainly, and linguistic and musical facility, but not these alone. What makes the calypso so attractive is its topicality, its engagement with current politics, social issues, local scandal, and international events. One could enter a tent in the late 1980s and hear a calypso about Tiananmen Square followed by one about a local newscaster, then one praising Trinidad as the most peaceful and racially diverse nation on earth. In calypso: branché sur son lieu, attentif aux rythmes du monde.

41   *Soca and Social Formations*

the 1990s, one could hear about Trinidad's own brief coup, about the rise of crime, or about a minister's tryst, all in one evening. Forty years ago one could have listened to a calypso about the Suez crisis. This is, of course, the found material that scholars of the cultural and social find so alluring. But a night at the calypso tent is only a partial glimpse of life in Trinidad. The people listening to calypso that night get up the next morning and go to work in the Canning's beer and soda bottling factory or the National Bank at the Trincity mall, or they might not have work at all. Perhaps they get up the next day and plan a "lime," a picnic, by the river out in Toco, a rural area of rivers, beaches, and great beauty, or try to think of a way of getting two thousand dollars into their bank account temporarily so they can apply for an American tourist visa and work illegally in a section of Brooklyn that will make them dream of Toco. Perhaps they will head for the University of the West Indies to lecture on contemporary literature. The theorist who does not accompany these people from the calypso tent to their next destination risks missing a great deal, perhaps even developing a false impression.

Nor does ethnography alone protect the theorist. My argument is not that cultural forms are less reliable than the people who employ them. A comparison of two recent ethnographies of Trinidad is helpful here. Kevin Yelvington's very good study of working-class Trinidadian women is an ethnography grounded in both local and global struggles. Daniel Miller's ethnography of celebrations and reading of modernity gives much less sense of the conflicts out of which various forms arise (Yelvington, *Producing;* Miller, *Modernity*). To accept uncritically the accounts of people in their daily routine in Trinidad is often as dangerous as accepting the account of Trinidad in the calypso. People go to the market for produce surrounded by a history. They go to work amid the institutions and practices of a political economy. To all of these they bring, of course ideologies, a habitus, and sometimes resistance and contention. The sites of action vary, as does the "continuity or transformation of structures," as Anthony Giddens puts it (*Social*). An analyst attempting to say something about a society must be alert to as many of these sites as possible. Much may be going on outside expressive cultural forms, and much may be hidden not just in but from the action of daily life. I contend that in Trinidad much else outside the calypso, and often contradictory, demands our attention.

Of course this is not to say there is not much going on inside the calypso. There is: ideology, for one thing. In analyzing some of what is happening, I will focus on ideology in the calypso. By ideology I mean, following Jürgen Habermas (*Theory*), ideas that legitimize certain kinds of domination. Or as Giddens writes, "how structures of signification are mobilized to legitimate the sectional interests of hegemonic groups" (84). I want to identify in particular two ideological constructs and one counterideological construct in the current calypso. Two of these embedded ideologies might be interpreted as harmful and regressive and one as potentially empowering—as counterhegemonic. For this argument, all three are to be viewed with considerable caution. The first element I want to investigate is the ideology of gender, taking the form of an objectification of women, especially in the so-called party soca songs. The second element is the ideology of nationalism, inscribed with a racial hierarchy particular to Trinidad's history. Both of these ideological strains can be identified as reinforcing the sectional interests of hegemonic groups. The third element is the counterideology of the political outsider, an image of the calypsonian as a critic of politics as usual, and concomitantly the idea of the calypso as a site of meaningful resistance or "liberation." If the calypso does contain all three of these ideologies, then from the outset we can see that it is a contradictory form.

The calypso in Trinidad has long been the site of larger social formations in race, class, gender, and nationhood.[2] But although the calypso may be an autonomous site of social construction. other evidence suggests that these constructions are not hegemonic. This evidence suggests also that it may not accurately reflect either a hegemonic bloc or a counterhegemonic force in the Caribbean. Again, this is not to suggest that calypso cannot reflect or influence Caribbean life, cannot be a site where we glimpse struggle or resistance. But how much of our attention does it warrant in practice, and what other areas of investigation suffer from insufficient intellectual capital—are maldeveloped by our commitments to culture?

### Ideology and Gender

Let me begin with a couple of examples of the ideology of gender hierarchy in the calypso, manifested in the following instances by an objectification of women in prominent calypsos. I should say first of all that there are structural conditions of domination in the administration of the form. Men run the calypso tents, staff the judging tables, own the recording studios, and order the performance line-ups. They still dominate the government, whose heavy hand is never far from funding, judging, and invitations. Stage antics, dancers, and symbols tied to carnival performance represent another field of play, another matrix of male domination. But here I will make only a specific analysis of some typical lyrics. Two prime examples are Crazy's "Nani Wine" and "The Dollar Wine" by Colin Lucas. Both these calypsos were massively popular, one in the late 1980s and one in the early 1990s. They were both contenders for "Road March"—the people's choice on the carnival days themselves. But they were also favorites throughout the carnival season, running from just after Old Year's (New Year's Eve) to Carnival Tuesday. Both calypsos and both calypsonians then made the rounds of the satellite carnivals that run through most of the year. The calypsonian Crazy, known for the stunts of his early days such as swinging out onto the stage "like Tarzan," is what Trinidadians call a dougla. In the language and dialect spoken by descendants of Trinidad's indentured Indian workers this translates as bastard, but in contemporary Trinidad the word has lost some of its social sting. Nani, on the other hand, has picked up some meaning. Not only does it mean grandmother, it also is slang for vagina. (A subsequent calypso by a fifteen-year-old Indian Trinidadian woman called "I Love My Nani" was banned from the airwaves as obscene.) When Crazy sings "Drupatee and she nani in soca tassa city," calypso goes ideological. I want to focus here on the objectification of the woman Drupatee's body, in fact its separation, but another point needs mentioning. Crazy is also writing ideologically against a racial hegemony in the calypso form that privileges the bass of soca over the Indian tassa drums. "Soca tassa city" does not exist. There is a place called "Soca City," and it is dominated by African Trinidadians. On the other hand, Crazy's objectification of an Indian woman, even the accompaniment of a chaperon figure (in the double entendre), is an all too familiar calypso image used by African Trinidadians in characterizing young Indian women as innocents locked away by Indian elders and hiding a secret rapacious sex drive, one that can be unlocked only by the Afro-Trinidadian calypsonian.

Colin Lucas's "Dollar Wine" is a classic Trinidadian party song, complete with its own dance. "Leave off the small change, give me big money wine," sings Lucas, repeating what his female dance partner has said to him. The slang "wine" means a rhythmic gyration of the hips in dance, but the gyration is read by others as variously socially and sexually challenging depending on its degree and on the social and class setting of the dance. Colin Lucas attempts in his song to titillate the audience as much as possible. His hip thrusts increase in intensity as he obligingly "gives her the dollar wine." Here again great sexual desire is attributed to the woman and becomes only a site of Lucas's "heroic" obligations. Moreover, like "Nani Wine," in the thirty or forty times I heard it played throughout the season in 1993, the first notes of the song inevitably drew virtually all the women at the fete onto the dance floor, and most of the men. There are certainly grounds for a case of pervasive gender denigration in these very typical calypsos.

But what of contestation and resistance? In confining ourselves to the calypso, we find little. Consistently the two most popular female calypsonians of the past fifteen years have been Drupatee and Denyse Plummer. The former, an Indian Trinidadian who performs at both chutney fetes and calypso fetes, could be said to contest some aspects of the Afro-Trinidadian cultural hegemony. She maintains an Indian instrumental presence and sometimes uses lyrics referring to Indian culture in Trinidad. But in all of her popular hits she conforms to the standard themes of calypso, including the notion of the woman as sex object. Denyse Plummer, a French Creole, unlike Drupatee, refrains from either suggestive dancing or self-referential sexual lyrics. She sticks to a classic part of the calypso genre—what I will describe later as the ideology of the national form. Both have produced slower calypso—that is, songs that are not designed to be their big hits for the season—as have a number of less well known women. But the dominant messages of the calypso remain firmly those produced by men. The gender hierarchy in the calypso form remains secure.[3]

But does this interpretation help us understand the place of women in Trinidad and its diaspora, or do we risk distortion? If the observer were to conclude from an analysis of the calypso that this expressive form reflected gender relations in Trinidad, would this conclusion be accurate, or would it misrepresent gender relations in contemporary Trinidad? In fact, there is some evidence that such a conclusion would be a distortion. But this is evidence accumulated outside a study of expressive cultural forms in Trinidad. I will offer three pieces of evidence here. First is the presence and impact of Hulsie Bhaggan in Trinidadian politics in the past three years. Second is a UNIFEM study on the state of women in the world. And third is the result of my ethnographic work on the recent Trinidadian diaspora (of the post-oil-bust years). All three seem to point to change, resistance, and contention not captured in the expressive form. All three point to the danger of a cultural reductionism.

Trinidad's most vital political movement of the past few years has been led by an Indo-Trinidadian woman. Hulsie Bhaggan, like most Indian Trinidadians interested in politics, had a choice. Join either the United National Congress Party (UNC) or the reformist National Alliance for Reconstruction (NAR). But the NAR had roots in elitist, French Creole, and upper-strata Afro-Trinidadian professional classes interested in prying leadership away from a deeply corrupt independence party, the People's National Movement (PNM). Some Indo-Trinidadian intellectuals and professionals do belong to the NAR, but few working-class Indians from Central (as the belt of largely Indo-Trinidadian communities is known) belonged, in every sense of the word. Bhaggan joined the UNC. But the UNC too, like its rival PNM, had grown more corrupt and rigid over the years. Bhaggan eventually rebelled against the leadership of UNC in several theatrical ways. These included a one-woman sit-down strike in the middle of Trinidad's main east-west highway and a similar hunger strike on the steps of the supreme court building. For these and her challenge to the UNC leadership she received both praise and condemnation. She was condemned by much of the traditional Indo-Caribbean community, party, and religious leadership for the stated reason that she was driving a wedge through a community that was finally posed to take over the reins of power in Trinidad (and subsequently did) and for the unspoken reason that she was a woman challenging a male hierarchy. She was praised widely by Trinidadian women of various backgrounds for her courage. She was also praised by some Afro-Trinidadian leaders whose glee at the UNC's division left them barely able to hide their racial bias and their sense that here was proof of the corruption in the Indian community (a charge leveled so effectively by that community at the Afro-Trinidadian-dominated government bureaucracies). Eventually Bhaggan was expelled from the party, ran as an independent, and lost. But she remains a force in the Trinidadian politics.[4]

Nor is Bhaggan's presence an anomaly. UNIFEM's conference report from the fourth World Congress in Beijing places the Caribbean well ahead of many other developing regions on women's issues. And though Cuba leads the region in gender equality, the Caribbean as a whole has made two decades of progress in income and women's health (UNIFEM, *World Conference*). The indicators are always problematic, but are they as problematic as the calypso form, which has shown no movement in gender relations in the past two decades?

My own current ethnographic research in Toronto and New York has to be considered in the context of migration and its forces, but I think it is revealing (Harney, *Nationalism*). The calypso form is also a diasporic form now, so it may not be a mismatch to look at some evidence from the diaspora. What I have found in interviews with families and with local colleges and universities is extraordinary participation in higher education among Trinidadian women. In New York City nearly half of the women between the ages of twenty and forty I have questioned are in school or have recently completed some form of further education. Perhaps because aid is available, the rate is even higher in Toronto. These rates are more than double the rate in Trinidad, a rate that has also been rising steadily in the past twenty years. As one informant declared, "When I go to my lecture all I see are other women from Trinidad, not too many men, mostly women." One would want to investigate the role of systemic racism on gender relations in the migration process in the United States and elsewhere to have a full understanding of this female enterprise. How are Caribbean men excluded? But the education of women remains a story not captured in the calypso form.

Moreover, to this outside evidence we may offer countering testimony: Jacqui Alexander's groundbreaking work on homophobia in the Caribbean state ("Not Just"). Some forms, like dancehall, may quite accurately reflect the kind of state violence Alexander uncovers. Calypso's form of homophobia is mockery, when it touches on the subject at all. But as Alexander points out so well, state-sanctioned homophobic repression is widespread, and the social formation around it is characterized not by familiar mockery, but by rabid fear. And thus again the calypso appears to be a poor prism for seeing these issues.

Both heterosexual and homosexual women in Trinidad, especially working-class women, often suffer physical and psychological abuse. But they also resist, not in the calypso very often, but in daily life, in higher education, in leading migration chains, in political strategies against the consolidation of local property and state enfeeblement. We could not label these aspects of the calypso ideological under this definition if they did not in fact represent some kind of power relationship. In general, men do exercise a degree of abusive power over women in Trinidad. But I would argue this power is highly provisional. Anthropologist Michael Lieber once wrote, "To witness the Trinidadian man's typical attitudes and actions toward women, together with the abuses generated by economic greed and rapacious lust for status at the expense of others, is most ugly in Trinidadian life" (*Street*, 110). But Lieber's research was done before the women's movement took hold (at least in Trinidad).[5] It is still ugly in places, but is it possible that the changes in gender relations are running ahead of their representation in soca? If so, why does this disjuncture exist? Why is the calypso not a site of more resistance, and why is it not more representative of change?

When these other levels of analysis are brought to bear on the subject, it seems that new questions and new voices come through. The limited voice of the occasional dissenting female calypsonian is augmented and amplified by the everyday resistances of Trinidadian working women. The question that arises becomes not how calypsos embody oppressive gender relations and sometimes their contention, but why the calypso is not an accurate picture of gender relations in Trinidad and its diaspora. In other words, Why is the social not reflected in the cultural, and why is the calypso not a decisive site of social construction of gender?

### Ideology and Nationhood

As should already be apparent from the discussion on the ideology of gender hierarchy, little can be discussed in Trinidad without reference to race. It is not surprising that Stuart Hall found race in Trinidad a classic example of overdetermination ("Negotiating"). Just as fierce as the calypso's objectification of women is its privileging of African- and Creole-based culture in the nationalist discourse. Infamous calypsos like Black Stalin's "Caribbean Man" sparked controversy in this regard (Deosaran, "Caribbean"). But the more general calls in many calypsos for everyone to participate in carnival and "come together as one" also privilege, in a less assertive but still ideological way, cultural forms and political histories that have been dominated by non-Indian parts of the population. Still, this ideological formation is complex. It could not be said to be an Afro-Trinidadian hegemonic discourse in any straightforward sense. The 20 or 25 percent of Trinidad's population who would not describe themselves simply as black or Indian influence if not dominate the nationalist discourse

(Yelvington, *Producing*). Many of them, light-skinned African Trini-dadians and the so-called French Creoles most of all, denigrate any black culture based on an African return. They, like many other mixed peoples and numbers of Syrians, Portuguese, and Chinese, pre-fer a national myth of Trinidadian origins in which forms like carni-val, steel band, calypso, and several foods and many phrases begin in Trinidad, not in Africa. Of course they would be even less likely to call something Trinidadian or national that clearly comes out of India. Nonetheless, they mediate any talk of an African/Indian division. Class enters the picture too, with many of the groups I have mentioned oc-cupying positions where they can produce and reproduce their vision of the nation. I have written at length on this nationalist discourse elsewhere (*Nationalism*); here I only want to mark the complexity be-fore moving on to a reading of several calypsos about the nation.

Let us again choose two popular calypsos: Sparrow's classic "Model Nation" and Superblue's "Bacchanal Time." These two calypsonians reached the pinnacle of popularity, Sparrow in the 1960s and 1970s and Superblue (first as Blueboy) in the 1980s and 1990s. The two ca-lypsos are emblematic of the two eras in several ways. Sparrow's clas-sic is infused with the spirit and hope of the independence era and the earnest nation building that accompanied it (Oxaal, *Black*). Superblue, back from a cocaine habit that seemed to represent the excesses of the early 1980s with its oil revenue–fueled consumption, became a peren-nial Road March contender in the 1990s. These two calypsos are very different. Sparrow's calypso is a medium-tempo piece. Superblue's is a party song, and in fact several informants have confided to me that Superblue uses some kind of Obeah to render crowds so entranced.[6] They also differ in the way they reinforce an Afro- and Creole-Trinidadian dominance in the concept of nationhood. Sparrow's idea of every race and creed together in the model nation is underpinned by the assumption that these races and creeds are willing participants not only in independence but also in a nation building that privileges the newly created, the uniquely Trinidadian, over the traditional, the preserved, the continuous. This confronts Indians in Trinidad in two ways. First, Indo-Trinidadian culture relies in part on a strong strand of traditionalism. Second, the Indo-Trinidadian community was largely excluded from the independence movement and subsequently from a share of power, especially during the period of Sparrow's song.

Superblue's party anthem represents in some ways the result, the consolidation, of this dominance thirty years on. Now Trinidad and

Tobago are "breaking away" (dancing wildly) without reference to race or creed. Trinidad the nation is presumed to be absolutely synonymous with carnival, an Afro-Creole-Trinidadian form. To the extent that Indo-Trinidadian culture is referenced in these calypsos or hundreds of others like them, it is as a contribution to archetypal Trinidadian forms like the calypso, carnival, and even cricket. The innocence of Superblue's party anthems hides a deeper confidence that the nation is a carnival nation.[7] Indo-Trinidadian culture is reduced to the efforts of an Indian spin bowler or the pepper sauce in a national dish.

But does the calypso help us understand race sufficiently in Trinidad? Does a study limited to expressive forms leave us asking the wrong questions? Again, there are strong reasons to answer yes to the second question, and perhaps no to the first. I suggest that in Trinidad today the interesting story is not the persistence of racialized narratives, but the defiance of them in its political institutions. For against the backdrop of these narratives, not to mention decades of racial oppression in Guyana, the United States, and elsewhere in the hemisphere, Trinidad's most recent election saw the peaceful transfer of power to the UNC and the first Indo-Trinidadian prime minister, Basdeo Panday. My argument of course is not that racial hierarchy is unimportant or even that it has greatly receded. My argument is that the calypso, or any other expressive form in Trinidad at the moment, does not capture the story, does not help the analyst ask the really vital question: What is the nature of the stability of Trinidadian institutions (if this is what is responsible) that such a transition should be possible while the cultures remain deeply inscribed with racial bias and hierarchy and even the concept of nationalism itself is inscribed with these defects? How has racism in popular sentiment been contained? It is not too bold to claim that this question is of more immediate interest (not least to people in the region) than the question of where and how the popular forms contain racist and racialized ideologies. I suggest, moreover, that cultural studies is not capable of answering this particular question in the Caribbean on its own. After all, now that Basdeo Panday is prime minister, he is bringing chutney into carnival, as *Billboard* magazine, of all sources, reports (Ferguson, "Carnival"). It is emphatically not the case that chutney came into carnival first and Panday into the Red House (the national parliament of Trinidad) second.

## Ideology and the Weapons of the Weak

The pitfall of cultural reductionism leads also to another defect, the romanticism of resistance and "liberation" in cultural forms. If culture becomes the principal field of study, then those who insist on some level of voluntarist analysis are forced to find it amid cultural forms. This analysis may locate voluntarism in carnivals, for me a notorious example, or in other parts of performative culture—in beliefs, language, daily practices. Sometimes it can be found there. But what about in the calypso? By restricting ourselves to the form, are we forcing an interpretation in this direction? The calypsonian often fosters a view of himself (rarely herself) as an outsider, especially in the world of politics. Political calypsonians like Sugar Aloes, Cro Cro, and Watchman often insist in the lyrics of their calypsos on their status as outsiders. We have seen already that this outsiderly pose is modified immediately by the calypsonian's complicity in at least two kinds of domination, gender and racial. There are noteworthy exceptions to this complicity. David Rudder is one. But in general the calypsonian is a vehicle for these two ideologies. But the third ideology I want to discuss is located not in the calypso alone, but also in Western academe. The calypsonian promotes an exaggerated sense of the challenge his or her art poses to the state and political order. Calypsonians are fond of the bravura exhibited in insisting that they will speak their minds no matter what the consequences. They are also fond of referring to themselves as the voice of the people. In these assertions they have some support from recent scholars of the Caribbean, who also exaggerate the challenge that some cultural forms pose and make much of the cultural form as a site of resistance, of playful subversion, of disappearance, and so forth.

The recent collection titled *Liberation Cricket* (Beckles and Stodardt, eds.) is a prime example. Although this book takes as its inspiration the work of C. L. R. James, like so much recent work about James it chooses its inspiration selectively. The collected essays all have as their theme the idea of West Indian cricket as a site of the invention of West Indian identity and often the site of transgression—of disindentification, cooptation, resistance to the way the game was played in England, to colonial rule, to neocolonialism, and so forth. But is this a description of liberation? James would not regard this as the same as "the self-mobilization of the masses," to use Cornelius Castoriadis's description of James's politics ("C. L. R. James," 296).

Liberation requires breaking people's chains. In *Beyond a Boundary* James gives us an analysis of the social formations in cricket. But elsewhere he gives us revolutionary politics, even while he was writing this book. In 1958 James was also writing in *Facing Reality* that "the valuable elements in all fields of contemporary culture can be preserved and made available only in light of a new vision of the world, and of humanized relations throughout the length and breadth of society. . . . To do this, if only ideologically, demands an assimilation of this culture in the light of both the experiences and activities of the proletariat. All those who do not proceed from this basis end up as whining or utopian snipers at capitalist culture, even when they do not actually defend it" (102). And further: "The nationalist struggle is not only for independence but to liberate new forms of social organization" (173). There is no new vision of the world and no search for new social organization in *Liberation Cricket*. But that is what James meant by liberation. There is, unfortunately, a lot of sniping.

Yelvington again shows the most caution in his contribution to this collection, warning us not to reduce Caribbean social formations to cricket. But most other contributors seem content to write under a revolutionary banner about a decidedly nonrevolutionary activity. The point may be turned against them; to paraphrase James, What know they of liberation cricket who only liberation cricket know? In Trinidad liberation has been helped by a firm understanding of social formations and the analysis of cultural sites like cricket. I would argue, however, that in the search for liberation political actions such as the 1937 oilfields labor riots, the 1970 Black Power revolution, and the Muslimeen coup in 1990 are more fruitful sources of inquiry than cricket and calypso.

Starting with the last of these, we start with a man, unlike the calypso pretenders, who really is feared by the state, Abu Bakr. Abu Bakr and his Muslimeen followers—numbering only an officially reported 134—took over Trinidad for a brief period in 1990. The coup was provoked by the government's refusal to make concessions on disputed land. Although it is hard to have much sympathy for the coup plotters because of their indiscriminately violent tactics, the issue of land reform behind their claim is far more relevant than the platitudes of harmony mouthed by many a calypsonian. The role of calypso in Bakr's radical movement has been one of assimilating his actions into a status quo framework, as Kevin Birth nicely shows us in his ethnographic article "Bakrnal: Coup, Carnival, and Calypso in

Trinidad." The calypsonian here plays the role of trying to reintegrate a break with tradition into that tradition. But in fact rebellion, not parliamentary order, is as much a tradition in Trinidad as in Jamaica and elsewhere. The calypsonians may sing of peace, or harmony, or every creed and race, and of parliamentary democracy, but Trinidadian people have not acted in accordance with this conservative narrative.

Troops joined students in 1970 and nearly overthrew the government then too. At that time McCandle Dagger and his NJAC (National Joint Action Committee) party spoke of liberation and acted on it. Uriah Butler and Adrian Cola Rienzi, leaders respectively of the unions of oilfield workers and cane workers, frightened the Colonial Office witless in the late 1930s by bringing African and Indian workers together, and the office responded with its customary brutality (Jacobs, *Butler*). This was also a liberation movement. When calypso and carnival integrate these events into their traditions, then, as Kevin Birth demonstrates with Abu Bakr, they are not playing a liberatory role. In fact it is not too much to say they may be playing a counterliberatory role.

I want to term this counterideology, somewhat awkwardly, the ideology of the weapons of the weak (Scott, *Weapons*). Again I pose the question, What do we gain and what do we lose from an analysis based on an expressive cultural form? In this last case, I believe we lose twice—once from missing the richness of dissent and rebellion outside the form, and again if we make the mistake of exaggerating the liberatory importance inside the form. These struggles are recorded in some calypsos, but they do not emanate from the calypso form. They are not hatched in calypso tents. To wait for the struggle in the calypso tent is to miss much of their power.

In fact, most calypsonians recognize and support a system of competitions that rely on current state sanctions and approvals. Moreover, the vast majority support one of two parties, either the independence movement party, the PNM, or the reformist NAR. Few if any express support for the Indian-based UNC, and only one or two are for the socialist–Black Power party, NJAC. (Watchman is an exception here. But although his suggestions to vote NJAC evoke momentary screams of approval from the crowds at the concerts, NJAC languishes at election time.) Most important, critiques emanate from a bourgeois framework, rarely offering radical reform as an articulated response and in fact often taking the very reactionary position that politics always has been corrupt and always will be and that there is nothing the people can do but laugh. Is it possible that this music, like cricket and like carnival, is not a weapon for the weak, but an opiate? As much as it is a forum for the construction and reconstruction of identities, it may also be the forum for the reproduction of passivity, pessimism, and bourgeois political ideology. Researchers who insist on its importance risk not only misleading themselves but also choosing a liberal capitalist form and excluding other social contentions and formations that might challenge that capitalism.

The calypso, like cricket and carnival, has been important for establishing and maintaining the social relations of a bourgeois democracy and citizenry in Trinidad. Typical of such democracies, Trinidadian social relations contain articulation of systemic racism and sexism, something reflected in the calypso. But also typical of such democracies are antiracism, antisexism, and liberation movements. With rare exceptions, the calypso in Trinidad does not usually help us to see these latter features. The analyst who seeks to understand Trinidad through the calypso will discover soca's role in the social formations of the former but will miss the larger invention and consolidation of other movements and institutions outside this expressive cultural form. The analyst who presumes that a popular form like the calypso must by definition embody the liberatory features will seek to promote the calypso form to the disadvantage of some of these same movements and institutions in Trinidad. If cultural studies is to continue to help us understand and change the world, we will have to regain a sense of the expressive form as the site, as Gayatri Spivak contends, where what is left out is marked ("Gayatri"). But simply substituting what is left out as a new truth will not do. It will merely reconstitute domination in its own image.

### Notes

1. At the risk of singling out any text from within a very large body in cultural studies, I suggest that for an example no worse than any other one look at anthologies such as Foster, Siegel, and Berry, *Bodies of Writing, Bodies in Performance* (1996), or Parker, *Nationalisms and Sexualities* (1992), or my own work *Nationalism and Identity* (1996). All place great faith in the ability of cultural texts to reveal social and political life.

2. I am taking my use of social formation from Nicos Poulantzas, "Social."

3. That neither woman is of African descent leads us into the interlocked fetishisms of color, culture, and sexuality. On the other hand, before their ascendancy, Calypso Rose—an African Trinidadian—was the most prominent calypsonian.

4. David Rudder, Trinidad's most thoughtful, if not most popular, calypsonian, sang her praises in his calypso hit "Go Down" (1996), asking everyone to "Go Down with Hulsie," reenacting her sit-down strike.

5. Lieber writes in his introduction, "I conducted the fieldwork upon which this book is based in Port-of-Spain, Trinidad in 1969 and again in 1970–71" (xiv). However, his book was published in 1981.

6. Obeah, a kind of magic, is loosely connected in the minds of many Trinidadians with the practices of Shango Baptists, a Christian sect with heavy African religious influences.

7. I believe that in my book *Nationalism and Identity* I overstated the theme of the carnival nation, as Daniel Miller also does, partly because of the seductiveness of these images in the hands of Superblue and other artists.

## Works Cited

Alexander, Jacqui. "Not Just (Any)Body Can Be a Citizen: The Politics of Law, Sexuality, and Postcoloniality in Trinidad and Tobago and the Bahamas." *Feminist Review* 48 (autumn 1994): 5–23.

Beckles, Hilary, and Brian Stoddart, eds. *Liberation Cricket: West Indies Cricket Culture.* Manchester: Manchester Univ. Press, 1995.

Birth, Kevin, "Bakrnal: Coup, Carnival and Calypso in Trinidad." *Ethnology* 33, no. 2 (1994): 165–78.

Castoriadis, Cornelius, "C. L. R. James and the Fate of Marxism." In *C. L. R. James: His Intellectual Legacy*, ed. Selwyn Cudjoe and William E. Cain, 277–97. Amherst: Univ. of Massachusetts Press, 1995.

Deosaran, Ramesh. "The Caribbean Man, a Study of the Psychology of Perception and the Media." In *India in the Caribbean*, ed. D. Dabydeen and B. Samaroo. London: Hansib, 1987.

Ferguson, Isaac. "1996 Carnival Laden with Festivity, Social Change." *Billboard* 108, no. 12 (1996): 9.

Foster, Thomas, Carol Siegel, and Ellen E. Berry, eds. *Bodies of Writing, Bodies in Performance.* New York: New York Univ. Press, 1996.

Giddens, Anthony. *Social Theory and Modern Sociology.* Stanford: Stanford Univ. Press, 1987.

Habermas, Jürgen. *The Theory of the Communicative Act.* Cambridge: Polity Press, 1986.

Hall, Stuart. "Negotiating Caribbean Identities." *New Left Review,* January–February 1995, 3–14.

Harney, Stefano. "Bacchanal Time: Class and Citizenship in the Caribbean World." Manuscript, 1997.

———. *Nationalism and Identity: Culture and the Imagination in a Caribbean Diaspora.* London: Zed Books, 1996.

Jacobs, W. Richard, ed. *Butler versus the King: Riots and Sedition in 1937.* Port-of-Spain: Key Caribbean Publications, 1976.

James, C. L. R. *Beyond a Boundary.* London: Pantheon, 1983.

James, C. L. R., Grace C. Lee, and Pierre Chaulieu. *Facing Reality.* 1958. Detroit: Bewick, 1974.

Lieber, Michael. *Street Life: Afro-American Culture in Urban Trinidad.* Boston: G. K. Hall, 1981.

Miller, Daniel. *Modernity, an Ethnographic Approach: Dualism and Mass Consumption in Trinidad.* Oxford: Berg, 1994.

Oxaal, Ivar. *Black Intellectuals and the Dilemmas of Race and Class in Trinidad.* Cambridge, Mass.: Schenkman, 1982.

Parker, Andrew, et al., eds. *Nationalisms and Sexualities.* New York: Routledge, 1992.

*Platt's Oilgram Price Report.* New York: McGraw-Hill.

Poulantzas, Nicos. "On Social Classes." In *Classes, Power, and Conflict,* ed. Anthony Giddens and David Held. Berkeley: Univ. of California Press, 1982.

Ramchand, Kenneth. *The West Indian Novel and Its Background.* London: Faber and Faber, 1970.

Renwick, David. "Government Encourages Private Ownership and Exploration." *Petroleum Economist* 63, no. 6 (1996): 32.

Rohlehr, Gordon. *Calypso and Society in Pre-Independence Trinidad.* Port-of-Spain: Gordon Rohlehr, 1990.

Scott, James. *Weapons of the Weak: Everyday Forms of Peasant Resistance.* New Haven: Yale Univ. Press, 1985.

Spivak, Gayatri. "Gayatri Spivak Speaks on the Politics of the Postcolonial Subject." *Socialist Review* 20 (1990): 25–32.

"Status of Women in the Caribbean." Bustamante Institute of Public and International Affairs, 1987.

UNIFEM. "The World's Women, 1995: Trends and Statistics." Report in preparation for the fifth World Conference on Women, United Nations, New York, 1995.

UNIFEM. *World Conference on Women.* New York: UNIFEM, 1996.

Yelvington, Kevin A. *Producing Power: Ethnicity, Gender, and Class in a Caribbean Workplace.* Philadelphia: Temple Univ. Press, 1995.

———, ed. *Trinidad Ethnicity.* Knoxville: Univ. of Tennessee Press, 1993.

## 3

# Trinidad Romance: The Invention of Jamaican Carnival

*Belinda J. Edmondson*

Like many of the black middle class, to my mother a calypso
was a matter for ne'er-do-wells and at best the common people.
I was made to understand that the road to the calypso tent was
the road to hell.

C. L. R. James, Beyond a Boundary

C. L. R. James's memories of the outrage the black middle class of early twentieth-century Trinidad felt toward the "ribald ditties" (*Beyond,* 25) that emerged from the calypso
competitions for the annual carnival are instructive for contemporary
viewers of Caribbean carnivals. It reminds us that, contrary to the
popular images of Caribbean carnivals as "neutral" ground in these
rigidly stratified societies, this ritual has always been a site of class
conflict and negotiation. Perhaps even more critical for us to note is
that it is the *black* middle class that finds the carnival particularly offensive. As James observes, the black middle class at that time perceived the rituals of black peasant culture as a "mass of poverty, dirt,
ignorance and vice which . . . surrounded the islands of black middle-
class respectability like a sea ever threatening to engulf them" (17).

This historical perspective on the Trinidad carnival and its most significant import, the calypso, is a necessary preliminary to the ensuing
analysis of the recent creation of a Trinidad-style carnival in another
English-speaking island, Jamaica. Jamaica, more so than Trinidad, is
a heavily black Caribbean society whose entrenched middle class has
a particularly conflicted relationship with the rituals of an overwhelm-

ingly black working-class culture that still defines the national image. (For example, black, working-class reggae superstar Bob Marley is in a sense a metonym for the island at large in the global imagination.) In recent years soca music, the descendant of the traditional Trinidadian calypso, has made an unprecedented comeback in Jamaican society, where the dominance of ska and reggae music, and particularly the intensely nationalist worldview that went with the latter, had placed soca firmly in the musical-cultural rear. Indeed, loyalties to reggae—and its contemporary variant, the explosively popular dancehall—remain entrenched, significantly, in the Jamaican working class. However, the soaring popularity of soca among the Jamaican middle classes resulted not merely in the allocation of more radio and disco play but in an unprecedented event: in 1990, Jamaica instituted its first carnival.

The event was more or less modeled on the Trinidad carnival, and indeed several officials from Trinidad were asked to help oversee it. Indeed, not only were Trinidadian soca bands brought in to perform, but even the carnival costumes from Trinidad were on display at the Jamaica carnival ("No Reggae"). It seemed imperative that the "bacchanal" (as carnival revelries are referred to in Trinidad) had a high degree of "authenticity." However, in Jamaica the mechanics are different in two respects: the carnival begins on Easter Sunday evening rather than right before Lent so as not to compete with the Trinidad carnival, which attracts droves of middle-class Jamaicans as well as non-Caribbean tourists, and it is more or less confined to the capital city of Kingston, although in recent years it has expanded to include strategic precarnival revelries in Montego Bay and other rural Jamaican towns. Whereas in Trinidad the carnival is embedded in deep historical traditions dating back to the combined religious rituals of the slave population and the Spanish slaveowners, in Jamaica the birth of carnival was a prepackaged, intrinsically commercial event.

My focal point here is that the importing of carnival, one of the most potent symbols of "Caribbeanness" in both popular and intellectual discourse, represents an overtly political issue: the struggle for symbolic primacy between the working class and middle class in Jamaica, played out through the "war" between soca and dancehall music in that country. I intend to argue that classic romanticized representations of Caribbean carnival are being used in an *intra*-Caribbean framework to obscure a classic class struggle over the symbols of nationhood and cultural identity. Thus the invention of Jamaica carnival is part of a wider cultural project to redefine the parameters of Jamaican nationhood with particular configurations of race and class relations as its critical postulates.

There are three important qualifiers to note before I proceed. Jamaica has always had a carnivalesque tradition of celebration in the Jonkanoo, an African-based ritual dating back centuries in which members of the community dress in elaborate costumes and masks and dance in the streets around Christmastime. Not surprisingly, Jonkanoo—or John Canoe, its European name—was discouraged by the European elites of nineteenth-century Jamaica as an immoral and debauched example of "African barbarism" that threatened their political hold on the black community (Wilmot, "Politics"). The implicit political radicalism of the Jonkanoo tradition is, if anything, the antithesis of what Trinidad-style carnival has come to mean in the Jamaican context. It seems very clear that to Jamaicans, carnival is *not* an African ritual like Jonkanoo in the sense that African rituals are often associated with rural, traditional culture, itself associated with primitivism and "backwardness." By contrast, in Jamaica carnival has come to epitomize some of the most salient myths of modernity, as I mean to illustrate.

Second, by no means am I implying that the Jamaica carnival is inauthentic *merely* because of its commercial nature, or opposing its commercialism to the "authenticity" of the Trinidad carnival, which has long been a vehicle for commercial interests in that country, as have been almost all the carnivals in the region. Indeed, the European carnivals of the nineteenth century were deliberately reorganized as military processions to attract tourists, gradually submerging into the "classical body" of the state (Stallybrass and White, *Politics,* 177). Many cultural rituals in our world change, self-consciously or not, to reflect the new particularities of the era and the community. The rhetoric of "authenticity" that often accompanies academic discussions of cultural practice like this one tends to use the working class or rural peasantry as the validating badge for the cultural practice in question. Since it is assumed—particularly in discussions of cultural practices of the communities of the African diaspora—that the rituals are a direct reflection of working class–peasant culture itself, any adaptation by the bourgeoisie must therefore be a dilution or distortion of a static but presumably pure original. I do not necessarily subscribe to this view; it seems to me that there are many ways in which cultural practices are transmitted from the less powerful group to the more powerful that do not diminish the presence of the former or usurp its power. Nevertheless, such cultural transmissions can also be transformed into strategies of group containment. It is with this idea that I am centrally concerned.

Last, I do not mean to imply that the importing of carnival to Jamaica is a unique phenomenon:[1] Toronto has long held the pan-Caribbean Caribana carnival every summer, at first as a local event for its Caribbean community and eventually, after the city realized its moneymaking potential,, as a full-blown tourist event. Similar carnivals take place, among other places, in Notting Hill, London, and in Brooklyn, New York.

The dynamic nature of the transmission of carnival to various locales forces us to recognize culture as part of a system of commodity exchange. Culture that is mediated by and organized around systems of commodity exchange, if not exactly produced, by them, is endemic to late twentieth-century capitalism, with its attendant view of cultural artifacts as so many items for consumption. In other words, the commodifying of cultural practice has become an intrinsic part of that very Caribbean culture it commodifies. The issue here, then, is not commodification as such, but the means to which it is put. The principal question is, Which consumers are being targeted? For *whom* is this carnival being produced, and why?

The origins of the contemporary Jamaica carnival lie in the organization of the "private party" first known as the Orange Carnival. Started in the early 1980s by a group of young, wealthy, mostly "white"[2] Jamaican men from prominent Jamaican merchant families who regularly attended the Trinidad carnival, the Orange Carnival was an attempt to restage the Trinidadian version at home in the company of friends. The invited guests paid the equivalent of fifty dollars in United States currency to drink, dance, and wear costumes. In 1990 Jamaica's premier calypsonian Byron Lee (a "brown" Jamaican of Chinese extraction) joined forces with the organizers of the Orange Carnival—now known as the Oakridge Carnival—to make carnival a national event.

However, the two camps eventually split when the more democratically minded Lee decided that the final Road March would proceed through Half Way Tree, part of the "downtown"[3] area of Kingston, which would allow the revelers to be seen by the masses (the "massive" in Jamaican popular parlance), who for the most part cannot themselves participate—it costs about sixty dollars in United States currency just to buy a costume and join a band, thereby excluding most of the populace from joining in the festivities. The original Orange Carnival became confined to the wealthier areas of Kingston and eventually merged into the larger Jamaica carnival, which had taken precedence on the national stage.

At the outset the Jamaica carnival excited a great deal of conflict. The most prominent arguments against it, as they played out in the pages of the national newspaper, the *Jamaica Daily Gleaner,* were, first, that the carnival was a lascivious orgy that encouraged promiscuous behavior in the citizenry, and that its timing on Easter Sunday was a sacrilege against the Protestant Church; all of which was related to the second argument that the carnival was, in the words of an irate letter to the editor, a heathen ritual of a "damnable alien culture" introduced by the amoral members of the private sector. "I say let's leave carnival to countries and people who are living deads, and let us, on the other side, keep shining our light into the darkness, whether it comprehends us or not," the writer concluded. The peculiar mix of xenophobic nationalism and religious evangelism of that letter was reiterated in other letters to the newspaper espousing similar views. In another such, the author decried criticisms of evangelical American preachers who come to the island to hold crusades as invasions of American culture while the importing of another island ritual was lauded by those who presumably should know better: "I would like to know," the writer demanded indignantly, "if we are not being asked to be 'Trinidadized' by the filth called carnival" ("Special Forum").

The association of carnival with the philosophies of Roman Catholicism—the pre-Lenten carnival rituals are a hallmark of the Catholic communities of the Caribbean and Latin America—is fairly obvious in these diatribes. However, these attitudes can be understood only in the context of the relation of class and denominational affiliation on the island. In Jamaica there is a general perception that the Catholic Church—whose adherents are a minority in an overwhelmingly Protestant nation—has a heavily middle-class constituency, buttressed by the fact that the priests are disproportionately white and nonblack in a majority-black country. The prominent white Jamaican commentator of the newspaper, Morris Cargill, noted the silence of the Catholic Church on the clerical debates on carnival and opined that it occurred because "the Jesuits are subtle, well-educated men, highly versed in the sophistication of civilized life" who understand the "harmless" nature of "the rituals of the uncivilized" (Cargill, "Rising"). The image of the highly educated and therefore tolerant Catholic leaders is here being contrasted to the presumed intolerant puritanism of the not-so-sophisticated Protestant evangelical community—which is for the most part associated with black lower-middle-class and working-class constituencies on the island.[4] Cargill's discussion of Jesuit tolerance is part of a middle-class rhetoric linked to the kind of cosmopolitanism associated with urban modernity. By contrast, the puritanism inherent in the rhetoric of carnival's critics quoted above is associated with the traditional, usually rural, past. The religious debate over carnival in a sense became a debate over which constituency was to define the nation's moral parameters; the apparent "tolerance" of the middle-class community toward carnival—a class historically shown to be particularly *in*tolerant of the rituals of the peasantry—may have been perceived as an attempt to transcend the moral code, which is one of the more equalizing impulses in any society.

The third, and most significant, criticism of carnival was that the organized promotion of soca music through carnival was an attempt to squelch the primacy of dancehall and thus deny material success to its ghetto practitioners.[5] This argument was fueled by Lee's remark, reported in a Trinidad paper and reprinted in the *Daily Gleaner*, that reggae would have to take a "backseat" to soca during the carnival, which he later explained was necessary because reggae did not have the sort of rhythm that revelers could easily move along to in the streets ("No Reggae"),[6] this despite the fact that dancehall has had an ever-increasing presence in the Trinidad carnival. The perception here is about more than money or actual numbers of fans. A poll conducted in 1991 by the well-known Jamaican pollster Carl Stone revealed that 95 percent of dancehall fans do not attend carnival and soca events, and that the reverse is true of soca fans. Moreover, "there is usually a strong and visible presence of lighter shade people" compared with those who attend reggae events, and "the Soca people have almost twice the buying power of the Reggae crowd in spite of the fact that they represent only about some 10 percent of the Reggae masses," Stone concludes ("Soca"). Therefore it is evident that the two musical events operate fairly independently of each other in terms of economics and fan base.

Though, as we have seen, the apparently diffuse criticisms of carnival are fundamentally linked, it is the last one that reveals some of the core issues surrounding the production of Jamaica carnival.

To perceive the connectedness of these objections, it is important to understand the meaning of dancehall in the Jamaican social fabric. Reggae and all its variants have always existed in that society *despite* its social institutions and its upper and middle classes, never because of them. Bob Marley became an official national icon only after his ascent to fame in North America and beyond, and as with all commodities that are prized only as they are valued by the metropoles of London and New York, so too reggae and its stars. The irony is that Jamaica is now defined in the global market precisely by these products of black working-class "marginalized" culture.[7]

Dancehall is a product of the black urban ghetto—the racial qualifier is an important one—and the culture of dancehall contains a marked critique of hegemonic attitudes toward black ghetto people. (In its form, at any rate, if not always in substance. In recent years there has been a sustained criticism of dancehall by newspaper critics, who consider it as sleazily apolitical as its predecessor, the Marley era of reggae, was radically political.) In turn, a common view of the non-working-class population is, not surprisingly, that dancehall practitioners are "semi-literate and illiterate noisemakers masquerading as artistes" (Commentary, 6 November). Of particular concern to this constituency are the sexually suggestive lyrics, called "slackness" in popular slang—the moniker carries innuendoes of slothfulness and immorality—as well as the "bad" grammar used in the music, described in one account as "the language of Yahoolish and the song-dance of Baboonia" (Commentary, 17 July). Language carries particular weight as a class signifier in Jamaica and the English-speaking islands generally. The criticism of the grammar of dancehall therefore reflects an entrenched perception in these comments that the music is an atavistic African primitivism—"Yahoolish" and "Baboonia" are clearly code words for old racist stereotypes of blacks—that is dragging the nation away from the literate and the modern back into a preevolutionary, primitive state.

In 1991 the *Gleaner* produced a series of articles on the cost of dancehall finery, noting the "vulgarity" of the apparel and concluding with the implication that the poor who "indulged" in these accoutrements (many of which the middle classes could not afford, the reporter hastened to add) were responsible for their continuing state of poverty. In contrast, the lavish costumes displayed for carnival are consistently described by reporters in tones of admiration: "a rainbow of colours and bare sun-tanned bodies," one report called them

(Whyte, "Jamaica"), unlike the distaste evinced in Stone's observation of "the pervasive presence of people displaying gold and jewelry" to be found at the dancehall events (Stone, "Soca"). One such commentary critical of dancehall fans—titled "The Poor Ye Shall Always Have"—implied a biblical inevitability to the state of continuing poverty of the majority of Jamaica's population that was yet tied to its love of dancehall culture, even as it deplored what the author perceived as the complicity of the poor with their condition: "The poor must take responsibility for their poverty when their priorities are so skewed. For surely, giving these people money is only making hairdressers and higglers [the Jamaican term for the mostly female market vendors] wealthy, but not putting an extra scoop of rice on their children's plates" (Green, "Poor").

The tone of the commentary above implies that such a disproportionate share of the wealth should not go "only" to hairdressers and higglers, whose practitioners are overwhelmingly black working-class women. However, the money that wealthy Jamaican businessmen make from carnival is lauded by newspaper commentators as a much-deserved reward for helping to revitalize the tourism industry by instituting carnival (Stewart, "Tourism"). Oddly enough, there were no lengthy newspaper commentaries on the extravagance of the middle-class who, like dancehall fans, spend large sums of money to buy carnival costumes and participate in the various festivities. In fact the *Gleaner*'s senior editor mounted a stinging defense of middle-class extravagance: "Those who resent Jamaicans trying to develop a carnival should stop and think. It is useless wondering where people get the money from to go to the various carnival events. The fact is that some people have money, and it is no skin off anyone's back if they see prices escalating day by day and decide to enjoy themselves while they still can. Those who don't have the money simply stay away, watch the reports and enjoy vicariously" (Wint, "Joy").

Furthermore, the criticism that the carnival celebration was so expensive as to exclude the working class was met by newspaper commentators with scathing indictments of "fuddy duddies" and "left wing ideologues" who want to "control the fun of the people"—neatly reversing the familiar leftist rhetoric that opposed interests of the elite middle-class soca practitioners and the theoretically democratic principles of the state into the putatively democratic impulses of carnival and the supposed hegemonic imperatives of social egalitarianism: "The Government [is] trying to make us into what we are not, they would

Carnival organizer Byron Lee. *Daily Gleaner,* 1996; photographed by Winston Sill. *All photographs in this chapter courtesy of the Gleaner Co., Ltd., Kingston, Jamaica.*

This woman, dressed for church service and with Bible in hand, disapproves of the carnival march in Half Way Tree on a Sunday. *Daily Gleaner,* 1996; photographed by Rudolph Brown.

Jamaica carnival participants. *Daily Gleaner,* 1996; photographed by
Winston Sill.

Dancehall queen
Carlene. *Star*, 1995;
photographed by
Rudolph Brown.

Denyse Plummer performing at
the Jamaica carnival. *Sunday
Gleaner*, 1996; photographed
by Winston Sill.

have us abandon Dynasty and Dallas to watch some black and white Latin American left wing propaganda film or listen to Julius Nyerere talk rot about forming a trade union of the poor . . . Carnival will make money" (Wint, "Joy").

Another commentary titled "To Be Carnal Is Human" uses the most common defense of carnival sensuality: dancehall, with its lack of "gay abandon that soca engenders," divides by its "political and social message," thereby furthering class divisions in Jamaica. Further, according to the commentator, no one can dance to dancehall tunes (Wint, "Carnal"). (An extraordinary remark, given the innumerable dance crazes spawned by that musical genre.) One interview with carnivalgoers revealed that one of the key selling points for the occasion was the lack of violence, in contrast to the notorious displays of gunfire that accompany the dancehall events; this was attributed to the "happy" themes of soca music, as opposed to the presumably darker themes of dancehall that precipitate such drastic responses (Clarke, "Carnival").[8]

Despite its supposedly "light" themes, soca is perceived by the commentators to have a quasi-political function because, as the primary component of the carnival, its apparently happy and unifying themes allow for a powerful moment of democratic egalitarianism and racial unity. The multiethnic, multiclass dimension of carnival is its most celebrated feature, both in Jamaica and abroad. As one Jamaican commentator rhapsodized, "It was good to see Jamaicans from the upper reaches of St. Andrew [an upper-middle-class stronghold] and from the rat holes of the ghettoes forgetting their circumstances and coming together to let their hair down . . . to make love and to be people" (Wint, "Joy"), apparently forgetting that the people from the "rat holes" could not afford to participate. As if to further this particular vision of carnival as transcending color and political boundaries, the *Daily Gleaner* ran a series of short stories whose theme was love and sex at carnival. The protagonist of one such story, a red-haired tourist, dances among the "friendly locals" and feels "at one with . . . the Jamaicans and the city, all lively and sensual" (James, "Magic").

The combination of breathless coverage and overwhelmingly supportive commentary in the national newspaper illustrate its concerted interest in promoting carnival. In particular, its defense of the "gay abandon" of carnival carnality as the great social equalizer has had a powerful role in shaping the discourse of cultural ritual, class, and race in Jamaica. The redefinition of the "bad" carnality of dancehall to the "joyful" carnality of soca and carnival reroutes the middle class's discomfort with the social and racial meaning of dancehall into an easy division between violence (associated with dancehall and ghetto dwellers) and order (the orderly, business-savvy commercialism of carnival, which received an endorsement from Jamaica's premier white businessman, Gordon "Butch" Stewart); the immorality of "slackness" lyrics versus the playful erotic suggestiveness of soca lyrics; the vulgarity of ostentatious ghetto gold chains versus the "colorful" carnival pageantry.

In particular, the manipulation of images of women in both musical movements has become the lightning rod of the controversy over which one better defines the nation. The apparently "brazen" demeanor and deliberately explicit outfits of the female dancehall acolytes—who often serve as symbols of the music on record covers —are a defiant retort to middle-class attitudes toward poor black women. In the Jamaican social arrangement, poor black women should aspire to respectability, which usually means a "ladylike" (read submissive) comportment, modest attire, and a devoutly Christian faith, all of which translates into invisibility. The nostalgia for the mythical devout, maternal black woman is nowhere more apparent than in constant scolding newspaper commentaries about the flamboyance of female dancehall fans. There is the inevitable comparison of the dancehall vamp to the sainted "lowly woman, in that old dress":

> Nothing will come between her [the dancehall fan] and those soup bowl earrings or that new outfit she needs to wear to Super Dee [a popular dancehall event]. And if she can't pay her rent this month because she has to dye her hair pink, well, that is how it goes. . . . It is not shocking to see a boy in rags collecting bottles at 2 A.M. while his muma, she with the corn-coloured hair, does the down and dirty in [dancehall] fashions. . . . Sure there are women of abject poverty who love their children. Their hair is in tight little braids, covered by a piece of cloth. And in a clean, but very old dress, they walk door to door selling toilet paper or other goods. . . . They don't wear sneakers with lights on the back [or] . . . b[atty]-riders." (Green, "Poor")

It would seem that poor black women can be virtuous only by wearing "tight little braids" as opposed to "corn-coloured hair," an "old dress" as opposed to the criminal "batty-riders" (known as hot

pants in the United States and Europe). As Jamaican cultural critic
Carolyn Cooper puts it, "The black woman is often seen as the poor,
strong, suffering type, valiantly struggling to bear the massive chip
on her shoulder. She is definitely not sexy—at least not in public"
("Browning").

In the meantime, the brown-skinned women of the middle class are
very publicly showcased in beauty pageants and adorn travel posters
as the quintessence of Jamaican female pulchritude. The erotic dancing of middle-class, often brown, women in carnival is described by
newspaper commentators not as "down and dirty dancing" but rather
as "a natural therapy for physical expression" (Stone, "Church"). The
officially sanctioned public displays of brown, as opposed to black,
female sexuality suggest that, in order for the brown woman to be used
as a symbol of the nation, the image of the sexualized black woman,
ingrained even more deeply in Western consciousness, must first be
exorcized from the picture by the image of the desexualized black
maternal figure.[9] Accordingly, the Jamaica carnival's premier symbol
is a scantily clad brown woman, Queen Carlene.

Queen Carlene's ubiquitous presence in recent carnival celebrations
is an interesting crossover element much commented on in the *Daily
Gleaner,* as if to prove the harmonious convergence of dancehall and
soca. Queen Carlene is known as an "uptown massive," a middle-
class, nonblack woman who participates in the dancehall dance and
fashion contests and is, in the words of one *Gleaner* commentator, the
"exotic darling of corporate Jamaica" (Fairweather-Wilson, "Dance
Hall"). One commentator claimed that Queen Carlene has helped to
break class barriers by the simple fact that she wears dancehall fash-
ions (Soas, "Legitimisation"). Certainly the reverse cannot be true;
when a dark-skinned, black Jamaican radio personality wore her hair
in African-style knots on television, the television station was inun-
dated with a barrage of furious calls and letters from outraged viewers who were appalled at her audacity in wearing a fashion associated
with black working-class culture in the very middle-class medium of
national television (Hutchinson, "Bumpy-Head"). The difference in
response to these two examples of social integration suggests that the
movement of class and race integration is very much limited to one
direction: the cooptation of black working-class symbols by the brown
middle class might be seen as a dissolution of class barriers, but the
movement of black working-class symbols into the arena of the middle

class is perceived as invasive. The ideal of the classless, raceless society is in the hands of the middle class to dispense or withhold according to its own social belief system.

While at one level Queen Carlene's presence is supposed to signify precisely the happy melding of musical and class divisions, at another level it serves to further highlight the distinctions. Carlene is an anomaly; dancehall queens are overwhelmingly black and working class. That the organizers of the carnival saw fit to use a non-working-class brown woman whose features are more palatable to establishment notions of beauty signals the obscuring of dancehall's ghetto connections by exoticising it and containing it within carnival rituals.

Further, the acclaim for white and light-skinned Trinidadian and Barbadian calypsonians—Denyse Plummer of Trinidad and Emile Straker of Barbados—in Jamaica underscores the racial dynamics at play in the Jamaica carnival. In Trinidad Denyse Plummer has met with hostility from crowds who see calypso as the sole preserve of black men, in much the same way that dancehall is perceived as a black male entity in Jamaica. By contrast, the popular Trinidadian calypsonian Black Stalin, known for his black nationalist lyrics, though he has performed in Jamaica during carnival season, has never played *in* the Jamaica carnival (Henry, Entertainment Section). It would seem that Black Stalin's lyrics are uncomfortably close to the "darker" lyrics of reggae. And indeed, the image of calypso and calypsonians as a political medium of the black working class is a common one in Trinidad, memorably etched in the Trinidadian novel *The Dragon Can't Dance,* whose rebellious ghetto calypsonians are also members of gangs. However, in a country where the national motto, "Out of Many One People" has consistently been used to obscure the undesirable image of a black majority, the multiethnic image of the Trinidadian carnival is particularly appealing to Jamaica's brown middle class. Indeed, the United States rhetoric of "melting pot" democracy that so attends talk of Jamaican national unity might be read as a way of uniting and thereby transforming painful histories of white hegemony and black anger, this despite the fact that a considerable number of Jamaica's official national heroes are black revolutionaries who fought white political power: Marcus Garvey, Morant Bay Rebellion leader Paul Bogle, maroon warrior Nanny.

In recent years, as blacks enter the corporate world in ever-increasing numbers, Jamaican whites and near-whites have been complaining of "reverse prejudice." They charge that blacks refer to Jamaica as "black man country" and in turn perceive them as foreigners.[10] The grassroots rhetoric of black nationalism in Jamaica—always a presence since Marcus Garvey's "Back to Africa" movement of the 1920s, if not before—became enmeshed with the discourse of national independence and self-determination that accompanied the island's independence from Britain in 1962, such that a claim to a national identity was, in many quarters, a claim to a politicized idea of black identity. That is, in order to be Jamaican one must accept the inherently political idea that African-descended black culture defines Jamaicanness.

For Jamaica's white and brown population, Trinidad's relatively large populations of nonblacks offers a more ideal multicultural mix. If carnival functions politically as a symbol of Trinidad itself, then the performance of this particular cultural ritual allows all of the various ethnic groups to participate in the idea of Caribbeanness by diffusing the balance of power. However, economic and social power are different, if related, entities. Thus, whereas in Trinidad carnival means, at one level, a fantasy that inverts social power from high to low, from white and brown to black, in the performance of Jamaica carnival a black country becomes, momentarily, brown.

Here brownness becomes, in the Jamaican context, more than merely a prestigious skin color: it is a form of social philosophy that allows not only the brown but also the black middle classes to share in modernity—that is, in the values and consumptive patterns of "First World" technological societies, associated with a sort of sociopolitical "whiteness"—and yet retain an intrinsic Caribbeanness. C. L. R. James's mother feared and loathed carnival calypso culture in Trinidad because, for Trinidad's black middle class, the carnival was a symbol of social regression, an immoral African retention that would deny them a chance at the social mobility associated with modernity and "progress."

Similarly, because of dancehall's inescapable association with blackness and poverty, it is not, despite its commercial power, a viable symbol of Jamaicanness for this particular group. The Trinidad carnival is a high metaphor of West Indian culture and yet retains, for Jamaica, a seeming apoliticality. It melds a mélange of colors into a neutral "brownness" and racelessness, even as it serves to preserve the social distinction of brownness, in the arcane logic of Jamaican social relations. The hope for future brownness is nowhere more apparent than

72 *Belinda Edmondson*

in the critique of black identity politics by black *Gleaner* commentator Dawn Ritch in a piece titled "The De-culturation of Jamaica," where she argues, "Development comes from cross-pollination. . . . the issue of colour is really pointless because in a thousand years the whole world will be brown. As George Bernard Shaw said, 'The only final cure for the colour problem is to be found in bed.'"

In the final analysis, it is the myth of multiculturalism, with all of its corollary attributes of nationalism and modernity, that is the primary benefit carnival bestows on the Jamaican middle class. The black middle class can share in the social privileges of brownness; the brown and white middle classes may avail themselves of the associative images of an African-descended ritual without having to recognize its political dimensions as a product of poor, black culture: accessibility without contamination. Thus Ritch can argue, without a hint of irony, "Money and education render the colour of one's skin irrelevant. The real wickedness is that those black people who have benefitted from their money and education keep agreeing with the poor that black identity can offer any consolation at all. Identity is a product we sell."

In *The Politics and Poetics of Transgression*, Peter Stallybrass and Allon White argue that "repugnance and fascination are the twin poles of the process in which a *political* imperative to reject and eliminate the debasing 'low' [by the dominant order] conflicts powerfully and unpredictably with a desire for this Other" (5). The dominant class attempts to reject and eliminate the "bottom" only to find that it is dependent on it and actually "*includes* that low symbolically as a primary eroticized constituent of its own fantasy life" (5). Jamaica, always a paradox, both affirms and belies this statement, inasmuch as the symbolic "low" is itself in question. That is, the very issue of *what* constitutes the low and *who* will decide those parameters is central to this conflict of power to define and contain a larger contradiction that is at the heart of Caribbean identity: the desire for both modernity and "roots."

### Notes

I thank Hilma Brown of the *Gleaner* for her kind assistance in procuring all the photographs reproduced in this chapter.

1. Jamaica is not the only Caribbean nation to import the Trinidad carnival. St. Thomas, another overwhelmingly Protestant nation, similarly imported the Trinidad carnival in 1950. Like the Jamaica carnival, the St. Thomas carnival takes place at the end of April.

2. I use the term "white" here in its social and political sense; unlike the situation in the United States, where racial categories are rigidly drawn, in the West Indian context they are more nebulous; as such, people of mixed black and white heritage can be called "brown," "red," or "white" depending on the circumstances.

3. The term "downtown" in Kingston originally referred, technically speaking, to the old commercial district of the city near the wharf, of which Half Way Tree is not a part. However, the term has now come to encompass all the urban areas in which there is a heavy working-class or "ghetto" presence.

4. In all fairness, it should be noted that the Anglican Church, the official denomination of the island and the center of black and brown Jamaican middle-class respectability, also denounced carnival (see, for example, "Anglican Church Raps Carnival"). But it is the evangelical community that was most vociferous (see "Christians Say No to Carnival" and "Adventists Lash Carnival").

5. According to one Jamaican newspaper report, "The word on the street is that reggae is under pressure. Some people feel that soca is being pushed by certain class interests who are attempting to upstage reggae. It is felt in some quarters that those who like Soca do not want to identify with the crow. Thus class lines are being drawn. If you like Soca then you are an 'up-towner.' If you like reggae then you are a 'roots man'" ("Is There a Move to Suppress Reggae?").

6. Note, however, that Lee has subsequently made a concerted attempt to fuse soca with reggae in recent carnivals, and the result has been a musical combination called "soggae" (see "Soggae Carnival").

7. I am referring here to the response of the middle classes and the aspiring middle classes—the "massive" of Jamaica have always honored their heroes independently and in defiance of the opinions of the Jamaican "respectable" classes. I would emphasize, however, that the (white) American and European embrace of reggae, which is in large part responsible for its profit-making power, is also connected to a romanticizing of Jamaican ghetto culture.

8. However, Carolyn Cooper explains that the volley of gunfire displayed at dancehall events is a salute to the lyricism and creativity of the singer; see Cooper, "Lyrical." Moreover, I would suggest that the reason soca lyrics are perceived to be "happy" is that the soca songs with more overtly political themes are less likely to receive airplay in contemporary Jamaica.

9. The binary construction of brown women's sexuality against that of black women has an eerie parallel in the images of white female sexuality that are similarly constructed against black female sexuality in American and European culture. For example, see Gilman, "Black."

10. For one example of white perceptions of black racism in Jamaica, see "Racism in 'Black Jamaica'?"

## Works Cited

"Adventists Lash Carnival." *Daily Gleaner,* 23 April 1990, 1a.

"Anglican Church Raps Carnival." *Daily Gleaner,* 5 April 1991, 1c.

Cargill, Morris. "Rising Prices: Carnival." *Sunday Gleaner,* 21 April 1991, 8a.

"Christians Say No to Carnival." *Daily Gleaner,* 14 April 1990, 7a.

Clarke, Claire. "Carnival—the Ultimate Escape." *Daily Gleaner,* 8 April 1991, 3b.

Commentary. *Sunday Gleaner,* 6 November 1994, 5c.

Commentary. *Sunday Gleaner,* 17 July 1994, 3e.

Cooper, Carolyn. "There's a BROWNING in the Ring!! Tra-la-la-la-la?" *Lifestyle* 23 (November–December 1992): 25.

———. "Lyrical Gun: Metaphor and Role Play in Jamaican Dancehall Culture." *Massachusetts Review* 35 (autumn–winter 1994): 429–47.

Fairweather-Wilson, Jean. "Dance Hall . . . Sifting the Truths." *Sunday Gleaner,* 17 April 1994, 3d.

Gilman, Sander. "Black Bodies, White Bodies: Toward an Iconography of Female Sexuality in Late Nineteenth-Century Art, Medicine and Literature." In "Race," *Writing and Difference,* ed. Henry Louis Gates Jr., 223–61. Ithaca: Cornell Univ. Press, 1985.

Green, J. J. "The Poor Ye Shall Always Have." *Sunday Gleaner,* 21 May 1995, 5c.

Henry, Balford. Entertainment Section. *North American Daily Gleaner,* 27 February 1996, 12.

Hutchinson, Joan Andrea. "No Bumpy-Head Gal." *Sunday Observer* (Kingston, Jamaica), 28 April 1996, 7.

"Is There a Move to Suppress Reggae?" *Sunday Gleaner,* 8 March 1990, 8a.

James, C. L. R. *Beyond a Boundary.* London: Hutchinson, 1963.

James, Osmund. "The Magic of Carnival." *Sunday Gleaner,* 8 April 1994, 6d.

"No Reggae during Carnival." *Daily Gleaner,* 27 March 1990, 6c.

"Racism in 'Black Jamaica'?" *Sunday Gleaner,* 21 April 1996, 8-9.

Ritch, Dawn. "The De-culturation of Jamaica." *Sunday Gleaner,* 7 April 1991, 5c.

Soas, Norma. "The Legitimisation of Dancehall Style." *Sunday Gleaner,* 31 July 1994, 2.

"Soggae Carnival." *Sunday Gleaner,* 10 April 1996, 10.

"A Special Forum on . . . Post Carnival Reflections," *Daily Gleaner,* 11 May 1990, 7a.

Stallybrass, Peter, and Allon White. *The Politics and Poetics of Transgression.* Ithaca: Cornell Univ. Press, 1986.

Stewart, Gordon "Butch." "Tourism—Larger Than Life." *Sunday Gleaner,* 14 April 1991, 6c.

Stone, Carl. "The Church and Carnival." *Daily Gleaner,* 10 April 1991, 6c.

———. "Soca Kill Reggae? Absolute Rubbish." *Sunday Gleaner,* 8 April 1991, 6c.

Whyte, Justin. "Jamaica Carnival '94: . . . Bigger, Better with Breathtaking Costumes, Revelry." *Sunday Gleaner,* 17 April 1994, 6c.

Wilmot, Swithin. "The Politics of Protest in Free Jamaica: The Kingston John Canoe Riots, 1840 and 1841." *Caribbean Quarterly* 36, nos. 3 and 4 (1990): 65–76.

Wint, Carl. "The Joy of Carnival." *Sunday Gleaner,* 7 April 1991, 6c.

———. "To Be Carnal Is Human." *Sunday Gleaner,* 1 May 1990, 9d.

# 4

# All That Is Black Melts into Air: *Negritud* and Nation in Puerto Rico

*Catherine Den Tandt*

Esta criolla pelinegra y ojinegra,
boquirroja y dientiblanca;
esta cerrera, briosa,
resollante potranca,
temblorosa en el pecho,
temblorosa en las ancas,
me relincha una rumba en el oído,
y sobre el corazón un son me piafa.
Esta semisalvaje mediasangre,
ibera y antillana,
merece que la corra a todo escape
en la pista de llamas
sobre la mar Atlante
tendida entre ambas razas.

This dark-haired and dark-eyed Creole,
red mouth and white teeth;
this untamable, spirited,
panting filly,
trembling breasts,
trembling buttocks,
she neighs a *rumba* in my ear,
and paws a *son* upon my heart
This semisavage half blood,
Iberian and Antillian,
deserves to be ridden at a gallop
on the track of flames
upon the Atlantic Ocean
spread between both races.

Luis Lloréns Torres, "Copla mulata"

It is perhaps unfair of me to begin this discussion of cultural politics and race in Puerto Rico with an epigraph taken from the first verses of Luis Lloréns Torres' (1878–1944) poem "Copla mulata." A particularly offensive example of the *negrista* tradition of Hispanic Caribbean poetry that appropriates blackness in a burlesque or exotic fashion, "Copla mulata" represents one early twentieth-century attempt to celebrate a creole, mestizo Puerto Rico. The figure of the *mulata*, "spread between both races," provides the poet with a pornographic fantasy of identity as he rides his "caliente potranca . . . / la cuesta de la noche a la mañana" (hot filly . . . / from dusk to dawn) and proclaims her, at the end of his poem, "digna de ensangrentar en sus ijares / mis espuelas de plata" (worthy of staining my silver spurs / with the blood from her flanks) (Morales, *Poesía,* 43; see Depestre, "Aventuras," for a discussion of the *negrista* aesthetic in Latin America).

The violence of Lloréns Torres' metaphor, so difficult to read and so very pleasurable to attack, makes it particularly quotable for my purposes. For this canonized national poet and cultural figure is also the author of the much better known poem "Canción de las Antillas," an ode to the Antilles written in a grand epic style. Gone are the thinly veiled rape fantasies. The poet mentions "Indias bravas, libres" (savage, free Indians) and "etiópicas bahías" (Ethiopian bays), but mostly he calls upon ancient Greece and Rome, a Judeo-Christian heritage, and the riches of Caribbean geographies (still in a sexualized discourse) to sing, in paroxysms of patriotic lyricism, the glories of the Caribbean and of Puerto Rico (Barradas, *Para entendernos,* 194–98). It is for his contribution to this brand of conservative, Hispanophile, and elite nationalism that Lloréns Torres was elevated, during his lifetime and long afterward, to the status of national poet and patriot.

I disinter these two poems as representative artifacts of long-standing competing and complementary desires of identity in the Caribbean and most especially in Puerto Rico. It is the ambivalence dramatized by the juxtaposition of "Copla mulata" and "Canción de las Antillas" that interests me—on the one hand, to bracket race and *mestizaje* within a dehumanizing and degrading *negrista* poem is perfectly commensurate with the goals of white, Europhile nationalism; on the other hand, "Copla mulata" signals a kind of schizophrenic consciousness, a black and African presence that consistently undermines a white discourse always, in the end, under siege.

Pointing to this ambivalence and tension is hardly a startling critical feat. In Caribbean studies, and in the wider sphere of colonial and postcolonial studies as well as cultural studies, there now exists an established tradition of analysis that reads the construction of identity as the interplay and erasure of difference. One notable and very recent example of such work is Joseph Roach's *Cities of the Dead: Circum-Atlantic Performance,* where he notes, "Without failures of memory to obscure the mixtures, blends, and provisional antitypes necessary to its production, for example, 'whiteness,' one of the major scenic elements of several circum-Atlantic performance traditions, could not exist even as perjury" (6). In the Hispanic Caribbean, difference and erasure have most often been played out among the categories of blackness and Hispanicism, along with a sprinkle of *indigenismo* and various elaborations of *mestizaje.* Vera Kutzinski's work on race in Cuba, Doris Sommer's analysis of the foundational fictions of the Dominican Republic and Cuba, and Jorge Duany's discussion of the politics of race and the history of merengue in the Dominican Republic are just three examples of readings that display the inner workings of difference and identity in these specific national settings.

In Puerto Rico there exists a long history of this type of exploration, and it is really this history of critique and analysis that I was referring to when I opened with a comment about fairness. For to showcase "Copla mulata" is in a sense to circumvent, pass over, the work of writers, historians, and cultural critics who have, since the 1950s and even before, made mincemeat of the racist discourse displayed in the poem, as well as the brand of elite nationalism it served. But in spite of the massive project of cultural and political revision and excavation that characterizes these explorations of race in Puerto Rico over the past thirty or forty years, most especially what Juan Giusti Cordero calls *antillanismo* and *afroantillanismo*—that is, the concerted effort across disciplines and in various artistic media to claim Puerto Rico as an Afro-Antillian space ("Afro-Puerto Rican," 62)— race continues to be a highly contested category in Puerto Rico, particularly as it intersects and conflicts with nation and the ongoing dilemma of Puerto Rico's political status vis-à-vis the United States.

This contention was made very clear recently when a group of black Puerto Rican artists displayed their work in an exhibition titled *Paréntesis: Ocho artistas negros contemporáneos.* The exhibition opened in San Juan on 7 May 1996, and it featured the work of Edwin Velázquez, Ramón Bulerín, Gadiel Rivera, Awilda Sterling, Daniel Lind Ramos, Liz D. Amable, and Jesús Cardona. On the whole, reviews were appreciative of the mixed-media exhibition. It was the artists' decision to foreground race in *Paréntesis* that caused some controversy. Jorge Rodríguez of *El Vocero* ended his review with the following comment: "I think that what I saw was an exhibition of Puerto Rican artists, and not of any color. As Puerto Ricans, we are the synthesis of three races" ("Exhiben," 39). The reviewer for *Claridad* felt the need to explain that "the fact that in the United States blacks and Puerto Ricans are identified as disadvantaged minorities, almost equally, within the political and cultural context, does not make this exhibition the torch of racial separatism" (Maldonado Reyes, "Paréntesis," 24). Other reviewers accepted the premise of the exhibition and wrote sympathetically of the artists' desire "to see their reflections, their expressions in the face of the *Patria*" (Routte-Gómez, "Artistic," 27; see also Alegre Barrios, "Ocho," 72–73).

There is a great deal to be said about this exhibition and the reactions it engendered. On the one hand there is the veiled and not so veiled accusation that calling yourself black in Puerto Rico is unpatriotic, that it invokes a United States model of racial politics (segregationist) that does not correspond to Puerto Rico as a *mestizo* space. On the other hand is the artists' insistence that the discourse of *mestizaje* in Puerto Rico is just that, a discursive construct that reifies black culture in folkloristic celebrations of Afro-Caribbeanness and hybridity while obscuring the inequalities experienced by black Puerto Ricans. In a letter to *El Nuevo Día*, Daniel Lind Ramos, one of the participating artists, writes that "in our country we are constantly being reminded of our *negritud* (with all that this implies), but to say publicly that we are [black] is 'disapproved of'" "Un planteamiento," 148). There is a great deal of irony in Lind's comment, irony that, in some sense, takes us back to "Copla mulata" and "Canción de las Antillas," to the ambivalence and tension expressed by the juxtaposition of these two poems.

In the following pages I will return to some of the foundational moments of what I am calling Puerto Rican *negritud,* a narrative of blackness that weaves its way through the history of contemporary Puerto Rico in literature, cultural criticism, historiography, popular music, and other artistic media, often folding imperceptibly into hybridity and *mestizaje*. Puerto Rican *negritud* is under fire these days, from black Puerto Ricans themselves as well as from competing discourses of Puerto Rican identity. Dealt a severe blow by the populist politics of the Partido Popular Democrático (Commonwealth Party) and the institution of the Estado Libre Asociado in 1952, as well as by the ensuing emergence of *afroantillanismo* throughout the 1960s,

1970s, and 1980s, Hispanophile nationalism went underground to some extent, but it never disappeared. With the Partido Nuevo Progresista (Statehood Party) firmly in power (March 1997) and the Young Project to sponsor another plebiscite on the issue of status having successfully passed a congressional vote in February 1998, Hispanophile nationalism is set to move again, especially in the context of linguistic identity and the preservation of Spanish in Puerto Rico.

Finally, although they do not abandon the discourse of *negritud,* a new generation of artists and cultural critics such as Mayra Santos Febres, Juan Flores, Teresa Hernández, and others have moved away from the metaphor of race in their varied articulations of Puerto Rican identity. In general, these figures call for models of identity that take into account migration patterns to and from the United States and within the Caribbean itself, as well as the cultural context of Puerto Ricans living in the United States. The hybridity they envision is a more postmodern version of hybridity, one that foregrounds movement and discontinuity rather than race. Instead of representing popular culture in literary works (a prominent and very forceful feature of *antillanismo*), they turn to popular culture itself—salsa, Puerto Rican rap, MTV, performance art, Nuyorican poetry, cross-switching and cross-dressing—to celebrate the multiplicities and contradictions that characterize contemporary Puerto Rican culture. But as *afroantillanismo* loses ground, so too does its political project, one closely allied to a politics of decolonization and regional empowerment. Another plebiscite is just around the corner. And Puerto Rico floats, between the colonial and the postcolonial, "at once postnational and prenational," as Juan Flores, María Milagros López, and Nalini Natarajan describe it ("Dossier," 94).

## All That Is Black

In 1898 the United States invaded Puerto Rico and very effectively disempowered the ruling class of the previous Spanish regime, the landowning *hacendados.* Its members fought back by developing and articulating a nationalist discourse that remained dominant throughout the first half of the century. Great nationalist figures such as Antonio S. Pedreira and Albizu Campos (who was himself *mulato,* or its Puerto Rican equivalent *trigueño*) first and foremost wanted independence for Puerto Rico, and the rhetoric of national identity that accompanied their political goals celebrated a European and Spanish heritage. The black or mixed-race component of Puerto Rican culture, very much present at the level of popular culture, was largely ignored or, as in the case of Pedreira, blamed for Puerto Rico's weakness and inability to achieve independence (see Pedreira, *Insularismo* [1934]).

This began to change in a startling way in the late 1940s and early 1950s. After the economic crisis of the 1930s (which unleashed the beginning of large-scale migration to the United States) and two decades of social unrest (Albizu Campos's Nationalist Party turned militant in 1932), Operación Manos a la Obra (Operation Bootstrap) was implemented in 1947, followed by its political partner the Estado Libre Asociado (the Commonwealth) in 1952. Both were conceived and launched by the Partido Popular Democr tico and its populist leader Luis Muñoz Marín. Operation Bootstrap was the project to industrialize the island and create a new middle class (and for the United States a showpiece of successful North American capitalism), and the ELA would grant Puerto Rico a certain amount of local autonomy while maintaining its status as an overseas territory of the United States. The ELA was very much a Puerto Rican invention. Luis Muñoz Marín sold the idea to the United States along with the plan for Operation Bootstrap. As Silvia Alvarez-Curbelo demonstrates, Muñoz Marín saw the Partido Popular as a party for the people, in the tradition of Latin American populism, and the *estadolibristas* fought successfully to wrest political power from the landowning class (whose economic power had already been severely weakened by the United States occupation), campaigning on a platform of agrarian reform, antipoverty, and modernization through industrialization (Alvarez-Curbelo, "La conflictividad").

Alvarez-Curbelo's essay, along with a series of essays that appeared with it in a collection on nationalism and populism in Puerto Rico, argues convincingly that the Partido Popular very consciously went up against nationalism as a discourse that served the interests of a specific elite class (Alvarez-Curbelo and Rodríguez Castro, *Del nacionalismo*). In its attempt to industrialize the island and create a new native bourgeoisie, the Partido Popular opposed nationalism to "the people." As economic historian James Dietz explains, a revolution at the level of production and culture was necessary in order to support the project of industrialization ("La reinvención," 183).

Race was effectively erased from the populist discourse of the Partido Popular during this period of revolutionary change and transition. Instead, intellectuals and politicians of the Partido Popular spoke of "the defense of culture and of democracy, and one greater integrating metaphor: the 'great/er Puerto Rican family'" (Rodríguez Castro, "Foro de 1940," 77). But this *gran familia* whose power and energy would be harnessed in the project of modernization included not only the white working and agrarian class but also, and perhaps most important, the mixed-race and black population. If race was absent at the level of political discourse proper, it exploded at the level of cultural representation, spawning the emergence, within the cultural realm, of a new foundational discourse—the notion that Puerto Rico is fundamentally African and *mestizo.*

There were efforts before 1952 to claim a space for blackness in Puerto Rico beyond representations in the *negrista* vein. The poetry of Luis Palés Matos, although often exoticizing *lo negro,* is one salient example, as is Julia de Burgos's "Ay, ay, ay de la grifa negra," published in 1938. The poetic voice in Burgos's poem proclaims herself black—"Negra de intacto tinte, lloro y río / la vibración de ser estatua negra" (Black [woman] of a pure tint, I cry and laugh / the vibration of being a black statue)—and celebrates this blackness in a poetic language that recuperates words like *grifa* and *cafrería,* perjorative terms referring to blackness in Puerto Rican slang. Although the poem begins with an invocation of blackness, it ends by calling for *mestizaje:* "que mi negra raza huye / y con la blanca corre a ser trigueña" (that my black race flee / and with the white [race] become *mestiza*) and in its grace and power it leaves our bareback rider of *mulatas* permanently disabled, at least rhetorically (Morales, *Poesía,* 157). As Juan Giusti Cordero notes, it is in "music and dance that *lo afro-puertorriqueño* gained a preeminence, and more genuine expression, that it was denied in literature" ("Afro-Puerto Rican," 60). Giusti Cordero gives the example of *plena,* a working-class musical expression with strong Afro-Caribbean components that, by the 1930s, had come to represent Puerto Rican music in Puerto Rico and in New York (60; see also Flores, *Divided Borders,* 85–91). It was *plena* musicians like Ismael Rivera, Rafael Cortijo, and El Gran Combo who would lead the Afro-Antillian cultural explosion of the next decades.

Nonetheless, it was not until after 1952 that a sustained cultural project of national redefinition began to take shape. In 1954 José Luis González published his short story "En el fondo del caño hay un negrito," narrating, in the dialect of working-class Puerto Ricans, the story of a little boy who lives in the water slums on the outskirts of San Juan. The family is hungry, and the father leaves to find piecemeal work in the city while the little boy stares at his face reflected in the water. By the time the father arrives home at night with a little food and some milk, the boy has once again discovered his own reflection in the water: "Entonces Melodía sintió un súbito entusiasmo y un amor indecible hacia el otro negrito. Y se fue a buscarlo" (Then Melodía felt a sudden enthusiasm and an undefinable love for the other little black boy. And he went to find him [Marqués, *Cuentos,* 94]). So ends the story with the unspoken suicide of the hungry little boy who so loves his own reflection that he slides into the murky water to join it.

In its choice of subject matter and use of dialect, the story broke radically with patterns established by another literary great of the period, René Marqués, who was still writing nostalgically of a lost Hispanic identity. When Melodía looks into the water, he sees a black face looking back at him, a metaphor for the argument that González would develop more fully in his 1979 essay "El país de cuatro pisos": that Puerto Rico's foundational people were the enslaved Africans brought to work the sugar plantations and that Puerto Rico in the twentieth century is fundamentally an Afro-Caribbean nation. González went on to argue that Puerto Rican culture was popular culture, that the nation resided in the popular, and finally, in the face of traditional *independentista* ideology arguing the opposite, that this culture had not been assimilated to United States culture but was in fact strong and coherent (González, "El país," 11–42). González's principal enemy in "El país de cuatro pisos" was not the United States, although he was an ardent *independentista* (until his death in December 1996, he lived in exile in Mexico and was for a long time barred by the United States government from entering Puerto Rico), but rather elite structures of power he was happy to see disintegrate as one result of United States presence on the island.

González was a pivotal figure in the elaboration of Puerto Rican *negritud*. He conceived of himself, at least at the time he was developing this essay, as a Gramscian organic intellectual. Unlike traditional intellectuals, who are distanced from the people, the organic intellectual could "des-retorizar" (deconstruct) culture and nationalize it, make it authentically national (11). At times González's position was precarious precisely because he dropped his analytical stance just as he proclaimed himself an authentic representative of the *nación-pueblo* (nation-people) (11). At one point in the essay, as he argued that African slaves were the first true Puerto Ricans, he made the point that they, unlike soldiers, entrepreneurs, and other transient colonials, were forced to remain on the island. As such, theirs was the constant presence that shaped what would become the Puerto Rican nation. He countered his own argument by saying that one could argue against him by pointing to the vast numbers of slaves who were continually attempting to escape to Santo Domingo where they would be free. Although that might be true, said González, those who were doing the revolting were the *bozales* (slaves born in Africa) and slaves brought from other islands, not (loyal) *criollo* slaves (20–21).

The implication that slavery can be read as a healthy nation-building institution represents a moment of excess in González's analysis, that moment when the national prerogative becomes overwhelming. Race, although supreme in González's powerful rearticulation of Puerto Rican history, fades away in the last instance. As critic Juan Gelpí shows very convincingly in his *Literatura y paternalismo en Puerto Rico*, the generation of writers that followed José Luis González, especially in their earlier writings of the 1970s and 1980s, forged a new Puerto Rico. Writers such as Luis Rafael Sánchez, Ana Lydia Vega, Edgardo Rodríguez Juliá, Rosario Ferré, and others, to varying degrees, talked back to patriarchal and conservative (read elite, Hispanophile) representations of the nation-space by dismantling prior canons and depicting an urban and Afro-Caribbean Puerto Rico. As Juan Flores points out in his critique of "El país de cuatro pisos"— he objects to the essentialist nature of its Afrocentric vision—these writers did provide a more flexible and complex version of *afroantillanismo* (*Divided*, 92–107). Within the confines of the literary, *afroantillanismo* remains a concrete political project. However, reactions to the exhibition *Paréntesis: Ocho artistas negros* speak both to the troublesome success of this redefinition of Puerto Rican identity in the public sphere (we are all mestizo/*mulato* here), and to the way this redefinition may have contributed to yet another process of erasure.

### Melts into Air?

Not surprisingly, some of the ambiguities and contradictions that characterize the interplay of race and nation in Puerto Rico are most obvious at the level of popular culture, especially popular music, and salsa in particular. A great deal has been written about salsa, and I merely want to highlight how, from the moment of its advent in the 1960s in the barrios of New York, salsa became a powerful metaphor of Puerto Rican identity. In 1984 Jorge Duany wrote, "When a group of youngsters gathers to listen to, sing, and dance *salsa,* it is celebrating and re-creating the values, beliefs, and practices of its cultural heritage. When new *salsa* orchestras invade Puerto Rican TV and radio stations . . . they are expressing and reaffirming a staunch collective will not to assimilate, not to lose themselves within the Anglo-Saxon cultural orbit" ("Popular," 200). Duany went on to mention the well-known battles, during the 1980s, between the *salseros* or *cocolos* and the *rockeros,* the latter signifying an Americanized, assimilated youth as opposed to the *cocolos,* who listened to salsa and proclaimed themselves Caribbean and Puerto Rican.

What was it that made salsa so Puerto Rican? It emerged from the Puerto Rican neighborhoods of New York and expressed in its origins an urban, working-class ethos (see Leymarie, "Salsa," who cites Cortés, Falcón, and Flores, "Cultural"; see also Rondón, *El Libro*). But salsa's Afro-Caribbean component was perhaps its most salient feature, not only in its hybrid mixtures of Afro-Caribbean rhythms (of which the Cuban *son* was the most important), but also because many of the early *salseros* consciously evoked this heritage in their lyrics ("Salsa," 344, 351). The word *cocolo,* for example, connoted blackness. Salsa was Caribbean, it was working class, it was urban, and it signified blackness. Without a doubt it presented, as Angel Quintero argues in a recent article, a challenge to "what the sonorous organization of occidental modernity considered 'normal'" ("La gran," 38). As such, it was an appropriate marker for Puerto Rican and Caribbean difference, this time in opposition to the threat of North American assimilation.

But salsa, like race in Puerto Rico, is difficult to grab onto. Critics such as Juan Flores and Isabelle Leymarie insist on stressing its hybridity in ways that take us beyond the Caribbean proper, back to the barrios of New York and to processes of cultural exchange that occurred there, including exchange with African American culture (Flores and Yúdice, "Living," 199–224). In a 1996 review essay Duany argues that "the symbolic boundaries between Puerto Rican and U.S. culture have been drawn clearly, perhaps even exaggerated. For instance, musical conflicts during the 1980s pitted *cocolos* (lovers of salsa music) against *rockeros* (those who preferred U.S. rock music), as if they were completely opposed, notwithstanding the fact that salsa was conceived and marketed in New York" ("Imagining the Puerto Rican Nation," 265).

In Puerto Rico these distinctions are at times difficult to sustain, and Lucecita Benítez's hit song in 1973, "Soy de una raza pura," is a good example. Lucecita, one of Puerto Rico's most beloved singing stars, began her career interpreting a Puerto Rican version of rock 'n' roll, known as *nueva ola,* that, in spite of its immense popularity during the 1960s, has received very little critical attention. The author of one book on Puerto Rican *nueva ola,* Javier Santiago, recounts in his introduction the reactions his proposed book received: "Man, you're crazy! The only thing that was done here was to copy the Americans" (*Nueva,* xvii). There is no doubt that *nueva ola* was a transplanted version of American rock 'n' roll, and Santiago describes its introduction to the island by Puerto Rican producer and promoter Alfred D. Herger as "an Operation Bootstrap-type program" (*Nueva,* 25). But ignoring its fabulous popularity as well as the ways *nueva ola* contributed to the growth of an island recording industry, and in some sense paved the way for the salsa craze that was to come, ironically, from New York, seems a fragile position to sustain.

Lucecita was one of *nueva ola*'s biggest stars in Puerto Rico and throughout Latin America. By 1973 she had varied her repertoire considerably, and "Soy de una raza pura" marked a period that Santiago describes as characterizing Lucecita's affirmation of her national identity ("Lucecita"). In her musical interpretation of David Ortiz's poem, Lucecita sings out that she is "de una raza pura, pura rebelde" (of a pure race, pure rebel). She is of a race that escaped the lash: "Soy un ritmo negro que a las cadenas hace sonido" (I am a black rhythm that makes the chains resound). Rhythmically, the song is pure 1970s rock, and in her powerful voice, Lucecita calls out that she is of a rebel hybrid race: "Soy borincano, negro y gitano / Soy taíno y soy l grimas y también dolor / por los siglos que he vivido / por lo mucho que he sufrido" (I am *borincano,* black and gypsy / I am Taíno and I am tears and also pain / for the centuries I have lived / for all that I have suffered) ("Lucecita"). The song once again invokes Puerto Rico as a *mestizo* space (here the Taíno Indians are recuperated as well) and turns toward blackness to signify the national body, Borinquen. "Soy de una raza pura," however, transgresses the very cultural categories it invokes. In genre and musical composition, it is indeed a hybrid production, and its hybridity is far more complex than the formulaic mixture of black, Taíno, and "gypsy" that dominates the song's lyrical composition.

At a 1997 conference on Caribbean regional and national definitions and identities held at the University of Puerto Rico in Río Piedras, performance artist and actress Teresa Hernández performed a piece titled "Isabella diserta," in which the character Isabella, with searing humor, dismantled the *conjunto* of narratives of Puerto Rican identity that cloud the contemporary nation-space. Although her disquisition was itself a most postmodern event, Isabella showed no mercy toward more recent attempts to address Puerto Rico's modernity, its uneven and disjointed relationship with global capitalism, within the paradigms of contemporary postmodernist and poststructuralist critical thinking. Her ironic invitation to the audience to join her in a moment of silence for "lost utopias" was especially resonant in the context of a debate in Puerto Rico between the "postmodernistas pesimistas," as Luis Fernando Coss has termed them in his defense of nationalism *La nación en la orilla,* and those who call for abandoning essentialist discourses of Puerto Rican national identity (Pabón, "De Albizu").

It was precisely this multiplicity of competing discourses that Teresa Hernández's performance highlighted. It seems clear that this multiplicity takes us far beyond the categories of *hispanidad* or *mestizaje* or *negritud.* Operation Bootstrap and the United States colonial experiment in Puerto Rico failed as projects of economic modernization and transformation. However, their mobilization of a new native bourgeoisie and of a new industrial and urban working class, with the patterns of massive migration and uneven industrial development they engendered, have made Puerto Rico a singularly complex modern, premodern, and possibly postmodern not-quite-a-nation-space (see Flores, López, and Natarajan, "Dossier," for a groundbreaking series of essays along these lines). Most important is the recognition that debates about status and national identity must also confront Puerto Rico's role as a metropolis within the Caribbean. North American and Puerto Rican rap music, technopop, and Dominican and now Puerto Rican merengue compete with salsa and Puerto Rican pop music on car radios and in San Juan clubs and bars. As Raquel Rivera points out in her defense of rap music in Puerto Rico, "At this point Puerto Rican culture is a major mixture that goes from Daniel Santos to Lisa M., from Celia Cruz to Vico C., from Brillantina Alka to Right Guard, from Toño Bicicleta to Alexis the Boxer, from young kids passing through Burger King and arriving at Mangú #3 [Dominican food establishment]" ("¿Que el rap?" 26).

But what of race? Puerto Rican rap, for example, is also racially and class marked, in ways that explode the folklorization of blackness in Puerto Rico. As Mayra Santos Febres argues, rap is a synthesis of distinctly Afrodiasporic and African American musical genres, arising from the same Puerto Rican, Dominican, and Cuban communities that gave birth to salsa, coming together with African American and Jamaican communities in New York ("Geografía," 352–53). Santos Febres points out that if salsa was the musical revolution of Operation Bootstrap and the patterns of circular migration it provoked, then Puerto Rican rap is the musical expression of the failure of Operation Bootstrap, both in the context of migration and on the island (353). The failure of economic development in Puerto Rico, coupled with the legacy of the Reagan years in the United States and in Puerto Rico, forced an alliance between poor, urban Puerto Ricans and inner-city communities in the United States (353). The policing and criminalization of rap in Puerto Rico that Santos Febres chronicles in her article (ironically by Governor Pedro Rosselló's pro-statehood administration) testifies to the threat of this alliance.

Although always present, race, along with the category of nation itself, seems to continually melt away, only to appear again, reinvented over and over as critics and artists scramble to find ways to address the complexities of contemporary Puerto Rican life. As such, it seems highly fitting that Teresa Hernández's "Isabella diserta" should be followed immediately by another mesmerizing performance by Puerto Rican actor Javier Cardona. In his "You Don't Look Like" (1997), Cardona mimics the confusion of a black Puerto Rican actor who goes to New York and is told that "he doesn't look like a Puerto Rican." Back in Puerto Rico, he is called up for an audition for a television commercial and realizes, as he arrives at the audition and sees his fellow competitors, that a black face is required for this particular commercial—the reason he was called. In a series of large-screen photographs that are both deeply comical and deeply troubling, the character takes the audience through a variety of "black types" he has been required to play: the *salsero,* the frilled maid, the *rasta,* the Latin beauty, the *rapero,* the machete-wielding cane cutter, the mammy, the basketball star, the drug dealer. After having blacked his face onstage, the character exits asking, "Ahora, ?me habre visto lo suficientemente negro? (Now am I black enough for you?)

## Notes

I thank the Caribbean 2000 Rockefeller Residency Project at the University of Puerto Rico, especially Lowell Fiet, Janette Becerra, Javier Enrique Avila, and Annette Guevárez. Janette Becerra was especially helpful with translations. Ana Lydia Vega and Robert Villanua brought "Soy de una raza pura" to my attention. My title is taken from *All That Is Solid Melts into Air* by Marshall Berman, who took it in turn from Marx.

## Works Cited

Alegre Barrios, Mario. "Ocho artistas negros." *El Nuevo Día* (San Juan), 7 May 1996.

Alvarez-Curbelo, Silvia. "La conflictividad en el discurso político de Luis Muñoz Marín: 1926-1936." In *Del nacionalismo al populismo: Cultura y política en Puerto Rico,* ed. Silvia Alvarez Curbelo and María Elena Rodríguez Castro, 13–35. Río Piedras: Hurac n, 1993.

Alvarez-Curbelo, Silvia, and María Elena Rodríguez Castro, eds. *Del nacionalismo al populismo: Cultura y política en Puerto Rico.* Río Piedras: Hurac n, 1993.

Barradas, Efraín. *Para entendernos: Inventario poético puertorriqueño, siglos XIX y XX.* San Juan: Instituto de Cultura Puertorriqueña, 1992.

Benítez, Lucecita. "Soy de una raza pura." In *Lucecita: Los años Hit Parade/1966-1973.* Disco Hit, CD XX13 (H.P. 070, 1973), 1993.

Cardona, Javier. "You Don't Look Like." Performance. Text: Javier Cardona. Slides: Miguel Villafane. Music: Wilfrido Vargas and Willie Colón. El segundo simposio anual del Proyecto Caribe 2000, 11–13 February, Río Piedras, Universidad de Puerto Rico, 1997.

Cortés, Felix, Angel Falcón, and Juan Flores. "The Cultural Expression of Puerto Ricans in New York: A Theoretical Perspective and Critical Review." *Latin American Perspectives* 3, no. 3 (1976): 117–52.

Coss, Luis Fernando. *La nación en la orilla: Respuesta a los posmodernos pesismistas.* San Juan: Punto de Encuentro, 1996.

Depestre, René. "Aventuras del negrismo en América Latina." In *América Latina en su ideas,* ed. Leopoldo Zea, 345–60. 2d ed. Mexico City: Siglo Veintiuno, 1981.

Dietz, James L. "La reinvención del subdesarollo: Errores fundamentales del proyecto de la industrialización." Trans. Blanca I. Paniagua. In *Del nacionalismo al populismo: Cultura y política en Puerto Rico,* ed. Silvia Alvarez Curbelo and María Elena Rodríguez Castro, 13–35, Río Piedras: Hurac n, 1993.

Duany, Jorge. "Ethnicity, Identity, and Music: An Anthropological Analysis of the Dominican Merengue." In *Music and Black Ethnicity: The Caribbean and South America,* ed. Gerard H. Béhague, 65–90. Miami: North-South Center, University of Miami, 1994.

———. "Imagining the Puerto Rican Nation: Recent Works on Cultural Identity." *Latin American Research Review* 31, no. 3 (1996): 248-67.

———."Popular Music in Puerto Rico: Toward an Anthropology of *Salsa.*" *Latin American Music Review* 5, no. 2 (1984): 186–216.

Flores, Juan. *Divided Borders: Essays on Puerto Rican Identity.* Houston: Arte Público, 1993.

Flores, Juan, and George Yúdice. "Living Borders/*Buscando América*: Languages of Latino Self-Formation." In *Divided Borders: Essays on Puerto Rican Identity,* by Juan Flores. Houston: Arte Público, 1993.

Flores, Juan, María Milagros López, and Nalini Natarajan. "Dossier Puerto Rico." *Social Text* 38 (1994): 93–95.

Gelpí, Juan. *Literatura y paternalismo en Puerto Rico.* San Juan: Editorial de la Universidad de Puerto Rico, 1993.

Giusti Cordero, Juan. "Afro-Puerto Rican Cultural Studies: Beyond *Cultura Negroide* and *Antillanismo.*" *Centro* 8, nos. 1–2 (1996): 57–77.

González, José Luis. "El país de cuatro pisos." In *"El país de cuatro pisos" y otros ensayos.* 7th ed. Río Piedras: Hurac n, 1989.

Hernández, Teresa. "Isabella diserta." Performance. Text with Viveca Vásquez, Eduardo Alegría and Taller de otra cosa. Partially taken from "Kan't translate—tradúcelo" by Viveca Vásquez and the Taller de otra cosa (1992). El segundo simposio anual del Proyecto Caribe 2000, 11–13 February, Río Piedras: Universidad de Puerto Rico, 1997.

Kutzinski, Vera. *Sugar's Secrets: Race and the Erotics of Cuban Nationalism.* Charlottesville: Univ. Press of Virginia, 1993.

Leymarie, Isabelle. "Salsa and Migration." In *The Commuter Nation: Perspectives on Puerto Rican Migration,* ed. Carlos Antonio Torre, Hugo Rodríguez Vecchini, and William Burgos, 343–61. San Juan: Editorial de la Universidad de Puerto Rico, 1994.

Lind Ramos, Daniel. "Un planteamiento personal en torno al problema racial." *El Nuevo Día* (San Juan), 6 June 1996.

Maldonado Reyes, Vilma. "Paréntesis (ocho artistas negros contemporáneos)." *Claridad* (San Juan), 12–18 July 1996.

Marqués, René. *Cuentos puertorriqueños de hoy.* 9th ed. Río Piedras: Cultural, 1987.

Morales, Jorge Luis. *Poesía afroantillana y negrista.* 2d ed. Río Piedras: Editorial de la Universidad de Puerto Rico, 1981.

Pabón, Carlos. "De Albizu a Madonna: Para *armar* y *desarmar* la nacionalidad." *Bordes* 1, no. 1 (1995): 22–40.

Pedreira, Antonio S. *Insularismo.* Vol. 3 of *Obras completas de Antonio S. Pedreira.* 7 vols. Río Piedras: Edil, 1988.

Quintero, Angel. "La gran fuga. Las identidades socio-culturales y la concepción del tiempo en la música 'tropical.'" In *Proceedings, Primer simposio de Caribe 2000: re-definiciones: Espacio—global/nacional/cultural/ personal—caribeño,* ed. Lowell Fiet and Janette Becerra, 24–42. Río Piedras: Caribe 2000, Universidad de Puerto Rico, 1997.

Rivera, Raquel. "¿Que el rap no es cultura?" *Claridad* (San Juan), 4–10 March 1994.

Roach, Joseph. *Cities of the Dead: Circum-Atlantic Performance.* New York: Columbia Univ. Press, 1996.

Rodríguez, Jorge. "Exhiben ocho artistas 'negros' contemporáneos en el Arsenal." *El Vocero* (San Juan), 8 May 1996.

Rodríguez Castro, María Elena. "Foro de 1940: Las pasiones y los intereses se dan la mano." In *Del nacionalismo al populismo: Cultura y política en Puerto Rico,* ed. Silvia Alvarez-Curbelo and María Elena Rodríguez Castro, 61–105. Río Piedras: Hurac n, 1993.

Rondón, César Miguel. *El libro de la salsa.* Caracas: Arte, 1980.

Routte-Gómez, Eneid. "The Artistic Substance of Color." *San Juan Star* (San Juan), 7 May 1996.

Santiago, Javier. "Lucecita en Hit Parade: Un poco de historia." In *Lucecita: Los años Hit Parade/1966-1973,* Disco Hit, CD XX13, 1993.

———. *Nueva ola portoricensis: La revolución musical que vivió Puerto Rico en la década del 60.* Santurce: Del Patio, 1994.

Santos Febres, Mayra. "Geografía en decibeles: Utopías pancaribeñas y el territorio del rap." *Revista de Crítica Literaria Latinoamericana* 23, no. 45 (1997): 351–63.

Sommer, Doris. *Foundational Fictions: The National Romances of Latin America.* Berkeley: Univ. of California Press, 1991.

# 5

## Positive Vibration?
## Capitalist Textual Hegemony
## and Bob Marley

*Mike Alleyne*

In this chapter I address the textual transmutation of modern Caribbean popular music as a direct consequence of its distribution through multinational record companies. I examine Marley's music as a text, not merely lyrically, but I foreground the instrumental content in considering issues of power and ideology that determine recorded aural textual and cultural representation. Proposing that the overall textual character of recorded music is determined by the variable foregrounding and subsuming of its creative elements, I discuss the corporate manipulation of Bob Marley's music and the wide and varied aesthetic and political implications of its Western cooptation.

Marley's pivotal position as the first Caribbean artist to receive large-scale financial backing from the Western record industry makes assessing his career crucial to an examination of commercial transformation in regional popular music. Promotion of his work established notable precedents for the mass-market commodification of Caribbean music, though not entirely without ideological mediation by the capitalist forces that furthered his access to discourse.

One of my principal propositions here is that the capitalism of the international record industry has transformed the articulation and

representation of the Caribbean musical text to an extent grossly underestimated within the region. Accounts of major market penetration frequently celebrate the increased commercial possibilities of deals
with major label while ignoring or understating the stark, counterbalancing capitalist realities involved. The industry characteristically
has helped consolidate Western cultural imperialism by commoditiz-
ing Caribbean music. Furthermore, its economic profits sustain the
hegemonic imbalance in the global political economy, thereby reinforcing Caribbean marginalization (Negus, *Producing,* 14; see also
Tomlinson, *Cultural*).

My references to Gramsci's concept of hegemony principally apply
to the inseparability of culture from more obvious dimensions of
power and the subtle use of culture to exert ideological influence in a
variety of forms. In acknowledging the inextricable connection between representations of power, Ngugi wa Thiong'o contends that
"for a full comprehension of the dynamics, dimensions and workings
of a society, any society, the cultural aspects cannot be seen in total
isolation from the economic and political ones" (*Moving,* xiv–xv). In
the context of popular music, the Gramscian model identifies hegemony functioning as undisguised cultural cooptation that disarms
textual incisiveness: "The attempt would be made simply to incorpo-
rate the music safely within the domains of leisure and recreation.
With the music thus contained, any progressive edge of subversive
meaning would become background to the dominant (ideological)
functions of popular music—entertainment and relaxation in the service of consumerism and the reproduction of labour power. In the extreme, the idea of revolution itself would become a mere posture in
the hegemonic landscape" (Garofalo, "Autonomous," 89). The rami-
fications for the emergence and maintenance of Caribbean musical
counterdiscourse are serious if, through hegemony, subversive power
can be at least partially defused (Storey, *Introductory,* 119).

"Authenticity," as used here, applies primarily to the original form
of artistic representation by the creator of the work, rather than to its
use as a means of imposing monolithic, static, or one-dimensional parameters on Caribbean cultural expression. Although I acknowledge
in this context the innate eclectic fusions that gave birth to reggae,
here I identify external cultural and economic forces as reducing the
congruence between the internationally commodified form and its root
components. The issue of authenticity also clearly relates to characterizing norms in Jamaican popular music before Marley's ascension

on Island, from which divergence can be roughly measured. It is directly relevant to identification of modes and styles of textual expression that either are native to Jamaica (via Africa) or have been organically syncretized to form integral popular cultural components.

Generally speaking, dual thematic currents dominated Jamaican popular music in the 1960s. Mainstream love songs coexisted with songs of protest, whose frequency and intensity increased as the decade progressed and the potential of political independence remained largely unfulfilled (Brodber and Greene, *Roots*, 9; Alleyne, *Roots*, 118). The Wailers' own music drew on both currents, though ultimately the protest component came to dominate their texts as the group members adopted the Rastafarian faith. The seminal albums recorded with Lee Perry, *Soul Rebels* (1970) and *Soul Revolution* (1971), epitomized the antiestablishment critique characterizing Marley and the Wailers before the Island years. They focused on social injustice, inequity, and complacency and on the inevitable consequences of this human misconduct at the hands of Jah. The song "Corner Stone" on *Soul Rebels* both signified the essence of Marley's Rastafarian philosophy and implied the rootedness of reggae aesthetics within it. Although the element of romance was still apparent on Wailers' releases, Marley's later decision on *Kaya* (1978) to highlight love themes—after achieving popularity based primarily on antihegemonic lyrical militancy—heavily complicated his career, provoking accusations of overt commercialization.

Much of the published writing on the career and work of Bob Marley seems to subsume possibilities for critical reassessments and alternative readings. Analyses of his music have usually underemphasized the economic context within which his creativity flourished. In this essay I do not seek to diminish Marley's remarkable commercial and artistic achievements, but I do indict the practices of the Western record industry and the limitations it imposes in its commodification of reggae and other Caribbean music. I am suggesting that within the landscape of the record industry's political economy, commercialization and cooptation are closely connected (Garofalo, "Autonomous," 79).

Island Records' presentation of Marley and his work since 1972 features highly significant instances of textual reconfiguration, dictated by capitalist imperatives that have intervened in the representation of the original cultural texts.[1] Paul Gilroy aptly describes the general approach of Island Records, and in particular its head, Chris Blackwell, toward the representation of black musicians in the Western market. Gilroy points to the adjustment of music and image to fulfill the expectations of white rock audiences and cites the marketing of Marley as demonstrative (*Ain't*, 169).

Blackwell's targeting of the album market through the Wailers was motivated primarily by the urge to maximize profits from reggae, since mere hit singles limited long-term transnational potential (Jones, *Black*, 63). The precise nature of Blackwell's participation during Marley's career remains a point of controversy, but it is certain that he engaged in considerable postproduction textual manipulation to create a viable product on Western terms. In the historically controversial *Marley and Me*, Don Taylor, Marley's former manager, contests Blackwell's creative role, citing false production accreditation on Marley's early Island albums to gain more money (82). In any event, my description of Blackwell's role here emphasizes his capacity as a record industry entrepreneur holding the crucial economic power to effect textual intervention rather than portraying him as a creative avatar.

From the outset with *Catch a Fire* (1972), Blackwell was determined to culturally and commercially recontextualize the Wailers' music (and image). The seemingly anomalous retention of the group's explicitly political messages was in fact wholly congruent with Blackwell's commercial objectives, involving exploitation of their rebellious stance. The original recordings were made in Kingston, Jamaica, performed and mixed by the Wailers themselves. But this original representation became subject to textual revision in London under the supervision of Blackwell, who remixed and edited the Kingston sessions. Since the material was deemed inappropriate for the white audience toward which the album was to be commercially directed, the text underwent editing that arguably weakened the creative authenticity of the work by introducing musical statements divorced from its cultural context.

The range of adjustments featured the creation of a more treble-oriented mix at the expense of reggae's characteristic bass depth. Other alterations included recording overdubs with British and American session men, accelerating the speed of the tracks, and bringing Marley's voice forward in the mix (Hebdige, *Cut*, 80). (See also Davis, *Bob*, 104, 109–10; Jones, *Black*, 64; and White, *Catch*, 234–35.)[2] The transformation brought about by Blackwell was not merely a minor, cosmetic modification but a reformulation of the text of reggae in which the elements considered most appealing to the Western rock audience were foregrounded at the expense of its primary Afro-Caribbean characteristics. The aesthetic cornerstone on which reggae had been built was commercially shifted. The overdubs and other postproduction surgery performed on the original Jamaican tracks ignored any necessity for retaining a holistic textual authenticity. Despite initially low sales for this debut album, the postproduction established a mode of representation characterizing Marley's career with Island in which remixing and supplementary overdubbing featured consistently (Jones, *Black*, 64).

The events surrounding this album raise concerns regarding the actual extent of Marley's participation in the textual reorganizing of his work, both then and subsequently. His reported presence during the overall reshaping of *Catch a Fire* suggests he understood the inevitability of record company intervention and the probable commercial benefits that collaborating brought through wider dissemination.

We must also recognize, however, that economic incentives must certainly have figured prominently, and issues of cultural cooptation resurface even in this context of apparent artistic empowerment. Despite Marley's collaboration on *Catch a Fire* and his probable inclination toward some creative compromise, I am arguing here that the ultimate economic power to determine the final commodified recorded textual representation was hegemonically exercised by Blackwell, to great long-term effect.

A pronounced instance of ideological divergence between artistic and commodified representation in Marley's career surrounds the change of the 1974 album title from *Knotty Dread* to *Natty Dread* (Davis, *Bob*, 138; Jones, *Black*, 65). The conceptual differences between the two titles underscore the distance between hegemonic and counterhegemonic positions. Although linguistic questions might arise since "knotty" and "natty" probably cannot be distinguished aurally in Jamaican parlance, cultural and ideological distinction arises from the word choice in the context of its international commodified representation. The opposition of uptown "natty" and downtown "knotty" highlights the difference in perspective between Blackwell and Marley: Blackwell's spelling choice clearly embraced a metropolitan translation of the concept.

In effect, by this mediation Blackwell ideologically diluted the "dreadness" of the album title, like much of the music itself, and made it more culturally compatible with Western norms. Although the change of album title was a shock to Marley, he considered it one among many undesirable but inescapable vagaries of the music business. Nonetheless, a potently antiestablishment statement in the original title became a harmless affirmation of the status quo.

The Wailers' fifth Island album release, *Rastaman Vibration,* drew responses that underscored the general incongruity between commercial success and critical acceptance and provoked further considerations of Western textual influence. Commercially it was a major success in both the United States and England, where remarkably large advance orders were registered, but some fans felt it lacked militancy and was too commercial. Although most of the album eschewed overtly political discourse, other fans may have thought the political significance of "War," utilizing the text of a 1968 speech by Ethiopian emperor Haile Selassie, was adequate and exemplary recompense.

Conversely, the song "Roots Rock Reggae" openly proclaims Marley's desire to attain mainstream presence through Billboard singles chart status: "Play I on the R and B / I want all my people to see / We're bubbling on the Top One Hundred / Just like a mighty dread." In this text Marley does not detach himself from explicit association with the commercial process, though one may argue that distributing his message was his main priority. Neville Garrick, Marley's longtime art director and friend, states that "there's a part on the song that never go on the record because it fade out where him say 'I feel like preaching on the streets of Harlem, want all my people to see" (Whitney and Hussey, *Bob,* 161). In dislocating Marley's ideological unity with this politically pivotal component of the black American community, this lyrical exclusion further demonstrates the editorial power residing in Western textual hegemony. The lyric also signifies Marley's consciousness of both reggae's and his own relatively peripheral but potentially explosive position within the American commercial context of the time. Thus the distinctly counterhegemonic and anti-Babylonian lyrical broadsides of "Crazy Baldhead" did not unequivocally indicate steadfast ideological intransigence in view of the way *Rastaman Vibration* demonstrated Marley's commercial sensibility.

Far more controversial was the increased proportion of love songs on *Exodus, Kaya,* and *Uprising,* accompanied by much lighter melodies. Although these albums were not entirely dominated by romantic themes, the presence of even three or four such songs in a Marley collection contrasted starkly with the greater concentration on overtly political concerns in the early albums. The love songs and lighter material assumed even greater prominence through being released as singles (White, *Catch*, 336–40).[3] The clear implication is that Marley's texts evolved in a manner that privileged Western (and his own) economic imperatives, owing to overt and subtle commercial pressures.

His commercialization effected a narrative discontinuity with the themes and mood characterizing his earlier textual articulation. Negative reaction to *Kaya*, which was notably mixed like a rock record, appears to have been particularly strong, notwithstanding the inclusion of some songs (such as the title track) from Marley's pre-Island recordings (Davis, *Bob*, 196–97). Marley explained the dominance of *Kaya's* "themes of love, doubt and dance" by averring both an intent to avoid the appearance of profiting by exploiting mass social suffering and a desire to escape thematic stasis (197). In the context of the then recent attempt to assassinate Marley, one might also posit that he avoided creating more enemies by temporarily sidestepping overtly political issues. In addition, the romantic emphases of both *Exodus* and *Kaya* were influenced by his ongoing extramarital relationship with Miss World 1976, Cindy Breakspeare (Davis, Bob, 184–85, 196; White, *Catch*, 287). The criticisms of sentimentality and commercialism leveled at Marley over *Kaya* are seen by one critic as typically dichotomous for an international artist whose initial textual concerns highlighted political and cultural consciousness (Mulvaney, *Rastafari*, 101).

The expansion of Marley's thematic focus during this phase when formerly marginal love concerns were made more central raises several questions (see Cooper, *Noises*, 127–32). Prominent among them are how far commercial factors might have influenced this development and the actual gender implications of his lyrical texts exploring the politics of love relationships. Although this emphasis may not have been a premeditated commercial strategy, it undoubtedly broadened Marley's audience by counterbalancing overtly political intensity with matters that were less disturbing and challenging, even innocuous. Hence this focal shift enhanced Marley's marketability by capitalizing on his own aura of sexual potency, making his image as applicable to amorous conquest as it was to sociopolitical rebellion. The immediate commercial success of *Uprising* versus the moderate sales of its 1979 predecessor *Survival*, which was thoroughly politically focused, illustrates the market value of such duality (Davis, *Bob*, 228).

The Euro-American audience has continually demonstrated a propensity for adopting reggae-oriented material based on its aesthetically pleasing surface qualities rather than on explicitly political content. A cursory survey of the hegemonic landscape reveals that major chart successes by reggae artists and pseudoreggae songs by white pop artists utilize elements of the music's syntax while simultaneously divorcing it from the political polemics of Rastafari (Cushman, "Rich," 36; Winer, "Intelligibility," 36).[4] In these circumstances the emergence of love issues in Marley's texts accommodated the commercial conditioning of the Western audience.

Gilroy defends Marley's movement into the realm of pop stardom, suggesting that his primary objective was cross-cultural outreach aimed especially at uniting the threads of the black diaspora. Consequently, the argument continues, any commercial adjustments to the musical text involved in achieving this goal constitute an acceptable price (*Ain't*, 169–70). But Gilroy's proposition is surely only a partial representation of the scenario. The capitalist bases of the record industry and the economic fruits reaped by both Island and Marley in consequence of the music's assimilability are wholly deemphasized in Gilroy's critique. Furthermore, the textual alterations were hardly minor adjustments.

Western corporate promotion of Marley's work after his death is characterized by an astute raiding of the vaults for previously unreleased material. Of the many releases, the most significant in the context of this essay is the comprehensive *Songs of Freedom* compilation, released in August 1993, containing seventy-eight songs recorded between 1962 and 1980 (Newman, "Island," 10). Although the album includes three previously unreleased songs, the radically remixed and reconstructed single release "Iron Lion Zion" bears only a slight resemblance to the album version. Whatever the song's aesthetic merits, the exceptionally bright mix given to this work, allegedly originally recorded in the early 1970s, removes it from its original temporal context in an attempt to inconspicuously transplant it into the 1990s. The text has been transformed to fulfill commercial objectives, not cultural ones.

Furthermore, in relation to the folksy album version, original Wailers member Bunny Wailer vigorously asserts that his vocals (as well as those of the late Peter Tosh) were removed from the song's final mix for *Songs of Freedom*, and he contests the idea that it was a lost item miraculously discovered (interview with Roger Steffens, *Beat*,

44). Except for vocals, the album version of "Iron Lion Zion" differs almost entirely from the far more commercial version released internationally as a single. If the version on the *Songs of Freedom* CD set is the original, then the single has been totally transmogrified by overdubs artificially modernizing the text for commercial purposes while invoking an archival mystique to create a false aura of authenticity. The carefully annotated liner notes make no reference to the discovery of more than one version of the song.[5]

The circumstances of textual intervention surrounding "Iron Lion Zion" forcefully underscore the impression that both the release and reconfiguration of Marley's posthumous material is motivated not by benign, aesthetic considerations but by strictly capitalist concerns (made even more apparent since Island's 1989 takeover by Dutch-based transnational Polygram, for over $300 million) (Negus, *Producing*, 4; Campbell Robinson, Buck, and Cuthbert, *Music*, 51). Even after the compilation of *Songs of Freedom*'s seventy-eight songs, over two hundred more Marley compositions and performances remain available for commercial exploitation. Reportedly though, few of these can be classified as "genuine unreleased rarities" (Howell, "Songs").[6]

The 1996 release of vintage Marley pre-Island recordings on the JAD Records CD *Soul Almighty: The Formative Years,* volume 1, including various "remixes" reportedly sanctioned by and involving other members of his musical family, clearly indicates that Marley's creative catalog will continue to be commodified for many years. The central contradiction of reggae's commercial success both through and since Bob Marley is the way the counterhegemonic stance of Rastafari in popular music ironically fuels the hegemonic forces that promote its dissemination (Storey, *Introductory,* 122). Despite reggae's adoption of an oppositional political stance, the dominant power structure reaps direct economic benefit from this expression. Paradoxically, while reggae acts as a force for counterhegemonic change, it simultaneously consolidates the economic power base of the status quo.

This incongruity suggests that the perception of creative empowerment through the music's dissemination must be tempered by a consciousness of how far Babylonian forces are extracting oil from the well of reggae. This, of course, applies to the wide range of major label associations characterizing the current dancehall era in Jamaican music. The overall scenario reinforces the idea that access to discourse is inseparable from economic power. Consequently this power operates to rechannel and thereby partially defuse revolutionary potential.

Bob Marley was exceptional in many ways, including his ability to create art that largely transcends the rampant commodification of Western culture. He made reggae a musical force to be taken seriously despite the numerous ambiguities surrounding his textual representation, creating an enduring musical message successful in conveying artistic, cultural, and ideological meanings despite its extensive commercialization (Gilroy, *Ain't,* 170). It must also be said that Marley's career was not marked by an uninterrupted, linear decline into lyrically and musically unconscious commercialism. The 1979 album *Survival* strongly contradicts such a proposition in its incisive reiteration of anti-imperialist politics and cohesive, hard-edged music so characteristic of the early albums preceding Marley's commercial breakthrough. Thus with *Survival* he satisfied the more militant segments of his audience while also fulfilling the economic imperatives of the record company. The cornerstone, whose image surfaces in "Ride Natty Ride," was now restored to its rightful position after being moved early in his career with Island. This demonstrates that commercial success need not always preclude contribution to a culture of resistance (Garofalo, "Autonomous," 84). But while Marley can be said to have made such a contribution, for which he has been described as "the most politically influential recording artist of the twentieth century" (Shaar Murray, *Crosstown,* 95–96), a general correlation may still be drawn between his commercial success and the mediation of his lyrical and musical militancy.

In conclusion, the principal considerations are the long-term political, cultural, and economic implications and actual consequences for Caribbean music brought about by Bob Marley's career. Although it is generally accepted that the music constitutes a sufficient "positive vibration" and that his outstanding creative contribution is not in question, the dichotomies of operating within the economic parameters of Babylon are well worth examining. I hope this essay demonstrates that Caribbean people are being "remixed" out of autonomous cultural representation on the world stage, having creative exclamations defused and subsumed by a simultaneously foregrounded and historically resonant Western hegemonic agenda.

The transnational record industry's exploitation of Caribbean music should not, therefore, be examined in isolation, since it reinforces, at several levels, international power structures inimical to regional development and decolonization. In considering the hegemonic power wielded by the Euro-American record industry, one should underestimate neither the power to reinterpret a musical text through multitrack remixing nor the assimilative aspect of cultural imperialism as it reinscribes Caribbean cultural texts.

Although some analysts may contest my interpretation as neo-Marxist economic reductionism and point to the simultaneous influence of less easily defined factors contributing to this transcultural phenomenon, the economic element remains pivotal in this discussion. The seemingly paradoxical dominance of Western critical perspectives in this analysis is not an oversight but a conscious means of compensating for the relative marginalization of commodification consciousness in Caribbean cultural criticism. In any event, all the observations I draw on here are demonstrable from individual textual and contextual analysis and thus remain valid regardless of their geopolitical source.

### Notes

1. The Island era of reconfigured Marley material is predated by Johnny Nash's exploitation and dilution of several Marley songs on his 1971 hit album *I Can See Clearly Now*. Although the Wailers provided part of the instrumental backing, Marley's vocals were (naturally) not a feature of these texts. In addition, Marley reportedly considered the final product, which included many overdubs by session musicians on the Wailers basic and uncredited contributions, to have been overproduced (Davis, *Bob*, 91, 98).

2. Both Davis and White note that Americans also participated in recording overdubs on this album. Prominent contributions were made by southern guitarist Wayne Perkins, who had never previously played reggae, and Texas-born (though British-based) keyboardist-arranger John "Rabbit" Bundrick.

3. This section of the Bob Marley Island discography illustrates both the frequency with which the "love songs and softer melodies" were released as singles and their proportion on respective albums.

4. Cushman cites pop-reggae hits by Blondie, the Eagles, and especially the Police as examples of appropriation of the musical text minus its philosophical import. He also notes that newer reggae bands (for instance, Ziggy Marley and the Melody Makers) are "more often products of the Western culture industry" ("Rich," 37).

5. The technological transformation of the song is confirmed in Ian McCann's *Complete Guide to the Music of Bob Marley*, 24, 114.

6. The author is citing a comment by Neville Garrick, coordinator of the Bob Marley Museum.

## Works Cited

Alleyne, Mervyn. *Roots of Jamaican Culture*. London: Pluto, 1988.

Brodber, Erna, and Edward J. Greene. *Roots and Reggae—Ideological Tendencies in the Recent History of Afro-Jamaica*. Kingston, Jamaica: ISER, 1979.

Campbell Robinson, Deanna, Elizabeth B. Buck, and Marlene Cuthbert. *Music at the Margins: Popular Music and Global Cultural Diversity*. London: Sage, 1991.

Cooper, Carolyn. *Noises in the Blood: Orality, Gender and the "Vulgar" Body of Jamaican Popular Culture*. London: Macmillan, 1993.

Cushman, Thomas. "Rich Rastas and Communist Rockers: A Comparative Study of the Origin, Diffusion and Defusion of Revolutionary Musical Codes." *Journal of Popular Culture* 25, no. 3 (1991): 16–61.

Davis, Stephen. *Bob Marley*. Rochester NY: Schenkman, 1990.

Garofalo, Reebee. "How Autonomous Is Relative: Popular Music, the Social Formation and Cultural Struggle." *Popular Music* 6, no. 1 (1987): 77–92.

Gilroy, Paul. *There Ain't No Black in the Union Jack: The Cultural Politics of Race and Nation*. Chicago: Univ. of Chicago Press, 1991.

Hebdige, Dick. *Cut 'n' Mix: Culture, Identity and Caribbean Music*. London: Comedia, 1987.

Howell, Peter. "Songs of Freedom a Living Marley Tribute." *Toronto Star,* 18 October 1992, C6.

Jones, Simon. *Black Culture, White Youth: The Reggae Tradition from JA to UK*. London: Macmillan, 1988.

McCann, Ian. *The Complete Guide to the Music of Bob Marley*. London: Omnibus, 1994.

Mulvaney, Rebekah M. *Rastafari and Reggae: A Dictionary and Sourcebook*. Westport CT: Greenwood, 1990.

Negus, Keith. *Producing Pop: Culture and Conflict in the Popular Music Industry*. London: Edward Arnold, 1992.

Newman, Melinda. "Island Brings out Marley Box in Style." *Billboard,* 8 August 1992, 10.

Shaar Murray, Charles. *Crosstown Traffic: Jimi Hendrix and Post-war Pop*. London: Faber, 1989.

Storey, John. *An Introductory Guide to Cultural Theory and Popular Culture*. Athens: Univ. of Georgia Press, 1993.

Taylor, Don. *Marley and Me*. New York: Kingston, 1994.

Tomlinson, John. *Cultural Imperialism*. Baltimore: Johns Hopkins Univ. Press, 1991.

Wailer, Bunny. Interview with Roger Steffens, *Beat* 12, no. 3 (1993): 44.

wa Thiong'o, Ngugi. *Moving the Centre: The Struggle for Cultural Freedoms*. London: James Currey, 1993.

White, Timothy. *Catch a Fire: The Life of Bob Marley*. New York: Henry Holt, 1992.

Whitney, Malika Lee, and Dermot Hussey. *Bob Marley: Reggae King of the World*. Kingston: Kingston, 1984.

Winer, Lise. "Intelligibility of Reggae Lyrics in North America: Dread in a Babylon." *English World-Wide: A Journal of Varieties of English* 11, no. 1 (1990): 36–37.

## 6

## "Titid ak pèp la se marasa": Jean-Bertrand Aristide and the New National Romance in Haiti

*Kevin Meehan*

I n January 1995, two weeks before completing his term as president, Jean-Bertrand Aristide wed Haitian American attorney Mildred Trouillot at his residence outside Port-au-Prince. In response to popular complaints that Aristide had "divorced" the people of Haiti by marrying the lighter-skinned, foreign-born Trouillot, the couple's vows included the following exchange. It is a text that explicitly reaffirms the couple's commitment to political struggle on behalf of Haiti's impoverished masses: " 'When you see this ring, remember me and remember you are an advocate of the people,' Aristide told his bride. 'When you see this ring, remember that it is better to fail with the people than to succeed without them, and with the people there is no failure,' Trouillot responded." At the end of the service, going out of his way to reinforce the message that his legal marriage to Trouillot in no way threatened his symbolic marriage to the people of Haiti, Aristide commented in Kreyòl, "This business about divorcing the people, no way" ("Aristide"). That a presidential wedding could become so explicit a signifier of national politics suggests how far the emergence of Aristide and the Lavalas movement has been structured narratively as a national romance. It also reminds us that statecraft has its narrative aspects and that literary and cultural criticism can sometimes be helpful in understanding developments in national politics.

The thesis I propose in this chapter begins with the idea that, in fact, romance is one of the primary narrative forms through which Haitian writers and politicians have chosen to tell their stories of national identity. This is true, first of all, in the broad sense that Haitian nationality has from the start been grounded in a quintessentially romantic story of slave revolt followed by national liberation after heroic struggles against seemingly impossible odds. In a narrower, more literary sense, however, Haitian nationality is also tied to the romance, for Haitian writers—who frequently do double duty as the country's leading politicians—have made the romance a major generic ingredient in the Haitian novel, beginning with Emeric Bergeaud's *Stella* (1859), the text that inaugurates the novel tradition in Haiti, and continuing in canonized twentieth-century works such as Jacques Roumain's *Gouverneurs de la rosée* (1944), Jacques Stéphen Aléxis's *Compère Général Soleil* (1955), and René Depestre's *Le mât de cocagne* (1976). I suggest that by attending to this tradition of national romance we gain an important insight into the emergence of the Lavalas movement and its principal spokesperson, Jean-Bertrand Aristide. The mobilizing force of Aristide's rhetoric derives, at least in part, from its organic relation to the work of earlier writer-politicians, including Roumain, Aléxis, Depestre, and others. Like them, Aristide has expressed his political vision using elements of national romance. Part of the reason Aristide has been able to forge a successful cross-class popular movement (unlike his predecessors), I would argue, is his ability to transform the traditional language of popular democratic struggle. Aristide's new national romance, his "marriage" with the Haitian people, poses a model of collaboration and conciliation that challenges the combined gender and class elitism that limits the appeal of earlier efforts at national development in Haiti. Aristide repeatedly draws on the core tropes of Haitian national romance, but he consistently recasts motifs of romantic coupling and maternity that in the Roumain-Aléxis-Depestre genealogy are always encased in a pattern of erotic and biological depictions. Although numerous cultural and political factors make Aristide's revisions possible, I will focus mainly on the connections between his work and feminist liberation theology. The result is that, by mixing traditional nationalist rhetoric with perspectives forged through his work among historically marginalized social groups, Aristide has helped to articulate broader, more egalitarian political ideals that are particularly attuned to the inclusion of Haitian women.

First of all I shall lay the groundwork for a reading of Aristide's new national romance by characterizing, in broad terms, the framework of traditional romantic nationalism within which Aristide is operating. Doris Sommer's observations about the central connections between the romance genre and nationalism in Latin American cultural history are in many ways applicable to Haiti as well. For Sommer, nineteenth-century Latin American romances help consolidate the nation by articulating its history. In addition, romantic plots typically involve lovers whose desire reaches across social divisions of region, class, race, and religion. By imaginatively moving toward a resolution of such divisions, the romance potentially helps consolidate national communities still emerging from anticolonial battles and civil war. The centerpiece of the genre, what allows it to serve as nationalism's ideological glue, is a close interweaving of erotic and political registers of meaning. National romances, according to Sommer, "construct Eros and Polis upon each other" (*Foundational,* xi). This model works particularly well when brought to bear on canonical, male-authored Haitian novels from the twentieth century. In the work of Roumain, Aléxis, and Depestre, a repeating pattern emerges: the (male) revolutionary nationalist subject appears first as a (heterosexual) romantic hero; although the hero's fate typically entails revolutionary martyrdom, a political legacy endures through the relationship established with a woman in the romantic plot; erotic potency prefigures historical agency, and the successful "birth" of nationalist consciousness and projects (often allegorized in the literal birth of an heir) depends on a conversion of erotic energies into political energies.

Jacques Roumain concludes *Gouverneurs de la rosée* with a well-known scene in which the mother of Roumain's martyred hero, Manuel, reaches down to feel Manuel's unborn child stir in the womb of the widow, Annaïse (192). In itself this image of maternity carries an important political valence that symbolizes Haitian national development and general social renewal in the period following the United States military occupation of 1915–34. Yet it also represents the culminating moment of a larger pattern of eroticized romance that is central to Roumain's narrative project. Without the romance plot that unites Manuel and Annaïse, the dream of liberation for the rural community of Fonds Rouge would remain unrealized. The romance is a central factor in resolving the blood feud that divides Fonds

Rouge (the two come from warring clans), and Roumain develops it simultaneously with the story of Manuel's political struggle to reconstitute the *konbit,* or peasant cooperative. Manuel's physical union with Annaïse parallels his intimacy with and control over the rural landscape, while practically speaking it is in his conversations with Annaïse that he first works out many of his political schemes. I have written elsewhere about how Annaïse's character resonates in the novel as a vehicle for history—as a biological factory for the future that is waiting to be born rather than as an agent in the production of that history (Cottenet-Hage and Meehan, "Re-writing," 277–78).

Although feminist reading strategies reveal the limited place of women within Roumain's scheme for liberation, *Gouverneurs de la rosée* is basically a seamless blending of romantic and revolutionary nationalist plot lines. This pattern receives a more complicated treatment in canonized novels by Aléxis and Depestre. In contrast to *Gouverneurs de la rosée,* which is a classic peasant novel that confines its narrative to the countryside, *Compère Général Soleil* offers a more complete picture of Haitian life. Aléxis depicts urban as well as country routines while following the development of a central character, Hilarius Hilarion, as he struggles for daily bread, political freedom, philosophical insight, and emotional fulfillment. The climax of the novel presents Hilarion's involvement with Haitian cane cutters on strike against horrible working conditions in the Dominican Republic, his fatal wounding while trying to return to Haiti with his family, and a final speech delivered to his wife, Claire-Heureuse. Heterosexual romance occupies a smaller place in this fully elaborated tableau, yet at key moments the love affair between Hilarion and Claire-Heureuse becomes the central narrative device for conveying the novel's symbolism and explicit political message of social regeneration through the unity of workers and progressive intellectuals. In the end, moreover, Aléxis replays the scenario in which a male political hero's female lover becomes the vessel for his revolutionary legacy. The final message to Claire is an injunction to reproduce more radical heroes: "You must create another Hilarion, other Désirés. You alone can recreate them" (350).[1]

René Depestre's novel, *Le mât de cocagne,* translated as *The Festival of the Greasy Pole,* follows the revolutionary nationalist plot beyond the usual ending of martyrdom for the hero. Instead of concluding with the death of Henri Postel, Depestre traces the history of Postel's romantic-revolutionary female helpmate Elisa (Zaza) Valéry and even scripts the novel in such a way that Zaza gets to tell her own tale through the device of an embedded letter that concludes the novel. Rather than offering a transformation that might open new possibilities for women in a narrative of political liberation, though, *Le mât de cocagne* is a grotesque parody representing an end point in the canonical male-authored tradition of Haitian national romance. Like his predecessors Roumain and Aléxis, Depestre proposes a critical incorporation of vodoun. In particular, his novel turns on the use of zombification (represented in the novel as "electrification") as a metaphor for political terror, spiritual death, and ecological disaster.[2] Prompted perhaps by bitterness over the murder of his close friend Aléxis at the hands of Duvalierist agents, Depestre creates a fictional double of Haitian society in which oppression and resistance play out as nihilistic farce. President Zoocrates Zachary appears in public as the graveyard loa Baron Samedi (as did François Duvalier). Zachary's macoutelike deputy, Clovis Barbatog, oversees political terror as minister of the National Office for the Electrification of Souls (NOFES). Postel, a former political opponent of Zachary and current victim of "electrification," decides to enter the annual Festival of the Greasy Pole, in which men compete to see who will be the first one to climb to the top of a huge greased tree trunk. Postel's transformation from electrified-zombified victim to revolutionary hero is ensured through a closely described vodoun ceremony in which he is visited by the loa Erzulie Freda, who has mounted Postel's young neighbor, Elisa. Following strictly the logic of romance and revolution, Elisa-Erzulie embodies not only erotic rejuvenation but political opposition as well. Depestre writes: "Elisa was presenting him [Postel] with the complete opposite of Baron Samedi and his electrification of souls" (93). The day after the ceremony, Postel duly climbs the greasy pole, finding a pistol at the top. He fires on his enemies but only wounds them, while he himself is mortally shot by a sniper posted on a nearby rooftop. Elisa survives these events and flees into the mountains, becoming known as "the maroon angel of Henri Postel" (135). As the appellation suggests, the place of women in this liberation scheme remains derivative. Even though Elisa is writing her own testament, her essentially symbolic function remains the same as that of Annaïse and Claire-Heureuse: she is a repository of the male hero's revolutionary legacy.[3] The bitterness and nihilism of Depestre's parodic narrative stem, I suggest, not only from disgust at the degradation of vodoun and the continuing oppression of Haitians under neocolonial conditions: *Le mât de cocagne* also represents the end of the line for a dominant, masculinist approach to narrating Haitian national development as heterosexual fantasy.

However one estimates the compensations of Haitian national romance in terms of literary or aesthetic pleasure, I propose that the canonical texts of Roumain, Aléxis, and Depestre fail to accomplish the primary ideological task of the genre, which is to help consolidate an imagined national community by projecting conciliatory narrative closure on a range of disruptive social divisions. On the contrary, a reading of the traditional twentieth-century national romance in Haiti reveals an inability to resolve social hierarchies at the level of symbolic production. Even as writer-politicians work in their fiction toward mediating the splits between urban and rural, intellectual and peasant, rich and poor, mulatto and black, and so on, one of the basic, determining social problems—the stratified relationship between men and women—remains solidly intact. Men continue to occupy a privileged role as historical subjects, or primary political actors, while women function as objects, as supporting players who watch, listen, follow, and frequently are reduced to the biological role of sexual partner or mother. Given the central place of heterosexual eroticism in the romances of Roumain, Aléxis, and Depestre, the subordination of women seems to be almost a built-in blind spot of the national romance as a genre. Against the backdrop of this intense patriarchal stratification, Jean-Bertrand Aristide's writing and speeches in the context of the Lavalas movement are remarkable both for how they follow in the tradition of national romance and for how they alter the language of that tradition in ways that reinscribe Haitian women as subjects of national history.

*Lavalas* is a Kreyòl word for the rushing stream of water produced by tropical rainstorms in Haiti. Thundering down mountain roads and ravines like an avalanche, the flood sweeps up everything in its path, even huge boulders that may have clogged a pathway for decades or centuries. Appropriated as a figure for social change in Haiti, the torrential force of the water represents the will of Haiti's impoverished majority joined with progressive intellectuals and sympathetic members of the Haitian bourgeoisie. This vision of unity as a mobilizing force is expressed succinctly in the movement's anthemic Kreyòl slogan, "Ansanm ansanm nou se lavalas": "All together, we are a torrent." Working together, the disparate groups that make up Lavalas represent a social and political avalanche with the potential to clear away the obstructions placed in the way of popular democracy by two centuries of neocolonial corruption stretching back to the moment of Haitian independence in 1804.

In simple terms, then, the social movement that bears the name Lavalas is a loose-knit collection of organizations assembled in the fight to bring down the most recent expression of entrenched neocolonialism in Haiti; that is, the thirty-year spectacle of Duvalierism. Lavalas has been galvanized by the diverse projects of Haitian liberation theology, but the movement in its entirety includes a wide range of social forces, and many of the groups under the Lavalas banner predate the historical birth of the popular church in the Americas in 1969.[4] Peasant associations, for instance, are contemporary extensions of the traditional Haitian peasant work group, or *konbit*. Women's organizations have existed at the grassroots level among market women for centuries in Haiti, while elite-sponsored attempts to forge cross-class alliances among women can be traced to the 1934 founding of the Haitian Ligue Féminine d'Action Sociale (Chancy, *Framing*, 40). The most important social unit developed specifically as a part of liberation theology is the ecclesial base community, or *ti kominote legliz* (TKL) in Kreyòl. TKLs are cornerstones of the social change process that culminates in Lavalas, and Aristide describes a typical one in his testimonial narrative, *In the Parish of the Poor*:

> The one room inside the little shack is crowded with young people, and a few who are not so young. It's hot. A young woman standing at the back is directing the discussion. What are those words we hear people saying? *Libète*. Liberty. *Dwa moun*. Human rights. *Teyoloji liberasyon*. Liberation theology. A pot of hot rice and beans is being distributed, paid for by contributions from everyone present. What is this place, what is this group, why are they gathered here under the light of one bare bulb to talk about liberty? You know what this is, brothers and sisters, as well as I do. This is an ecclesial base community; in Haiti, we call them *ti kominote legliz*. Today you can find groups like this all over Latin America; there are more than 300,000 of them in our hemisphere. I work with them, brothers and sisters, and so do you. (13)

The official political arm of the Lavalas movement in the early 1990s, FNCD (National Front for Change and Democracy), historically represents the effort to build an effective lawmaking instrument based on a coalition of TKLs, peasant associations, and women's organizations, as well as youth groups, neighborhood vigilance brigades, human rights groups, trade unions and journalists' organizations, associations of the unemployed, and more. At the heart of this political project is a cultural challenge of finding the symbolic means to imagine such a coalition and articulate its will in concrete public utterances. Aristide's writing and his oral statements (mainly sermons, radio broadcasts, and political speeches, though he has also recorded an album of music) function precisely as symbolic vehicles for imagining coalition. In the rest of this essay I trace both how Aristide's rhetoric of coalition and conciliation is grounded organically in earlier expressions of Haitian national romance and how he produces a new version of the national romance that is more cognizant of the experiences and historical agency of Haitian women.

Romantic coupling retains much of its force as a symbol of social unification and popular mobilization in the contemporary Haitian scene, and the legacy of linking romance and revolutionary nationalism is evident in much of Aristide's own work as well as in the public discourse surrounding his career. "Haïti Chérie," a popular song that is the country's unofficial second national anthem, depicts the nation as the beloved of the singer, and throughout Aristide's tenure as president, public ceremonies were frequently framed by a recording or even a live performance of this song. The force of the song as a vehicle for expressing Haitian nationalism was made clear, for example, when Aristide returned to Haiti on 15 October 1994 after three years in exile. Before any speeches or official demonstrations, two women singers led the crowd and assembled dignitaries in a rousing rendition of the song while United States secretary of state Warren Christopher sat rigid in his seat of honor, not singing, oblivious to or uncomfortable with this manifestation of nationalist sentiment. In his writing, Aristide incorporates the chorus of the song—"Haiti chérie, je t'aime" —as the conclusion to his theological treatise *Théologie et politique* (142). Aristide's autobiography, meanwhile, comments explicitly on the popular practice of constructing his relationship to the Haitian people in terms of a "marriage." He writes: "The people thought of me as a shield, a free and disinterested spokesperson. We had been companions for a long time; we were 'twins,' as the people had said, or 'spouses.' *Titid ak pèp la se marasa*" (Titid and the people are married) (*Autobiography*, 120).

As I noted at the outset of this chapter, that the issue of Aristide's symbolic marriage to the Haitian people surfaced in the events surrounding his and Mildred Trouillot's wedding ceremony points to the staying power of romance tropes in Haitian public culture and underscores how far Aristide and Lavalas have popularized and begun to realize the popular democratic aspirations of previous generations of Haitian writer-activists who worked with and through discourse of romance and revolutionary nationalism.

Even while reanimating the national romance legacy as it is handed down through Roumain, Aléxis, and Depestre, though, Aristide alters it to emphasize new roles for women as historical agents. These modifications, I believe, help illuminate why Aristide and the Lavalas movement have been able to take hold of the Haitian popular imagination —and Haitian political history—in ways that earlier activists only dreamed about.

At a general level, liberation theology provides the obvious point of departure for thinking about Aristide's pursuit of cross-class alliances through the framework of Lavalas. A more comprehensive analysis of his intellectual and political development would consider the writing and activism of Gustavo Gutierrez, Leonardo Boff, and others and would, in particular, focus on how liberation theology offers an approach to popular religion that breaks through the impasse of spiritual life that continued to divide Roumain and Aléxis, as elite intellectuals, from the religious culture of everyday Haitians.[5] Generally speaking, though, liberation theology is consistent with, or an extension of, the attempts of earlier Haitian writer-activists to break through class divisions and establish bonds of solidarity with the suffering masses. If, however, we continue to stress the problem of *gendered* social divisions, the work of liberation theology appears much more transformative. Whereas gender elitism, as we have seen, remains unresolved in the canonical version of the Haitian national romance, liberation theology sustains Aristide's attempts to modify the status of women within the national romance. In both of the examples I am about to consider—when Aristide offers allegories of national renewal through the familiar figure of the pregnant mother and when he writes in a more theoretical vein about the role of women in the base ecclesial communities, or TKLs—his depiction of women as subjects of historical change draws directly from the daily world of Haiti's popular church.

Nowhere is the revisionist aspect of Aristide's work more evident than when he engages with the maternal discourse we have seen operating at the center of canonical narratives of social renewal and progressive change in Haiti. Male-authored texts in the Haitian novel tradition focus on women as recipients of male ideology, revolutionary plans, and frequently, sperm to produce a revolutionary heir. Female characters occupy these positions with little or no complication. Rarely if ever is there any consideration of what motherhood might mean from the female character's point of view. Women writers in Haiti and elsewhere across the Caribbean who choose to engage with maternal discourse (rather than displacing or rejecting it altogether) present much more troubling and ambiguous images of motherhood as painful and traumatic. When Aristide takes up this piece of the national romance tradition, as he does in *In the Parish of the Poor,* his work is much more in line with that of these Haitian novelists, particularly Marie Chauvet, Marie-Thérèse Cólimon-Hall, and most recently Edwidge Danticat.

The passage I shall focus on in Aristide's writing is an anecdote narrated at the beginning of *Parish.* A car has run out of gas in downtown Port-au-Prince, and the narrator watches as the driver gets out to assess the situation. Aristide writes:

> Then I saw another face, the passenger. A woman. She looked out of the back window with tears in her eyes, and the driver looked around the street at the unemployed loungers who are always there, and said to them, "She is going to have a baby right here." He told them that he had taken the woman from her home because the midwife was unable to help her. The pregnancy was difficult, and the woman needed to go to the hospital to have her baby. Now the tears were coming down the woman's cheeks. "If we do not get to the hospital, she will die," the man told the loungers. "Her baby will die, too."
>
> The loungers—hungry young men who had never had a job and who never will have a job if my country goes on as it has done for the last half century—looked at the car and heard the man's voice and saw the woman's tears. Their backs straightened, their cigarettes fell to the ground, their eyes cleared. They approached the car, eight of them, leaned over, and put their shoulders to the chore. The driver steered. The woman lay back. Down one long dusty road, a left turn, and down another, through the green and white gates of the State Hospital, and she had arrived.
>
> That was the force of solidarity at work, a recognition that we are all striving toward the same goal, and that goal is to go forward, to

advance, to bring into this world another way of being. Even if the motor has died, even if the engine is out of gas, that new way of life can be brought into this world through solidarity. The loungers are an awakened populace, the driver brings them the words to awaken them, and the woman carries within her, on her seat in the old beat-up car, the new life, the new Haiti. (4)

Aristide returns to this image of traumatic but ultimately successful childbirth later in the narrative when he relates the story of a woman wounded in an infamous state-sponsored attack on St. Jean Bosco Church where Aristide served as pastor throughout the mid- to late 1980s until he was removed by papal decree. The woman is rushed to a hospital, where she delivers a healthy child despite having been bayoneted in the stomach during the assault, and Aristide revisits this image several times throughout the text when he speaks about the possibilities for social rebirth. Whereas Roumain ends *Gouverneurs de la rosée* idealistically with the protagonist's unborn child stirring in the womb of the wife-mother in order to suggest the coming birth of the new society, Aristide's more realistic vignette acknowledges the troubled passage such historical upheaval actually entails. By presenting the picture of suffering female bodies as central to the work of imagining a transformed national community, *In the Parish of the Poor* signals an awareness of the gender politics of liberation struggle and the images used to encode that struggle. By attending to the complications in maternal discourse, then, Aristide alters the narrative formula for the national romance to make it more reflective of women's lived experiences.

Another way Aristide reworks maternal discourse in the Haitian national romance is by drawing on feminist strands of liberation theology that theorize pregnancy and maternity as principles of divine creativity. Pregnancy as a figure for imminent historical change is, in fact, a motif that runs through the work of many prominent liberation theologians, though often I take this to be a variation on the Marxist theme that the seeds of a future social order are contained in the present.[6] Working somewhat on the margins of liberation theology, though, feminist thinkers have taken the pregnancy motif much further. Writing about the Christian doctrine of the Trinity, for instance, Brazilian theologian María Clara Bingemer argues for a concept of deity that recovers core female attributes in all three aspects— "Father," "Son," and Holy Spirit. Bingemer writes:

The thinking being done in Latin America today seeks to recover from the biblical root of the experience of God, which uses the word *rahamin,* "womb," female entrails, to refer to God's love. Countless Old Testament texts, especially in the prophets, refer to God by this part of the female body. The effect of this is that in theology—feminist or not—God the Father is being called also Mother, or, better, Maternal Father or Paternal Mother. These divine female entrails, pregnant with gestation and birth, which have been identified in the Father, also appear in the incarnate Son, who in the Gospels is driven to cry out in frustrated maternal desire to gather under his wings the scattered an rebellious "chickens of Jerusalem" (Luke 13:34). . . . Once God is experienced, not only as Father, Lord, strong warrior, but also as Mother, protection, greater love, struggle is tempered with festivity and celebration of life, permanent and gentle firmness ensures the ability "to be tough without losing tenderness," and uncompromising resistance can be carried on with joy, without excessive tension and strain. God's compassion, flowing from female and maternal entrails, takes on itself the hurts and wounds of all the oppressed, and a woman who does theology is called to bear witness to this God with her body, her actions, her life. ("Woman," 484–85)

Even without engaging the doctrinal issues raised in this passage, it is evident that Bingemer is using the tools of theological reflection to develop a more liberating perception of women. Her exegesis of the Hebrew word *rahamin,* "womb," as a principle of divine creativity and by extension of female historical agency takes us straight into dialogue with the narrative tradition of using images of pregnancy to suggest coming historical change. Here, though, women are not figured as mere biological objects fulfilling the role of procreative vessels for male-authored desires for a revolutionary heir. Instead, *the idea of procreation* becomes an occasion for thinking about women as liberatory subjects, that is, the direct producers of human history.

Aristide develops something very similar to Bingemer's commentary when he analyzes women's creativity as a moving force within the base ecclesial communities, or TKLs, in *Théologie et politique.* Asserting that women represent a qualitative as well as a quantitative force in Haitian society, Aristide focuses on the *creativity* manifested by and within the liberation church. It is this creativity that distinguishes liberation theology and, at the same time, is constructed by Aristide as most indicative of women's gendered identity. Considering examples that range from various types of liturgical celebration to the maintenance of secular organizations such as Solidarite ant Jèn (Youth Solidarity, an umbrella youth organization) and Lafanmi Selavi (The Family Is Life, an orphanage), Aristide refers to "the values of creativity that live in women" (123). He recognizes women's labor in the TKLs as a politically liberating intervention, one that produces "instruments of struggle" 123) that are "capable of breaking certain barriers in order to open themselves up and enter into relation with each other and with those who inhabit their world" 123–24). Aristide writes:

> These are above all these festivals where, through dance, through invented and imagined dances, through choreography, participants vibrate in every dimension of the being that springs forth [ce qui jaillit] from their life and the lives of others. The women express the struggle, the hope, the resistance, and those who come to mass find themselves in a festival animated in large part by women. . . . All of this has allowed us to create instruments of struggle geared to unite men and women against misery, against injustice and exploitation. . . . This culture [of women] necessarily implies a celebration. One can not exclude celebration from culture, this celebration that realizes itself in vodoun, Protestant and Catholic ceremonies. In vodoun as much as in the other religions, we rediscover this woman who dances, who celebrates life against death, life that is tied to liberation. One cannot be chained if one is to live; one must free oneself in order to live! The celebrations carry the cry of a woman chained by the structures [of repression], by misery, by hunger. The celebrations carry the cry of a woman thirsty for liberty, justice, love, and equality. These celebrations explode the mental structures of a society constituted in judgment, which condemns the woman who has the freedom to dance in spite of being already condemned by a reality of misery and hunger. (*Théologie*, 124, 131)

These comments, although they may seem to takes us out of the realm of symbolic or literary production and into sociological theory, are in fact not a separate issue from the narrative history we have been examining. In addition to the fact that he is representing here the cultural sources of radical social change (and in this context one might juxtapose Aristide's discussion of liturgical dance with the famous passage from *Gouverneurs de la rosée* in which Manuel joins in the ceremonial dance for Legba), we also have to reflect on how this passage engages the theme of women's creativity as a central part of the struggle for liberation in Haiti. For Roumain, Aléxis, and Depestre, the liberatory logic of their writing hinges at some point on a recognition of women's creativity, though they limit this potentially revolutionary gesture by encasing it in stock devices such as eroticism and maternal figurations that emphasize biological reproduction. In writing about women's dancing and other forms of celebration and festivity, then, Aristide is situating himself in relation to a thematic issue that is deeply rooted in the Haitian tradition of national romance. Yet he is writing about this theme in a way that transforms traditional stock aspects and opens up Haitian national romance to the narrative task of constructing women as subjects of historical change as well as recording women's real contributions to the historical process. Echoing Bingemer's assessment that "uncompromising resistance can be carried on with joy," Aristide's feminist liberation theology politicizes women's creativity and envisions women not as biological factories for the revolution but as productive makers of history whose work is a central mediating force in the ongoing process of national development.

Aristide's contribution to the history of democratic struggles in the hemisphere needs to be understood, then, from the vantage point of language and narration as well as other aspects of statecraft. His importance as a political figure is inseparable from his successful efforts, as writer and speaker, to revitalize the narrative traditions for expressing nationalist sentiment in Haiti. While not completely discarding the canonical approach to national romance handed down in the Haitian novel through Roumain, Aléxis, and Depestre, Aristide's written and spoken interventions shift the grounds of passionate patriotism in decisive ways. In the new national romance, one might say, the Haitian *polis* is built upon *agape* rather than *eros*. I have focused mainly on the discursive roots of this shift in liberation theology, and though the cultural and political sources of Aristide's rhetoric extend further into the complex of Haitian cultural history, the scope of this essay permits me to make only cursory gestures toward these other influences. Aristide's openness to vodoun iconography is a complex issue that deserves more commentary. Although trained and ordained as a Roman Catholic priest, Aristide has always been something of a religious syncretist who refers sympathetically and inclusively to the history and cultural practices of vodoun. As more than one commentator has noted, vodoun affords women a much more egalitarian social space, less determined by the patriarchal and heterosexual values that mark dominant religious and political life, and the importance of vodoun as offering an alternative language for expressing the national romance tropes should not be underestimated.[7]

While, as we have seen, the canonical national romance tradition in Haiti valorizes eroticism and biologism, there are also countercurrents in less canonized literature that also may have had an impact on Aristide. In some ways, for example, Aristide's deeroticizing of the national romance represents a return to Haiti's early foundational fictions, including Bergeaud's *Stella,* and perhaps even the prenovelistic discourse of Toussaint L'Ouverture's correspondence, which could be considered founding *texts* of Haitian nationalism and global decolonization. In these earlier texts, romantic patriotism is coded through filial affection (Toussaint) and sibling devotion (Bergeaud), rather than the intense eroticism of twentieth- century writers.[8] Perhaps in response to the concern with physical differences that partially constitutes color and caste divisions, the early Haitian romance decorporealizes its protagonists, and the ideological challenge of national reconciliation is filtered through channels other than physical heterosexual love.[9]

Finally, behind these and other specifically literary developments are the numerous grassroots democratic movements whose activities during and after the ouster of Baby Doc in February 1986 prefigure the emergence of Lavalas as a hegemonic political force. These popular organizations, whose history has yet to be fully recorded, provide Aristide with a reading and listening audience and an activist constituency and therefore serve as enabling preconditions that his words depend on. His writing and speeches, meanwhile, codify and conjugate as public political discourse the more democratic nation-building energies initially nurtured in the TKLs, workers syndicates, women's organizations, neighborhood associations, students' unions, rural co-ops, and so on. In rewriting the national romance, Aristide has recast the language used to define the Haitian body politic and has been a central figure in forging a progressive hegemony that has not existed in Haiti since the days of the revolutionary alliance between black leaders like Toussaint, Henri Christophe, and Dessalines, mulatto affranchis like Petion and Rigaud, and the black masses of Saint-Domingue. Perhaps most radical is how far the new national romance in Haiti recreates the body politic as a more egalitarian space where women, and particularly poor, Kreyòl-speaking women, enter the scene of Haitian history as the principal producers of a liberating social praxis. Democracy is an unfinished project in Haiti, but this is equally true across the Caribbean and in the wider arena of pan-American societies (including the United States). Whereas most of the scholarly postmortems on Aristide's election, exile, and return focus stereotypically on how the radical firebrand was chastened by his sobering exposure to United States political culture, Aristide himself has constantly asserted that culture is a two-way street. Just as Haitians continue to learn from their experiences in the world system, so does the world have positive lessons to draw from Haiti. As other nations in the Caribbean and the Americas search for answers to their own political, cultural, and economic dilemmas, the revitalization of the Haitian national romance is one of the most important lessons any of us can derive from the history of Aristide and Lavalas.

## Notes

1. Unless otherwise noted, all translations are my own.

2. Looking down on Port-au-Prince (fictionally rendered as Port-au-Roi) from the heights of a mountain denuded of trees and vegetation, Postel reflects to himself: "Erosion and deforestation are, for our mountains, what zombification is for our people" (*Festival of the Greasy Pole*, 41). Subsequent references are to Carrol F. Coates's translation.

3. Elisa memorializes Postel as a progenitor of radical resistance: "Your death will nourish the actions and dreams of your people as your life fertilized my own" (139). Postel also continues to function as the central source of her own revolutionary resolve: "When the days go by too depressingly, I close my eyes and immediately feel Henri's vital energy correcting, lightening, refreshing my vision of things" (142).

4. Historically, the liberation theology movement grew out of two important conferences of Latin American bishops, at Medellín, Colombia, in 1969 and Puebla, Mexico, in 1979, where conferences attendees adopted the idea that the Roman Catholic Church, in all its activities, should exercise a "preferential option for the poor."

5. Roumain and Aléxis both embrace vodoun aesthetically but reject it politically as a mystifying "opiate" that constitutes an impediment to full liberation.

6. The following examples give some idea of the trend: "The praxis of liberation, in its deepest dimension, is pregnant with the future; hope must be an inherent part of our present commitment in history" (Gutierrez, *Theology*, 14); "For a Christian, it [history] is pregnant with God, and so must be interpreted by theological reflection. . . . Theology and martyrdom point to sanctity, lived in a new mode, appropriate to the new mode of being the church, and to *the new model of society developing in germ in the action of the poor*"

(Boff, "Originality," 44, 47; my emphasis); "The Latin America of today is pregnant with the Kingdom of tomorrow" (Bingemer, "Woman," 487).

7. For instance, the popular Kreyòl phrase that I have taken as a title for this essay, "Titid ak pèp la se marasa," invokes the vodoun figure of the Marasas, or twins. In his autobiography, Aristide himself interprets this phrase to mean he and the Haitian people are "twins" as well as "spouses," thus detaching the national romance somewhat from associations with the union of heterosexual lovers. For further discussion of vodoun and gender politics, see Patrick Bellegarde-Smith, *Haiti: The Citadel Breached,* 22–29; Myriam Chancy, *Framing Silence;* Gerald Murray, "Population Pressure," 300; and David Nicholls, *Haiti in Caribbean Context,* 121–29.

8. In his classic letter to the French Directory, dated 15 November 1796, Toussaint denounces the white planters' schemes to reinstitute slavery and declares himself a "better father" to the Haitian people: "You will see that they [the Saint-Domingue planters] are counting heavily on my complacency in lending myself to their perfidious views by my fear for my children. It is not astonishing that these men who sacrifice their country to their interests are unable to conceive how many sacrifices true love of country can support in a better father than they, since I unhesitatingly base the happiness of my children on that of my country, which they and they alone wish to destroy" (quoted in James, *Black,* 197).

Bergeaud's novel explicitly rejects eroticism in condemning the rivalry of Romulus and Remus for the affections of Stella (138–39). In contrast, Bergeaud celebrates the reconciliation of the brothers and champions their fraternal love as a political ideal: "How sweet it is to love one another! Had the men ever been disunited? Discord is a violent and unhappy state that exhausts individuals and ruins societies. When will discord be banished forever from our country!" (198–99).

9. I am adapting the notion of decorporealization from Carla L. Peterson. In *Doers of the Word: African American Women Reformers in the North (1830–1879)* Peterson uses the notion of "decorporealized voice" to describe the rhetorical strategy of Frances E. W. Harper's oratory in the nineteenth-century United States. According to Peterson, Harper strove to deemphasize her physical appearance through dress and posture in order to compel audiences to pay more attention to her abolitionist, temperance, and uplift ideas and less attention to her black female body (122–24).

## Works Cited

Aléxis, Jacques Stéphen. *Compère Général Soleil.* Paris: Gallimard, 1955.
Aristide, Jean-Bertrand. *In the Parish of the Poor.* Trans. Amy Wilentz. Maryknoll NY: Orbis, 1990.
———. *Jean-Bertrand Aristide: An Autobiography.* Maryknoll NY: Orbis, 1993.

————. *Théologie et politique.* Montreal: CIDIHCA, 1992.

"Aristide Weds Adviser, Irking Some Haitians." *Washington Post,* 21 January 1996, A27.

Bellegarde-Smith, Patrick. *Haiti: The Citadel Breached.* Boulder CO: Westview, 1990.

Bergeaud, Emeric. *Stella.* Paris: Duroy, 1859.

Bingemer, María Clara. "Woman in the Future of Liberation Theology." In *The Future of Liberation Theology: Essays in Honor of Gustavo Gutierrez,* ed. Marc H. Ellis and Otto Maduro, 476–87. Maryknoll NY: Orbis, 1989.

Boff, Leonardo. "The Originality of the Theology of Liberation." In *The Future of Liberation Theology: Essays in Honor of Gustavo Gutierrez,* ed. Marc H. Ellis and Otto Maduro. Maryknoll NY: Orbis, 1989.

Chancy, Myriam. *Framing Silence: Revolutionary Novels by Haitian Women.* New Brunswick: Rutgers Univ. Press, 1997.

Cottenet-Hage, Madeleine, and Kevin Meehan. "Re-writing Postcolonial Social Texts: Maternal Discourse in Chauvet and Lacrosil." In *Contemporary Women Writing in the Other Americas,* vol. 2, *Contemporary Women Writing in the Caribbean,* 277–92. Lewiston, Queenston, and Lampeter: Edwin Mellen Press, 1996.

Depestre, René. *Le mât de cocagne.* 1976. Translated by Carrol F. Coates as *The Festival of the Greasy Pole.* Charlottesville: Univ. Press of Virginia, 1990.

Gutierrez, Gustavo. *A Theology of Liberation: History, Politics, and Salvation.* Ed. and trans. Sister Caridad Inda and John Eagleson. Maryknoll NY: Orbis, 1973.

James, C. L. R. *The Black Jacobins: Toussaint L'Ouverture and the San Domingo Revolution.* New York: Vintage, 1980.

Murray, Gerald. "Population Pressure, Land Tenure, and Voodoo: The Economics of Haitian Peasant Ritual." In *Beyond the Myths of Culture: Essays in Cultural Materialism,* ed. Eric B. Ross, 295–321. New York: Academic Press.

Nicholls, David. *Haiti in Caribbean Context: Ethnicity, Economy and Revolt.* New York: St. Martin's Press, 1985.

Peterson, Carla L. *Doers of the Word: African American Women Reformers in the North (1830–1879).* New York: Oxford University Press, 1995.

Roumain, Jacques. *Gouverneurs de la rosée.* 1944. Translated as *Masters of the Dew.* Trans. Langston Hughes and Mercer Cook. London: Heinemann, 1978.

Sommer, Doris. *Foundational Fictions: The National Romances of Latin America.* Berkeley: Univ. of California Press, 1991.

7

# Shadowboxing in the Mangrove: The Politics of Identity in Postcolonial Martinique

*Richard Price and Sally Price*

Our space is the Caribbean . . . the estuary of the Americas

Édouard Glissant, *Le discours antillais*

During the past couple of decades, anthropologists have begun to understand the extent to which cultural criticism—particularly critiques that stress the constructedness of culture and tradition—runs political risks. As the title of a provocative essay by Jean Jackson asks, "Is there a way to talk about making culture without making enemies?" And an emerging literature makes patently clear that anthropological studies focused on nationalist ideologies face special challenges in this regard (see, for example, Linnekin and Poyer, *Cultural Identity;* Handler, "Fieldwork"). This essay, which is intended to complement other recent analyses of the reproduction of essentialist and masculinist notions in ostensibly antiracial and anticolonial discourse in the Caribbean (Williams, *Stains;* Segal, "Living"; Yelvington, *Producing*), offers a reading of some important recent texts from Martinique, which we attempt to historicize and contextualize ethnographically.

It may be useful for us to begin with a few words on our own subject position. As committed Caribbeanists, we share a vision of the region that was enunciated three centuries ago by Père Labat: "I have traveled everywhere in your sea of the Caribbean . . . from Haiti to Barbados, to Martinique and Guadeloupe, and I know what I am speaking about. . . . You are all together, in the same boat, sailing on the same uncertain sea . . . citizenship and race unimportant, feeble little labels compared to the message that my spirit brings to me: that of the position and predicament which History has imposed upon you" (quoted in Lewis, *Main,* 93). The great Caribbeanist Gordon K. Lewis—who quoted this passage not directly from Labat's *Nouveaux voyages* but from a 1957 radio script written by George Lamming—commented that "the prophetic vision of that passage has never been far from the conscious surface of the Caribbean imagination" (338).

In addition to focusing our research interests on the region for thirty-odd years, we have for the past decade made the Caribbean our home, living in a rural Martiniquan community we first knew through undergraduate fieldwork in the early 1960s. Like the Martiniquan writers whose ideas we consider in this chapter, we participate routinely in at least two realms of experience—that of the island's day-to-day realities (from yam gardens and wakes to traffic jams and French television) and a more internationally oriented intellectual sphere that operates through air travel, publishing, and far-flung academic networks. In short, we are not studying people out "there" from a home-base back "here" but rather engaging the intellectual agenda of people who are very much our peers in terms of their education, publishing involvements, and access to the media. Just as we comment on their work, they comment on ours (see, for example, Chamoiseau, "Les nègres"). The plea we make in these pages for a broadening of their vision, a fuller recognition of the region as an interconnected whole, does not advocate replacing one essentialism with another. Instead, we intend to point toward conceptual openings that could, we believe, both complicate and enrich their acclaimed literary depictions of Martinique's past and its place within the wider Caribbean.

### An Absence of Ruins

In the post-Columbian Caribbean, history begins with rupture and pain. Violence, torture, and blood course through the works of the region's great writers—from Carpentier, Césaire, and James to Lamming, Naipaul, Glissant, and Walcott. A character in one of Paule Marshall's novels explains to visiting anthropologists, "Ah, well, ah, history. . . . Any of you ever study it? . . . Well, don't if you haven't. I did for a time—West Indian history it was and I tell you, it nearly, as we say in Bournehills, set out my head. I had to leave it off. It is a nightmare, as that Irishman said, and we haven't awaked from it yet" (*Chosen,* 130).[1]

Colonized for more than five centuries, quintessentially Western, Caribbean peoples face the challenge of somehow recasting the modernist paradigm of progress, unashamedly triumphalist and Eurocentric. How at the same time to appropriate and subvert the central ideas associated with modernity? How to write in the colonizer's language and assert one's own vision of the world? How at once to represent and resist the March of History set in motion by Columbus? How to play off one part of oneself against another? Over the years, Caribbean intellectuals have rehearsed many of the difficulties, from the vitriolic queries of V. S. Naipaul: "How can the history of this West Indian futility be written? What tone shall the historian adopt?" (*Middle,* 29); or the pointed asides of Édouard Glissant about "the loss of collective memory, the careful erasure of the past, . . . the obscurity of this impossible memory" (*Le discours,* 277; *Poétique,* 86); to the stark assertions of Derek Walcott: "In time, the slave surrendered to amnesia [and] that amnesia is the true history of the New World" ("Muse," 4); or Orlando Patterson's conclusion: "The most critical feature of the West Indian consciousness is what Derek Walcott calls 'an absence of ruins.' The most important legacy of slavery is the total break, not with the past so much as with a consciousness of the past. To be a West Indian is to live in a state of utter pastlessness" ("Recent," 258).

But these and other Caribbean writers have also pointed the way toward possible escapes. Carpentier, in the famous formulation emerging from his confrontation with the Haitian Revolution, proposed that the history of the Americas, "por los fecundos mestizajes que propició," is nothing "sino una crónica de lo real-maravilloso" (that fertile mixings have made the history of the Americas a chronicle of magic realism ["Prologo," 12–30]). In this same regard, Lamming reminds us of the redemptive potential of Caribbean folk wisdom: calypsonian Lord Kitchener, commenting on the Soviet triumph in space signaled by the launch of *Sputnik,* sang "Columbus didn't need no dog"—at once, Lamming hints, wryly acknowledging the hegemony of Western History (the definition of Columbus as a Great Man) and effectively subverting it (along with its triumphalist narrative of Western progress) through carnivalesque ridicule (*Pleasures,* 77; see also Gikandi, *Writing,* 58). Similarly, Wilson Harris has criticized the intellectual West Indian perspective that stresses an absence of ruins or a sense of pastlessness in the folk thought of the Caribbean, calling on historians to seek out "an inner time," to break out of the traditional "high-level psychological censorship of the creative imagination" that has hamstrung critical Caribbean scholarship: "I believe," he writes, that "a philosophy of history may well lie buried in the arts of the imagination" (*Explorations,* 24–25, 28–29). Glissant, who conjures up the need for "a prophetic vision of the past," asserts that "the struggle against a single History, and for a cross-fertilization of histories, means at once repossessing one's true sense of time and one's identity. It also means posing in an entirely new way the question of power" (*Le discours,* 132, 159). Walcott's advice is complementary: "History remains for the Caribbean the territory of the imagination and memory, and that imagination is not innocent but experienced" ("History," 6); "The children of slaves must sear their memory with a torch" ("Twilight," 5); and "The truly tough aesthetic of the New World neither explains nor forgives history" ("Muse," 2).[2]

### Contextualizing the Créolistes

The tiny island of Martinique—which one recent student has dubbed the "Isle of Intellectuals" (Taylor, "Isle")—has already made a disproportionate contribution to these debates. Politically and economically, today's Martinique, like its sister territories Guadeloupe and French Guiana, stands out from its Caribbean neighbors by being part of Europe, lending its cultural politics a particular complexity. In the thirties, Aimé Césaire's explosive *Cahier d'un retour au pays natal* announced the birth of *négritude,* and a new poetics of resistance, written in what was at once extraordinarily powerful, masterful, and subversive French, began to spread its message wherever colonized peoples still suffered. One of Césaire's students in Fort-de-France's Lycée Schoelcher, although choosing prose rather than poetry, continued the literary assault in a yet more militant vein and was quickly heard round the world: Frantz Fanon.[3] And Édouard Glissant, a near contemporary of Fanon at the lycée, remains a major contributor to world literature and theory through his wide-ranging essays, poetry, and novels focused on neocolonial and postcolonial realities.

Nearly a decade has now passed since a set of newcomers announced their arrival on this scene. In 1986 Patrick Chamoiseau, a young Martiniquan writer, startled the French literary world with

*Chronique des sept misères,* generally considered the first work of the *créolité* movement.[4] That novel was soon followed by a manifesto, *Éloge de la créolité* (1989), coauthored by Jean Bernabé, Raphaël Confiant, and Chamoiseau, and then by a canon-fixing history of French Antillean literature (Chamoiseau and Confiant, *Lettres créoles*) as well as a flood of prize-winning novels by Chamoiseau and Confiant.[5] Most recently, the world premiere of *L'exil de Béhanzin* (Fort-de-France, March 1995), a film whose screenplay was written by Chamoiseau, elicited active local debate about the *créolistes'* perspectives, continuing the heavy mediatization (television, radio, magazines, newspapers) that has come to accompany every new contribution to the movement; in May 1995 *Béhanzin* was crowned with a prize at the francophone film festival in Montreal.

Despite the widespread—and in our view well deserved—praise for Chamoiseau's and Confiant's novels (see, for just one example, the articles collected in Arnold, *History*), little critical attention has been devoted to their ideas about the Caribbean and its past. Perhaps the time is ripe for a brief review of the *créoliste* agenda—particularly as it concerns the revisioning of history.

The *Éloge* is a praise song for a Creole identity that is not defined by someone else, an embracing of all the strands that have contributed to the making of the Antillean. The past, it argues, requires radical revisioning:

> Our History, or more precisely our histories, are shipwrecked within Colonial History. Collective memory must be our priority. What we once believed to be Caribbean history is no more than the History of Colonization of the Caribbean. Beneath the shock waves of French history, beneath the Great Dates marking the arrival and departure of colonial governors, beneath the uncertainties of colonial struggles, beneath the standard white pages of the official Chronicle (where the torches of our revolts appear only as tiny blotches), there was our own obstinate trudging along. The opaque resistance of maroons united in their refusal. The new heroism of those who confronted the hell of slavery, using obscure codes of survival, indecipherable means of resistance, an impenetrable variety of compromises, unexpected syntheses for living. . . . Within this false consciousness we had but a bunch of obscurities for memory, a feeling of bodily discontinuity. Landscapes, Glissant reminds us, stand alone as inscriptions, in their nonanthropomorphic way, of at least some of our tragedy, of our

will to exist. Which means that our history, or histories, are not totally accessible to historians. . . . It is no accident that, when it comes
to Caribbean history, so many historians use literary citations to try
to grasp principles that they can only graze with their usual method-
ology. . . . Only poetic knowledge, romantic knowledge, literary
knowledge, in short, artistic knowledge, can reveal us, perceive us,
bring us back, evanescent, to a reborn consciousness. (Bernabé,
Chamoiseau, and Confiant, *Éloge,* 36–38)

When the *créolistes* acknowledge intellectual antecedents at all,
their references are almost exclusively francophone. In this essay we
suggest that a consideration of their program within the context of a
broader Caribbean historiography may be useful. At the time the
*créoliste* movement emerged, in the mid-1980s, related perspectives,
many centered in the anglophone Caribbean just next door, had been
widely discussed for at least two decades. As a metaphor or model for
the development of Caribbean culture, "creolization" (a concept originally borrowed from historical linguistics) had long been debated and
proclaimed by Caribbean writers and artists as well as Caribbeanist
social scientists. (For a sampling of this extensive literature, see the
essays, dating from the 1950s onward, collected in Brathwaite, *History,* and for other British Caribbean references, Walmsley, *Caribbean;*
for the Hispanic Caribbean, see Fernández Retamar, *"Caliban,"* and
González, *El país;* for diverse pan-Caribbean antecedents, including
Martí and Toussaint, see Gikandi, *Writing,* 16–17, and of course
Ortiz, *Contrapunteo,* as well as Mintz and Price, *Birth,* which includes relevant social science bibliography.) Even within the bounds
of the francophone world, a model stressing the "interpenetration of
civilizations" had been used as early as the 1950s to interpret the cultural history of (Afro-)Brazil (see Bastide, *Les religions*), though the
*créolistes* do not acknowledge it. Not to mention the competing metaphors of hybridity, *mestizaje,* and so forth, that were being so hotly
debated by intellectuals from Ghana and Mexico to the Indian sub-
continent, and even in metropolitan France (see, for example, the essays collected in Appiah, *Father's;* García Canclini, *Culturas;* Bhabha,
*Location;* Todorov, *Human*), at the very moment when the *créolistes*
burst onto the scene. Setting their ideas within an insular intellectual
history of Martinique, the *créolistes* have been able to underscore
their difference from earlier generations. But in a more international

Caribbean context, the major programmatic claims of the *créolistes,* when first stated, were already widely acknowledged.

While the predominantly adulatory reception by metropolitan French critics of *créoliste* novels has tended to focus on their stylistically innovative contributions to French language and literature,[6] the writers themselves tend to emphasize, rather, their special vision— political, historical, linguistic, and cultural—of Martinique and its place in the world. In contrast to their collective father figure Aimé Césaire (whose *négritude* they criticize as an overprivileging of world-wide Africanity), or their elder brother figure Édouard Glissant (whose *antillanité* they characterize as focusing too exclusively on the mere adaptation of Old World peoples to a new Caribbean environment), the *créolistes* see themselves as stressing the historical interpenetration of peoples and cultures that created a truly new, syncretic, Creole culture. They argue, for example, that when the African migrants arrived, they were "naked" culturally, "with their only baggage nebulous traces lodged in the folds of their memory" (Chamoiseau and Confiant, *Lettres,* 37). They write of "all these peoples precipitated into the crucible of the Caribbean archipelago . . . in which no synthesis occurred but rather a kind of hesitant *métissage,* always contested, always chaotic, carrying anthropological densities across vaporous borders, bathing in a creole space that was almost amniotic. . . . [After a certain time, these people had become] *créole*—that is, already multiple, already mosaic'd, already unpredictable" (51, 38). And they proclaim themselves to be "neither Europeans nor Africans nor Asians . . . but Creoles . . . at once Europe and Africa, enriched by contributions from Asia, the Levant, and India, and including also survivals from Pre-Columbian America" (Bernabé, Chamoiseau, and Confiant, *Éloge,* 13, 27)[7]—thus disregarding Glissant's stricture that "creolization as an idea is not primarily the glorification of the composite nature of a people" but rather "a cross-cultural process . . . an unceasing process of transformation" (*Le discours,* 25, 52).[8]

In the service of their identitarian quest, the *créolistes* rewrite central aspects of the Caribbean past. For example, to highlight the processual importance of the "crucible" of the plantation (where, they argue, their new culture was forged), they deny that "immigrants"— whether African slaves or indentured Africans, Indians, or Chinese— had experienced any sort of "diversity" in their own homelands; for each such immigrant "group," their particular Old World is seen as a cultural monolith. Moreover, the French Antillean plantation is depicted as a relatively "gentle" institution in the broader Caribbean context: masters and slaves are said to have worked side by side, both suffering the deprivations of displacement and engaging in frequent cultural interchange; truly "harsh" slavery is displaced onto other colonial powers, like the Spanish, English, or Dutch (see, for example, Chamoiseau and Confiant, *Lettres,* 35–41).[9]

As for maroons (the rebel slaves who had been so heavily romanticized during the heyday of the *négritude* movement), the *créolistes* tend to view them as having in a sense taken the easy way out by abandoning the plantation hotbed of creolization and simply "Americanizing," adapting to a new environment rather than fully "creolizing" (Bernabé, Chamoiseau, and Confiant, *Éloge,* 30; Chamoiseau and Confiant, *Lettres,* 34, 39). Like the Anglo-Saxon colonists in North America, East Indian indentured workers in Trinidad, or Italian immigrants in nineteenth-century Argentina, they assert, the Saramaka and "Boni" (Aluku) maroons of the Guianas merely adapted to the new physical environment of the Americas without engaging, as their enslaved brethren did, in the much more complex cultural interaction with other parts of the population that constitutes, for the *créolistes,* the essence of creolization (Bernabé, Chamoiseau, and Confiant, *Éloge,* 30–32).[10] By understating the tremendous diversity of African cultures and languages represented in any early Caribbean colony—and in these very maroon communities at the outset—the *créolistes* obscure the ways in which these maroon communities were, in fact, the most thoroughly (and earliest fully) "creolized" of *all* New World communities. For the central creolization process in those maroon societies was inter-African syncretism (which is based on the multiplicity of African cultures and languages involved), combined with less substantial interactional contributions from Europeans, Amerindians, and others (see, for example, Price and Price, *Afro-American;* Price, *Alabi's*). The *créolistes,* however, depict maroons as somewhat uncultured isolationists "on the margins of general [historical] processes . . . spiritually mired in times past, with their loincloths, spears, and bows . . . their bamboo bracelets, eagle feathers, earrings, and designs traced in ashes on their faces" (Chamoiseau, *Texaco,* 107, 142).

For the *créolistes,* the real heroes of the historical narrative are the plantation slaves who, "secure in their secret dignity, often laid the groundwork for what we are today, and did so more effectively than many a maroon" (Chamoiseau and Confiant, *Lettres,* 61).[11] More specifically, it is the *conteur* (storyteller) who replaces the maroon as the heroic figure par excellence. The *conteur,* "among the most docile of slaves," has "almost the quality of an Uncle Tom, whom the master doesn't fear," which allows him to spread a subversive message of day-to-day resistance through all manner of verbal ruses (Chamoiseau and Confiant, *Lettres,* 56–64; see also Chamoiseau, *Au temps; Solibo;* and Confiant, *Contes; Les maîtres*). Here again we miss a pan-Caribbean perspective, for the *créolistes* fail to acknowledge that the *conteur* whom they enshrine has long been a central figure in the landscape of critical thinking about the Caribbean, a well-documented subspecies of what Roger Abrahams calls the man-of-words (*Man-of-Words*). It is perhaps no accident that the *créolistes* choose to portray their own literary activities as those of modern-day *conteurs* (*marqueurs de paroles,* "markers of speech") in much the same way that Césaire and his followers have viewed themselves as metaphorical maroons. If today's Martinique, with its deep imbrication in France and Europe, can be conceptualized in an analogous mode to a slave community within an all-encompassing plantation system, then a self-proclaimed *marqueur de paroles,* the agent of a ruse-based subversiveness comparable to that of the slave-era *conteur,* becomes a more appropriate contemporary figure of resistance than the fiery rebel of yore.

J. Michael Dash's 1995 study (*Édouard*) has helped to open our eyes to how very far the *créoliste* vision of the Caribbean past is directly indebted to ideas embedded in the novels of Glissant.[12] These include a privileging of the *conteur,* who resists imaginatively and from within the community, over the figure of the maroon, who tends to be inward turning and isolationist; an identification between *conteur* and narrator; an insistence on the impossibility of *marronage* in the Martinique of tourism and shopping malls; and the need to develop more generalized, modest forms of resistance. Dash emphasizes that Glissant's narratives are not about "a glorification of those who resisted over those who collaborated . . . [but about] mutual interdependence and the emergence of a composite, creole culture" (*Édouard,* 84), and he bluntly criticizes the *Éloge* for its "tendency to turn Glissant's ideas into ideological dogma . . . in terms that are suggestively reductionist" (23). He goes on to argue that this new dogma of *créolité*

is tempted to produce its own rhetoric, its own approved texts, its own hierarchy of intellectuals and a new heroics of *marronnage,* orality and popular discourse. It lacks the ironic self-scrutiny, the insistence on process ("creolisation" and not "*créolité*") that is characteristic of Glissant's thought. Indeed, despite its avowed debt to Glissant, *Éloge de la créolité* risks undoing the epistemological break with essentialist thinking that he has always striven to conceptualise. (23)

### Diversalité

The *créolistes'* ideological agenda encourages them to depict Martinique—in both the past and the present—as brimming with diversity (often referred to in their writing as "*diversalité*" (e.g., Bernabé, Chamoiseau, and Confiant, *Éloge,* 54; Chamoiseau and Confiant, *Lettres,* 204). "*Créolité,*" declares the *Éloge,* "is the interactional or transactional aggregate of Carib, European, African, Asian, and Levantine cultural elements, which the yoke of history has harnessed together on the same soil. . . . We want, in the true spirit of *créolité,* to . . . explore our Amerindian, Indian, Chinese, and Levantine origins and find their rhythms in the beating of our hearts" (26, 40). Various markers (and discourses ) of color, class, race, and ethnicity—but not gender, see below—are enlisted in the service of this celebration of diversity. During a public debate broadcast in part on television (25 September 1993), for example, Confiant expressed pleasure at having grown up among "*békés* [white creoles of the planter class], *chabins* [people—like Confiant himself—whose physiognomy juxtaposes "negroid" and "European" features, such as kinky hair and broad nose with light skin and green eyes], *milats* [mulattoes, which is also a class designation], and *coulis* [descendants of Indians from the subcontinent]." In their historical schema, Chamoiseau and Confiant essentialize Martiniquan maroons and slaves as two "ethnic groups" (*Lettres,* 39) and trace social changes in mid-twentieth-century Martinique to the action of "everybody—white, black, mulatto, of Carib ancestry, *chabin,* or Indian" (44). In other words, they foster an illusion of diversity by peopling the island with a reified set of categories drawn from cross-cutting kinds of schemata (class, "race," national origin, etc.).[13]

From a broader Caribbeanist perspective, however, the society of Martinique looks anything but diverse. Even people from smaller islands might well be inclined to share Walcott's gaze on the place: "I memorize the atmosphere in Martinique / as comfortable colonial— tobacco, awnings, Peugeots, pink gendarmes . . . / their nauseous sense of heritage and order" (*Arkansas*, 75). Anyone with comparative experience in the Americas (and especially in such Caribbean places as French Guiana, Belize, Trinidad, or Suriname) would be hard pressed to see the Martinique in which Confiant grew up as especially differentiated internally—ethnically, racially, or culturally. In the context of other Caribbean settings—whether particular islands (even small ones like St. Croix or Sint Maarten/Saint Martin) or diasporic spaces like New York or Toronto, Miami, Paris or London—Martinique emerges culturally, racially, ethnically, and economically, rather, as *relatively* homogeneous.

The *créolistes'* lack of a pan-Caribbean perspective, in any but a superficial programmatic sense, combined with a (French-inspired) notion that one nation normally equals one culture, leads them to be genuinely intrigued when they discover that in the French Antilles things are different. The idea of multiple identities then becomes not the normal (human or Caribbean) state of affairs but a phenomenon in need of explanation and celebration: "Who could ever have imagined that the epic of the Ramayana, an ancient text thousands of years old, fixed forever in the canon of Indian literature, would be able to find an eagerly receptive audience among the young Creole-Indian storytellers of Martinique or Guadeloupe? Who would have thought that the mysteries of the long-gone [*sic*] Caribs would find a place in the words of the old Creole storytellers in Martinique, Guadeloupe, and Guyane? . . . Who?!" (Chamoiseau and Confiant, *Lettres*, 51). Meanwhile, Cubans with Andalusian ancestry or "East Indian" Trinidadians have, in the *créolistes'* vision of the Caribbean, "simply adapted" to a new environment, "without really creolizing" (Bernabé, Chamoiseau, and Confiant, *Éloge*, 32). In claiming that "as Creoles," they are "closer, anthropologically speaking," to the people of the Seychelles, Mauritius, or Réunion than, for example, to Puerto Ricans or Cubans (32–33), they neglect to recognize the fundamentally creole and Caribbean nature of Puerto Rican and Cuban cultures. Moreover, their claim to "anthropological closeness" masks what might rather more directly be attributed to the workings of empire.

The *créolistes'* insularity—their willful nonengagement with both non-French Caribbean and nonfrancophone scholarship—colors their understandings of the Caribbean past in a number of domains.[14] The development of local language provides an apt illustration. (Given that one of the authors of the *Éloge*, Bernabé, is not only a linguist but a specialist in creole languages, this aspect of their project is particularly noteworthy.) In *Lettres créoles,* Chamoiseau and Confiant offer a revisionist explanation of the development of Martiniquan Creole (52–56). They posit that in the "beginning" (which they date as 1625 to 1675–80) colonists from the northwest of France, particularly Normandy and Anjou—at a time, they remind us, when the "French" language was still largely confined to the Île-de-France and Racine had difficulty making himself understood beyond Lyons—confronted Africans who spoke different languages. They then "destroy the myth" that the absence of *r*s in Creole stems from blacks' not being able to pronounce that sound, asserting instead that "this phonetic trait [of Creole] stems from the Norman colonists—solely from them—and not from the Africans, since, as everyone knows, whatever their native language, they roll their *r*s almost like Arabs." To support this claim, they cite a 1908 dictionary of Anjou speech that gives *pourmener* for *promener, célébral* for *cérébral,* and *flamaáon* for *franc-maáon* (54–55). Their explanation of why Antilleans allegedly cannot pronounce *s* when followed by a consonant again draws on the Anjou dictionary, which, through examples such as *espirituel* for *spirituel,* allows them to derive the trait from that part of France. After further examples of this sort, they conclude that "four-fifths of all so-called anomalies of Creole pronunciation, compared with French, are due not to the blacks but simply to the dialects of the first white colonists," and that the same holds for lexical contributions (55). They argue that "the language of the Caribs, the languages of West Africa, and the Tamil of the Indians also contributed to Creole, particularly on the lexical plane" and cite a handful of Amerindian botanical lexemes, magicoreligious African ones, and a few "from the cuisine transported from south India" (55), concluding, "Thus, this language born on the plantations reflects in its phrases the diversity of the world" (56).

Although Creole linguistics is hardly devoid of controversy, there are certain basics that can be safely stated. One is that for scholars who, like the *créolistes,* adopt a historicist (rather than a bioprogram) explanation, the role of African languages on both syntactic and phonological levels is fundamental. Furthermore, the very common substitution of *l*s for *r*s in a wide range of non-French-related creole languages (such as Ndyuka or Saramaccan) can in no way be explained by recourse to the pronunciation patterns of Normans. In their discussion of the development of Creole, the *créolistes*' insularity limits their ability to arrive at a persuasive narrative of the Caribbean past.[15]

The *créoliste* vision stresses, as part of its depiction of *diversalité*, that Martinique is neither monolingual nor diglossic but rather truly "multilingual" (or "polyglot"): "*Créolité* itself is multilingual. . . . Its domain is Language. Its appetite: all the languages of the world" (Bernabé, Chamoiseau, and Confiant, *Éloge*, 48). Building on this linguistic claim, and insisting that Martinique is "intrinsically multicultural," Confiant, for example, evokes

> the illiterate cane cutter who, to cure a malady, goes to Catholic mass in the morning, participates in a Hindu ceremony in the afternoon, and consults a black *quimboiseur* in the evening. . . . [as well as] the semiliterate fisherman who inscribes "Ecce homo," "Agnus Dei," or "Kyrie eleison" on his fishing craft, showing that he possesses the intuition of multilingualism. . . . All this amid a population of fishermen who speak only Creole, in a [French] *département* where the official language is French! (*Aimé*, 61)

"The whole world," proclaims the *Éloge*, "is evolving toward a condition of *créolité*," toward a "new dimension of man of which we are the prefiguration in silhouette" (51, 27).[16]

## Modernization and "Pastifying" in Martinique

In contrast to most literary critics, who accept the *créolistes'* self-definition as intellectual rebels (see, for example, Burton, "Idea"; Scarboro, "Shift"), we would argue that much of the ideology of the *créolité* movement, from its emphasis on the role of French (as opposed to African languages) in the development of Creole to its championing of ethnic diversity, fits comfortably within its historical moment. Indeed, we believe that, in terms of cultural politics, the kinds of specificities championed by the *créolistes* are in step with a rapidly modernizing Martinique in which people are, with considerable coaching from France, adjusting to their new place within a greater Europe.

Since the 1960s, the island world of Martinique has been undergoing a fundamental transformation, responding to French-mandated programs designed to bring it and its sister neocolonies into line with Europe in terms of roads, electricity, telephones, piped water, airports, hotels, golf courses, marinas, social programs (a panoply of welfare benefits, pensions, unemployment insurance), residential construction (tripling the standard size of houses even as family size began to plummet), cars (bringing the per capita ownership to levels rivaling that in the United States), supermarkets, appliance stores, and other large-scale consumer offerings (INSEE, *Tableaux*). Agriculture has atrophied while service industries and the civil service have mushroomed. As the landscape has been transformed, the environment has suffered fierce degradation. The media have been modernized, making the French language an omnipresent part of everyone's daily life. Greater Fort-de-France has grown to represent nearly half the island's population, and massive numbers of Antilleans have been lured to the metropole by official French programs designed to fill particular employment niches, with the result that some 40 percent of the "Antillean population" are now settled in the hexagon (Marie, "Les populations").

This unusually rapid modernization, imposed from the metropole, is profoundly assimilationist in spirit. And it demands the concomitant rejection of much of Martiniquan culture as it had developed during the previous three centuries—at least as a viable way of life for today's forward-looking generation. One television advertisement ridicules the country bumpkin, visiting his bourgeois cousins, who grates fruit to make juice rather than buying it ready made in a carton at the supermarket, and another ridicules the simpleton who hacks at trees with a machete when a gasoline-powered brushwacker could fell them at the touch of a button. Such promotional campaigns have successfully created a whole range of "needs," such as electronic front gates, home security systems, travel agents, and canned dog food, that were virtually unknown just two decades ago. And in terms of values and self-perception, Martiniquans have been encouraged to situate themselves as thoroughly modern, bourgeois members of the First World (and Europe) and to look with benevolent condescension on, say, Haitians, Saint Lucians, or Brazilians as their disadvantaged and backward Third World neighbors.

Despite all this, Martiniquans (most Martiniquans) do not feel fully French. Nor, of course, do most Frenchmen consider them to be. At best, they are Frenchmen with a difference, because of the racial discrimination they confront at every turn. In Paris, Antilleans are routinely confounded with, for example, illegal Malian immigrants in police sweeps of the subway. And at home, where white immigrants from metropolitan France now constitute more than 10 percent of the island's residents, the battle for who "owns" Martinique is played out through hundreds of minor confrontations each day: a retired metropolitan gendarme complains to the police about the loud music at a Martiniquan restaurant next door and a highly politicized court case centered on charges of racism ensues; a Martiniquan protests that a tourist has blocked the entrance to his house with his rented car and a fistfight breaks out; and disputes flair up with regularity over the hiring of metropolitan workers for local construction projects or in civil service positions. For Martiniquans, these kinds of incidents are tremendously charged and leave unresolved the personal tension inherent in being simultaneously Martiniquan and French.

France's modernization project has also created an avid thirst in Martinique for representations of "the traditional society we have forgotten in our rush to modernity . . . *la Martinique profonde*" (E. H.-H., "Le premier," 44–45), and attempts to quench it are visible everywhere. Two recently opened museums are devoted to depictions of life in the 1950s, thus "permitting the new generation to discover the scenes their ancestors knew"—one even bringing the scenes to life through Sunday appearances by a folkloric dance group who play the part of traditional villagers from "that bygone era" (Staszewski, "Images," 48–50). Celebration of the *patrimoine* permeates the local press, radio, and television, animated by artists, musicians, dancers, tale-tellers, writers, theater groups, and cultural associations (see Cottias, "Société"). Mass media publications, whether directed at Martiniquan households or at tourists to the island, promote a nostalgic image, in words and pictures, of a sterilized "traditional" way of life. The current telephone directory, for example, includes a heavily illustrated five-page section on "traditional housing" in Martinique (France Telecom, *Les pages*, 55–59) that is very similar to the much more detailed folklorized depiction of the island in the lavish *Guide Gallimard* (1994). In the same spirit, commercialized folklore is available at every village fete and large hotel, and it floods the airwaves.

Two decades ago, Glissant argued that cultural symbols of Martiniquan identity—music and dance, the Creole language, local cuisine, carnival—take on remarkable power in such contexts by fostering in people the illusion that they are representing themselves, that they are choosing the terms of their "difference," while at the same time obscuring the rapidity and completeness of the assimilationist project. This focus on "*le culturel*" and "*le folklore*," he wrote, serves both the assimilators and the assimilating, by lulling the latter into complacency and helping mask the crushing force of the *mission civilisatrice* (*Le discours*, 213). Richard Burton, following Glissant (*Le discours*), describes how the agricultural (and in some communes, fishing) base on which traditional Creole culture was founded "has been eroded beyond all possibility of restoration, leaving that culture —where it survives at all—increasingly bereft of any anchorage in the actual lived experience of contemporary French West Indians and, as such, subject to a fatal combination of folklorization, exoticization, and commodification" ("Idea," 7–8). The modern Martiniquan, he argues, is "as much a spectator of his or her 'own' culture as the average tourist: 'culture,' like everything else in Martinique today, is, it seems, something to be consumed rather than actively produced in a living human context" (7–8).

In our view, there is a tendency for the literary works of the *créolistes*[17] to be complicitous with the celebration of a museumified Martinique, a diorama'd Martinique, a picturesque and "pastified" Martinique that promotes a "feel-good" nostalgia for people who are otherwise busy adjusting to the complexities of a rapidly modernizing lifestyle.[18] Confiant's Creole-language novel "*Kòd yanm*" (1986), recently translated into French as *Le gouverneur des dés* (1995), may serve as an illustration. The novel presents a virtual tableau vivant of a picturesque 1950s Martinique. All the cultural diacritics of a soon-to-disappear local culture are foregrounded, including (and this is a selective list): the *major* ("the braggart respected by every segment of this multiethnic island society—the great white planters, the petit bourgeois mulattos, the black and Indian sugarcane workers") with his four women (a legal wife and three others) and countless children spread throughout the island; men's ritual boasting-toasting (about a rival's relatives, including his momma); cockfights; rum shops; men's crapshooting at *fêtes patronales;* a wake, with its *conteurs;* snakebite and its non-Western cure; *séyansyé/séanciers* (specialists in *la magie antillaise*); Creole disease concepts (for instance, *blès*) that do not correspond to Western categories; charcoal making; *dìwlis* (a local incubus); the *koudmen* (communal work parties, with their call-and-response singing); a distinctive *couli* (East Indian) culture, with its rituals and, especially, its cuisine;[19] the characteristic behavior, dress, and speech of *bétjé/békés, milat/mulâtres, chaben/chabins,* white *jandanm-a-chouval/gendarmes-à-cheval,* and Chinese shopkeepers; martial arts combats (danmyé or *ladja*), with drumming;[20] as well as countless ethnographic details, duly explicated, such as the fact that, traditionally, Martiniquan men and women do not kiss or hold hands in public.

In terms of "pastifying," Confiant's novel is a veritable tour de force,[21] an illustration of Burton's comment that "Créolité is in practice often retrospective, even regressive, in character, falling back, in a last desperate recourse against decreolization, into the real or imagined plenitude of *an tan lontan* (olden times)" ("Idea," 23). Indeed, Confiant himself openly acknowledges what he refers to as his "patrimonial duty," his determination to preserve for posterity these disappearing or already disappeared institutions that give Martinique its cultural specificity (cited in Taylor, "Mediating").[22] But in this regard, the *créoliste* movement nonetheless seems ensnared in one of the traps of modernization, almost inevitably risking the kind of "patrimonialization" of which Walcott wrote: "Stamped on that image is the old colonial grimace of the laughing nigger, steelbandsman, carnival masker, calypsonian and limbo dancer . . . trapped in the State's concept of the folk form . . . the symbol of a carefree, accommodating culture, an adjunct to tourism" ("Twilight," 7).[23]

There is reason to believe that the *créolistes* would concur with the main lines of our description and analysis of the changes taking place in Martinique. From Chamoiseau's *Chronique des sept misères* (1986) to Confiant's *La savane des pétrifications* (1995), and in countless public statements, they have underscored the ongoing process that might be glossed as the consensual rape of Martinique. All this does not leave today's *engagé* writers as much room for maneuver as they might wish. Gone is the righteous anger of Césaire's anticolonialism; gone is the scalpel with which Glissant dissected the heart of 1960s-style French neocolonialism. "Our present," said Confiant recently, "isn't tragic like Rwanda's or Haiti's—no one is dying of hunger in Martinique. Nor is our situation pathetic or dramatic. It is rather comic and absurd" (quoted in Kwateh, "Raphaël"). And part of this "absurdity" is that, despite their quasi-independentist rhetoric, the *créolistes* by and large benefit from the several kinds of mystifications described by Glissant. For they remain at one and the same time social critics railing against French domination *and* beneficiaries of lucrative literary prizes from Paris, both the champions of a fast-disappearing "traditional" Martinique *and* unchallenged masters of the modern media, expertly harnessing local television, radio, and newspapers to promote their literary careers.

### Sexual Politics

The *créolistes'* "common sense" about gender strongly colors their representation of the island's past and present. In a recent set of reflections from the perspective of literary criticism, A. James Arnold takes the *créolistes* to task for their stance on gender and sexuality, arguing that their novels depict cultural production as an exclusively masculine activity, restricting the proper sphere of women to reproduction and venal sexual activity ("Erotics," 16-17).[24] He goes on to argue that the *créolistes* have backed themselves into a corner where the orthodoxy they preach leaves no room for the kind of creative freedom enjoyed by their less overdetermined sisters—writers like Maryse Condé or Simone Schwarz-Bart, whose novels are "characterized by greater openness to the wider world and [are] less dependent on sexual stereotypes" (19). This forces the *créolistes,* Arnold asserts, to conform to a particular "teleological project: a certain locale is required, . . . a certain use of Creole is mandated, . . . a certain gendering of characters, narrators, and even the symbolic geography of their fiction is rigorously imposed—and then theorized" (19).

From our own ethnographic perspective, we would suggest that the *créolistes'* masculinist position emerges directly—and uncritically—from the routine sexism of Martiniquan daily life. Men, backed by a relatively complicitous silence from most female Martiniquans, regularly relegate women to a nonproductive domestic sphere, as mothers and sexual partners, by denying them entry into such areas of authority as historical knowledge, political power, cultural interpretation, or public literary creativity. In the town where we live, at virtually every official holiday gathering—whether for Cultural Week, Emancipation Day, or the festival of the patron saint—the invited speakers take care to formally express the community's appreciation of local women, often by a hyperbolic poem especially composed for the occasion, and to ask rhetorically where "we" would all be if not for the love and care of the women who bore "us" and cared for "us" unselfishly in sickness and health, or those who raise "our" children with the same faithful devotion. A particularly pointed discussion along the same lines occurred at an evening round table on literature, held a couple of years ago on the occasion of the community's annual "Cultural Week." The invited guests, three literary figures accompanied by their wives, responded to a question from the audience about the lack of women authors in Martinique by saying that it posed no problem because their own novels were filled with female characters who actively expressed the women's point of view.

Periodically this perspective, in which the presence of novelized female characters is used to excuse the absence of novelizing female writers, is given voice in the Martiniquan newspaper's weekend supplement. As the title of one article (Party, "Femmes") declared with enthusiasm, "Women, the Writers Love You!" "Woman Is Half of Heaven" it remarked. "Whether as mistress, mother, or motherland, the many-faceted image of the woman is . . . omnipresent in our literature, contrary to what certain well-intended people imagine. One has only to see the multitude of characters that they incarnate in the work of both contemporary and past writers." To prove the point, the rest of the page was devoted to a selection of six Caribbean authors—all men, and including the European husband of the prolific Guadeloupean novelist Simone Schwarz-Bart, who herself received no mention in the article.[25]

Much the same dynamic characterizes television coverage of women's issues, where, for example, highly publicized programs on lesbianism and battered women are hosted by men who interview male physicians, psychiatrists, and sexologists on these phenomena, and where women make an appearance largely in the role of victims, anonymized by computer-scrambled faces and electronically disguised voices. A May 1995 meeting in Fort-de-France called by the organization "Elles Aussi" to "educate women about the complexities of political life and increase their active participation in political struggles" consisted of three male speakers addressing an audience of female listeners ("Les femmes"). And media coverage of the 1995 International Week of the Woman ran features on fashion shows (including extravagant millinery) and workshops devoted to new trends in cosmetics.

If, as Arnold argues, the *créolistes* tend, in their depictions of the past, to erase women as active agents of cultural production, and if they tend to depict themselves as heirs to the (male) *conteur* of slave days, it should not be surprising that they tend to deal with living female writers and critics by simply silencing them. And here again they are drawing on the familiar Martiniquan vision of gender roles in which women serve primarily as mothers and lovers, in which homosexuality is highly stigmatized or denied, and in which authorial authority is the exclusive prerogative of men. A recent literary encounter incited both Chamoiseau and Confiant to put some of their convictions in these regards on record. In the process, they inadvertently exposed both their general defensiveness toward scholarship that fails to conform to the *créoliste* orthodoxy as they have defined it and their more specific discomfort at the idea of female colleagues who dare to challenge it.

The commotion began with the arrival in Martinique of a metropolitan French writer who came to promote her new book, an adulatory work on Aimé Césaire (Lebrun, *Pour Aimé*). In a public lecture, Annie Lebrun, author of several books on psychoanalysis, feminism, and surrealism, spoke warmly about her appreciation of Césaire's work. Casting her net more widely over the Martiniquan literary scene, and criticizing Confiant's recent polemic about Césaire (*Aimé*), she then ventured that the *créolistes'* "exotic mediocrity" had turned their movement into "the Club Med of literature" (quoted in Kwateh, "Raphaël").

Every private club in Martinique has its hired bouncer at the door, and the *créolistes* are no exception. In normal times this role seems to fall to Confiant, more visible in the media than Bernabé and more rarely caught smiling than Chamoiseau. Meanwhile Chamoiseau, still basking in the glory of his Prix Goncourt, plays a role more akin to the establishment's friendly owner. But when the rather prim-looking Ms. Lebrun appeared at the door, both of them sprang into action, donning brass knuckles (figuratively speaking), and leaving her for dead in the gutters of local newspapers. A grim Confiant addressed his "comrades" in the press, counseling "courage" in the face of "la dame Lebrun," a second-rate invader from Europe behind whose skirts the local sponsors, men too cowardly to speak for themselves, were said (perhaps correctly) to be hiding ("Un peu"). It was particularly painful, he admitted, to realize that some of these men, as teachers, exert influence over high school and college students in Martinique and have responsibility for turning them into "real men, men standing tall in their britches, men standing up for their ideas" ("Un peu"). In a separate attack, he berated "this third-rate scrivener, French to boot, and hence in a poor position, a very poor position," to participate in a discussion among Martiniquans: "While I could accept the arguments you have presented if they had come from an Antillean, an African, or a black American, they are totally intolerable and unbearable coming from you, French woman, Westerner, overblown and wallowing in your colonial smugness. . . . You have no right—morally or historically—to enter into the debate about Martiniquan identity" ("Les élucubrations"). Chamoiseau also joined the fray, charging that Lebrun's "violent insults to the *créoliste* movement, her venomous insanities, stem more from a psychiatric disorder than from any literary analysis" ("Une semaine"). He described her as "an obscure, failed poetess" and her audience as the "denigrating, envious, bitter enemies [of the *créolistes*]—all that old *négriste* crowd that's now falling apart," viciously attacked the local bookstore owner who featured Lebrun's publication in his window (referring to him condescendingly as a "stationer"), and evoked with ridicule the "quivering of her ovaries" upon reading Césaire ("Une semaine")—prompting one Martiniquan journalist to compare Chamoiseau to an Iranian Ayatollah, a Haitian Tonton Macoute, or a Red Guard during the height of the Chinese Cultural Revolution (Laouchez, "Patrick").

The *créolistes'* treatment of women writers from their own part of the world provides an even more interesting window on their vision of Antillean society. While Martinique boasts relatively few women writers (Ina Césaire may be the best-known exception), the literature of the French Antilles more generally has been enriched by such contemporary authors as Dany Bébel-Gisler, Maryse Condé, and Simone Schwarz-Bart. The comprehensive *Lettres créoles* makes no mention of Bébel-Gisler (whose strongly expressed politics regarding the Creole language differ from theirs), mentions Ina Césaire just once and only to chastise her for writing about *contes* (folktales) without focusing —like them—on the figure of the male *conteur* (58-59), and dispenses in three paragraphs with Condé's substantial corpus (from Hérémakhonon [1976] and *Ségou* [1984] to *Moi, Tituba, sorcière . . . noire de Salem* [1986], and more), ending with a stunning appropriation of her work by depicting her 1988 "renunciation" of her concept of a "black world" as a sign that she was finally, in their words, "growing up" and seeing Antillean realities as they do (150–52).[26] But it is the authors' longer, adulatory discussion of Schwarz-Bart that is most revealing in terms of their naked sexism:

> A meeting with the Guadeloupean novelist Simone Schwarz-Bart
> is always a pleasure. Beautiful in her inalterable manner, the hair
> flowing free in the wake of former braids, the blasé look of her eye-
> lids, the wide smile, a simultaneous seductiveness and simplicity. . . .
> To reread, and reread once more, her *Télumée Miracle* (1972) is to
> be enriched each time. Who can pretend to have plumbed all the un-
> derstanding of creole life in Guadeloupe that this novel has devel-
> oped? Who can have exhausted the complexity of *Télumée Miracle*?
> What sociological study of recent years can tell us about the mental
> universe of the Antillean Creole woman with as much force, depth,
> and acumen? (182)

Regardless whether, as Arnold has suggested (*History,* 16), the *créolistes'* brief acknowledgment of these several women writers in *Lettres créoles* represents merely "a tactical necessity on their part," the radiant vignette of Schwarz-Bart is arresting in its choice of detail: her flowing hair, her eyelids, her smile, her inalterable beauty, her seductive allure.[27]

In sum, the way the *créolistes* theorize gender and deploy masculinist strategies in the practice of their profession erases and silences women. And this impoverishes their interpretations of the Antillean past and present alike. Carole Boyce Davies and Elaine Fido make a related argument for the Caribbean more generally:

> The concept of voicelessness necessarily informs any discussion of Caribbean women and literature. . . . By voicelessness, we mean the historical absence of the woman writer's text: the absence of a specifically female position on major issues such as slavery, colonialism, decolonization, women's rights and more direct social and cultural issues. By voicelessness we also mean silence: the inability to express a position in the language of the "master" as well as the textual construction of woman as silent. Voicelessness also denotes articulation that goes unheard. (*Out of the Kumbla*, 1)

Simon Gikandi, in a similar vein, demonstrates how two (very fine but by no means unique) anglophone novels by women (Zee Edgell, *Beka Lamb*, and Merle Hodge, *Crick Crack, Monkey*), share the premise that "the unveiling of the lives of Caribbean women not only recenters them in history as custodians of an oral tradition, but also functions as an indicator of sources of domination that might have been lost or repressed in both the colonial text and male-dominated nationalist discourse" (*Writing*, 201). Or to return to the French Antilles, Maryse Condé has insisted, with characteristic directness, that "the central role of women in the liberation struggles both before and after the abolition of slavery has been largely obscured. Frequently living on the plantation as cook, nursemaid, or washerwoman, it was often she who was responsible for the mass poisonings of masters and their families, for the setting of terrifying fires, for frequent *marronage*" (*La parole*, 4). Indeed, Condé's own *Traversée de la mangrove* (1989) provides a welcome complement to the *créolistes'* masculinist vision by defining "a narrative center that would effectively subvert not only patriarchal discourse but also the colonial discourse within which it is inscribed" (Crosta, "Narrative," 147).

### A King among the Creoles

*L'exil de Béhanzin* throws into relief many of the particularities of the *créolistes'* historical agenda that we have already mentioned.[28] This 1995 film might be seen as a comprehensive allegory of the *créolistes'* vision of the postemancipation history of Martinique: immigrants arriving from backward, monolingual, monocultural lands to discover a sophisticated creole world in the making that is bubbling with ethnic and linguistic diversity. Chamoiseau's screenplay is hung on the scaffolding of historical event—the exile of King Béhanzin of Dahomey, whose empire was crushed by French armies in 1894 and who spent a dozen unhappy years in Martinique, living through the devastating eruption of the Mont Pelée volcano in 1902. But despite director Guy Deslauriers's claim that "we tried to stick as close as possible to historical reality" (quoted in Thomas, "Guy"), the main story line is invented from whole cloth and the depiction of central psychological and sociological realities is historically ungrounded.

The lyrics of the theme song (written by Chamoiseau) express the heart of the plot, the redeeming power of *créolité:* "L'anmou rivé fè'y oubliyé péyi Dahomé . . . I fini pa enmen'y pasé tout péyi-a i té pèd la" (Love succeeded in making him forget the land of Dahomey. . . . He came to love her even more than the country he lost). The *belle créole* who, according to the film's fiction, instantly erases the African king's love of his country is the green-eyed Régina (played by France Zobda), first seen in a group of comely laundresses disporting themselves among the boulders of a tropical river. Their melodic chatter and rippling laughter could have served as the sound track for a nineteenth-century operetta, and their ruffled, off-the-shoulder blouses could have come straight off the racks of an upscale Parisian boutique—though a few capricious tumbles in the clear, rushing water quickly make their wearers look more like college coeds in a spring-break wet T-shirt contest, revealing that Ms. Zobda's physical charms consist of more than her sparkling eyes and radiant smile. Régina is *créolité* incarnate: "" (a composite of "all lands, all traditions, all cultures").[29] And her house, a prototypical *case créole* ("traditional" creole house), is a little stage set with a decor of the sort that can be found in modern Martiniquan museum displays, the lobbies of hotels that host *ballets folkloriques,* and pricey gift shops at the airport—neat as a pin, with attractively arranged tropical fruits in "traditional" basketry, ample

France Zobda as
Régina (Circuit Ciné-
matographique Élizé
S.A.). *Reproduced cour-
tesy of American Anthro-
pological Association.*

use of madras cloth, but none of the diacritics (for instance, walls
covered with pages torn from old newspapers) of a lived-in creole
house.

As depicted in the film, Béhanzin (played by the Jamaican-born
Delroy Lindo, with a francophone dubber providing his voice) embodies Africanity. Set next to photographs of the historical Béhanzin,
the actor's features are rougher and "blacker"—in short, more what
a present-day Martiniquan would call *nèg-congo* ("African" or sav-
age-primitive). And in virtually the only segment of the plot when he
takes the initiative, the otherwise passive Béhanzin awakens from an
oracular dream and succeeds in saving Régina from a deadly snakebite through mystical African lore. Early in the film Béhanzin confronts
the dilemma of modernity—via the anguishing question of whether
he should permit his son to be sent to *lycée* to learn Western ways.
His decision to permit the boy to attend school, in order to equip him
for the coming struggle, is made in the context of his shock upon dis-
covering cultural diversity. "In contrast to his African homeland, the
island of Martinique is inhabited by a diversity of people, who came
from Africa, Europe, and Asia—a melting pot startling enough to im-
press the African king, no matter how godlike" (Chapelle, "Dieu").
In Chamoiseau's own words (at the film's premiere, 28 March 1995),
it was a "tremendous mixture of peoples, of languages, of colors, that
Béhanzin discovered in America—epitomized by *la belle créole.*" Or as
the film's director put it, "Béhanzin arrived in a land in full efferves-

cence, boasting Arab, Chinese, East Indian, and white peoples.[30] . . . He is faced with the difficult question—difficult because he has no ready answer for it—of why this part of the world has such a fantastic mix of peoples. And what could it all lead to? A hundred years ahead of his time, he was pondering the *problématique* of intercultural encounters" (quoted in Thomas, "Guy," 36).

Suffice it to say that, in contrast to his movie version, the historical Béhanzin was a sophisticated, highly cultured god-king, who reigned over a large empire with numerous language and ethnic groups, a developed system of classes, and constant interactions with rival European—and African—powers (see, for example, Lombard, "Kingdom"). The acceptance of Western education for his son was hardly innovative; Béhanzin's own father, the redoubtable King Glélé (Gléglé), was formally educated in Marseilles. And as for choice of women, the Dahomean monarch probably had as wide a range as any man on earth. Historically, then, Béhanzin (like most of the Africans who arrived in the New World as slaves) was in fact far more cosmopolitan, in terms of linguistic and cultural *diversalité,* than the Creoles he encountered in Martinique.

The film's take on *marronage* is enunciated early on, after the horse-drawn carriage in which Béhanzin is being transported is accosted by a frenzied, nearly naked, spear-wielding black man. As our notes record the scene,

> "It's a *nègre marron!*" exclaims the driver. And he tells the maroon (in Creole), "Leave us alone, this is the king of Dahomey." Immediately the maroon prostrates himself, waving his arms up and down in movie-swami fashion and chanting "Béhanzin Ahydjéré, *rwa Dahomé, rwa mwen,* (etc.)" [B.A., king of Dahomey, my king]. B steps down from the carriage to raise up his subject, who runs off, shouting (presumably to his fellows in the forest): "The king has come! We'll kill the whites! We'll be free!" As the king's carriage continues, the driver explains to Béhanzin with marked disdain, "Those maroons! It was easier to just run away from it all than to stand firm and confront the white man in the canefield."

How wonderful to imagine, a half century after the abolition of slavery, a wild Martiniquan maroon—and a youngish one at that—who is up to date on current events in Africa! This same maroon returns at the very end of the film in a deranged state, wildly tossing volcanic ashes in the air so they fall onto his upturned face.

It is hardly surprising that Africans, including some of Béhanzin's direct descendants, who saw previews of the film at a festival in Burkina Faso reacted negatively. In those excerpts from their comments shown on Martiniquan television, the Dahomeans complained that Béhanzin, a powerful leader and national hero of resistance, was depicted in the film as a pitiable, broken man who lacked cultural credibility. "They're presenting him as a king who can't even speak his own language correctly," objected one.[31] They also complained about his patent passivity and undignified, instantaneous enthrallment to a Creole woman. (Even the Martiniquan audience sitting around us in the theater found this dimension of Béhanzin's film character ludicrous; when one of the four African wives who accompanied Béhanzin to Martinique sensuously unveils her spectacular body beside the king's bed and he simply turns his back, dreaming of the *belle créole* whom he has at that point laid eyes on only once, and briefly, the audience erupted in guffaws of incredulity.) As if to emphasize this perspective, the film's official poster miniaturized the whole African continent to fit into a small part of the map of Martinique. The *créoliste* image of the defeated African whose humanity was redeemed by his encounter with creoleness provides stark contrast with the postcolonial African vision of the last great Dahomean resister of European empire.

### Crossing the Mangrove

During the development of their movement, the *créolistes* have called on various metaphors to describe *creolité*, from *migan* (a breadfruit dish used in a variety of linguistic contexts to connote mixedness—see Price and Price, "Migan") to *mangrove*. The metaphor of the mangrove swamp has a long history in Antillean literature, from Césaire's ambiguous, sometimes negative invocations, which focus on fetidness, brackishness, malodorousness, and pestilence (see, for example, Césaire, "Moi," 116),[32] to its more recent adoption by the *créolistes* to emphasize recycling, regeneration, creation, fertility, and (following Glissant) the fundamentally rhizomic (rather than single-rooted) character of *créolité*—"submarine roots: that is, free-floating, not fixed in one position in some primordial spot, but extending in all directions of our world through its network of branches" (Glissant, *Le discours,* 134, and *Poétique;* see also Bernabé, Chamoiseau, and Confiant, *Éloge,* 28, 50). Lately the *créolistes* have sought to appropriate the metaphor for themselves: "This land is mangrove, Aimé Césaire! The people are mangrove. The language is mangrove" (Confiant, *Aimé*, 299; see also Chamoiseau, "Penser").[33]

This ecological model may indeed, as Burton has suggested ("Idea," 24–25), contain the potential to help the *créolistes* transcend the "nostalgic essentialism" that their movement otherwise risks. But more important, we would point to the potential of their moving from lip-service to practice in the recognition of Martinique's fundamental Caribbeanness. The *poto-mitan* of our argument, its spiritual center-post, has been that the *créolistes*' vision of the past would look radically different if they were to adopt a genuine, as opposed to merely programmatic, opening to the whole of the Caribbean (from Cuba, down through Trinidad, to Suriname)—both to its thinkers and writers and to its political-historical-cultural realities. Glissant, quoting first Walcott, then Brathwaite, in the dual epigraphs to *Poétique de la relation* (1990), has underlined that in the Caribbean, "Sea is History" and that "the unity is submarine." Venturing across apparent language and culture barriers to engage the region's writers and intellectuals would encourage the *créolistes* to focus less on the fact that in Martinique modernity has been "imposed from without" (Confiant quoted in Kwateh, "Raphaël," 38) and turn more attention to the unique ways that Martiniquans are making it their own and continuing to produce "culture" in the process (see Miller, *Modernity*, for the example of Trinidad). It would also permit them to engage more fully the debates surrounding the global phenomenon of postcolonial literature ("The Empire Writes Back"—see, for example, Gyssels, "Littérature").[34] This sort of opening could not but complicate and enrich the *créolistes*' view of the respective roles of men and women as producers and transmitters of culture, of maroons and what they have accomplished, of the development of creole languages, and indeed of the whole process of creolization including the special Martiniquan variant. And such a shift in perspective might permit the *créolistes* to situate within a broader Caribbean-international environment—and thus to represent yet more effectively—the unique riches of their very particular mangrove.

## Notes

A first version of this chapter was presented under the title "Repasando el pasado en las antillas francesas" at the conference "El malestar en la memoria: Los usos de la historia," Trujillo, Spain, June 1995. We thank various participants, especially Manuela Carneiro da Cunha, Manuel Gutiérrez Estévez, and Jorge Klor de Alva, for stimulating discussion. While revising the essay we read two just-published works that provide further support for many of our arguments—Dash, *Édouard Glissant,* and Condé and Cottenet-Hage, *Penser la créolité*—and have added citations from them as appropriate. We are grateful to Édouard Glissant, Harry Hoetink, Peter Hulme, Leah Price, Peter Redfield, Daniel A. Segal, and the anonymous reviewers for *Cultural Anthropology,* where the material next appeared, for their challenging and helpful comments. All translations are our own.

1. Significantly, Lamming and Walcott each use the same Joycean phrase, "History is a nightmare from which I am trying to awake," as an epigraph for major texts—respectively, *The Pleasures of Exile* (1960) and "The Muse of History" (1974).

2. In the present context, this sampling from Caribbean writers is intended merely to set the stage. It may be worth stressing, however, that in the Caribbean, literature and history are singularly intertwined. Indeed, Lamming has claimed that after "the discovery" and "the abolition of slavery," the third most important event in British Caribbean history was "the discovery of the novel by West Indians as a way of investigating and projecting the inner experiences of the West Indian community" (*Pleasures,* 36–37), and Césaire or Guillén or Walcott might well second his assertion for the poetry of the wider region. The broader historical-identitarian dilemmas faced by all these writers are finally beginning to get the attention they deserve—see, for example, Benítez-Rojo (*Repeating*), Gikandi (*Writing*), and Webb (*Myth*).

3. Walcott describes his own literary "discipleship" during this period to "the young Frantz Fanon and the already ripe and bitter Césaire [who] were manufacturing the home-made bombs of their prose poems, their drafts for revolution" ("Twilight," 12).

4. Raphaël Confiant (in Kwateh, "Raphaël," 37) calls it more precisely "the first work of the movement written in French." From 1979 to 1987 Confiant published five "*créoliste*" novels in the Creole language; in 1994 and 1995, two of these were published in French translation (as *Mamzelle Libellule* and *Le gouverneur des dés*).

5. Chamoiseau's books include, among others, *Chronique des sept misères* (1986, Prix Kléber Haedens, Prix de l'Île Maurice), *Solibo magnifique* (1988), *Antan d'enfance* (1990, Prix Carbet), *Texaco* (1992, Prix Goncourt), and *Chemin-d'école* (1994). Confiant's novels in French include, among others, *Le nègre et l'amiral* (1988, Prix Antigone), *Eau de café* (1991, Prix Novembre), *Ravines du devant-jour* (1993, Premio Casa de las Americas), and *L'allée des soupirs* (1994, Prix Carbet). For this chapter we restrict our discussion of the *créolistes'* work largely to the movement's two literary heavyweights, Chamoiseau and Confiant. In certain contexts they now place

the Guadeloupean writers Gisèle Pineau (whose *La grande drive des esprits* won the 1993 Prix Carbet) and Ernest Pépin (whose latest novel is *Coulée d'or* [1995]) in their corner.

6. The *créolistes'* literary experimentation, using the French language with strongly Creole rhythms and mixing lexical creolisms into the stream of French prose, was foreshadowed in Martinique by Césaire's call to reinvigorate the French language, which had, he said, become "burdensome, overused," by creating "a new language . . . an Antillean French, a black French that, while still being French, had a black character" ("Interview," 67). In the anglophone Caribbean, this sort of thing had long been part of the literary program (see, for example, Brodber, *Jane and Louisa Will Soon Come Home;* Mais, *The Three Novels of Roger Mais;* Reid, *New Day;* and for general discussions, Brathwaite, *History;* Cooper, *Noises*). Walcott charted the territory in 1970: "What would deliver [the New World Negro] from servitude was the forging of a language that went beyond mimicry, a dialect which had the force of revelation as it invented names for things, one which finally settled on its own mode of inflection, and which began to create an oral culture of chants, jokes, folk-songs and fables; this, not merely the debt of history was his proper claim to the New World. For him metaphor was not a symbol but communication. . . . It did not matter how rhetorical, how dramatically heightened the language was if its tone was true, whether its subject was the rise and fall of a Haitian king or a small-island fisherman, and the only way to recreate this culture was to share in the torture of its articulation. This did not mean the jettisoning of 'culture' but, by the writer's creative use of his schizophrenia, an electric fusion of the old and the new." ("Twilight," 17)

7. As Burton points out, these opening words of the *Éloge* were prefigured by René Ménil's 1964 statement, in *Action* (the journal of the Martiniquan Communist Party), that French Antillean culture was "neither African, nor Chinese, nor Indian, nor even French, but ultimately Antillean. Our culture is Antillean since, in the course of history, it has brought together and combined in an original syncretism all these elements derived from the four corners of the earth, without being any one of those elements in particular" (Burton, "Idea," 14). Madeleine Cottenet-Hage notes further, quoting Maryse Condé, that the *créolistes'* proclamation of being "*neither* Europeans, *nor* Africans, *nor* Asians" remains entrenched in "the same old categories—race, nationality, territory—so dear to us but which are fast becoming obsolete" (*Penser,* 11).

8. Glissant's original in fact uses *métissage* for what his friend and collaborator Michael Dash translates, like us, as "creolization" (see Glissant, *Caribbean,* 140). Later Glissant writes more specifically that "*la créolisation nous apparaît comme le métissage sans limites*" (*Poétique,* 46). Most recently he has begun to criticize the metaphor of *métissage* for its scientific and bio-

logical implications, preferring the term *créolisation,* which adds, he argues, the key element of *imprévisibilité* (unpredictability) (*Introduction,* 16–17, *passim*).

9. A similar soft-pedaling of the brutality of French colonial slavery, compared with that in neighboring colonies, is found in the projected Musée Régional de Guyane (see Price and Price, "Ethnicity") as well as in the *Guide Gallimard* for Martinique (1994). This is a view of the past that seems to fit the rapidly Europeanizing, relatively nonconfrontational, nonanticolonial mood of the 1990s in the former French Caribbean colonies. Indeed, the *créolistes'* revisioning of the Antillean past deserves detailed comparative analysis with other attempts, such as that of Gilberto Freyre in 1930s Brazil, to construct foundational mythologies.

10. Leaving aside questions of possible WASP creolization in New England, it may be worth recalling that one of the West Indian writers most interested in creolization, who used Creole rhythms in many of his novels, was Sam Selvon, an "East Indian" Trinidadian writing precisely about the ambiguities of creolization among his people (see Lamming, *Pleasures,* 45; Gikandi, *Writing,* 111–13, 131–32), and that one of the few creole languages that developed in Hispanic America was Cocoliche, the language of precisely these nineteenth-century Italian immigrants to Argentina.

11. It is beyond the scope of this essay to engage Arnold's provocative argument about the *créolistes'* literary-logical necessity to construct an imaginary maroon (the "Super-Male") within a particular erotics of desire (see Arnold, "Erotics"). But it may be worth pointing out—in contrast to the image in Martinique—that among Jamaican maroons, Grandy Nanny is considered primus inter pares of their warrior ancestors and has been officially elevated to the status of Jamaican National Hero, and that among Suriname maroons a number of female ancestors are individually remembered and honored as warriors and ritual leaders for their roles during the seventeenth- and eighteenth-century struggle for freedom (see Price, *First-Time*).

12. The *Éloge* includes repeated homage to Glissant (see Chamoiseau, "En témoignage"; Bernabé, Chamoiseau, and Confiant, *Éloge,* 59–68). Note, however, that once Glissant made critical statements suggesting that the concept of *créolité* risks, "more or less innocently," the same sort of essentialization as *négritude* (*Poétique,* 103), the *créolistes* began distancing themselves from him (see, for example, Confiant, Aimé, 260).

13. The ways in which the *créolistes* construct *diversalité* might be seen as an extreme case of what Daniel A. Segal, in an essay on nationalism in contemporary Trinidad and Tobago, has called "imagined pluralism," emerging from "a particular memorialization of the past, rather than . . . some unusual degree of social heterogeneity within contemporary society" ("Living," 224, 223).

14. In contrast, earlier generations of Martiniquan intellectuals have been

profoundly internationalist—Césaire with his African ties, Fanon in Algeria, Glissant in the United States. And the same contrast holds for the cosmopolitan literary allusions of these earlier generations (which continues, for example, in the recent work of Glissant (*Poétique*) through its engagement with the work of Henry James, Whitman, Walcott, Faulkner, Brathwaite, Borges, Naipaul, Carpentier, Lezama Lima, Pound, Michael Smith, and many others).

15. Even Glissant, in a work that otherwise considerably transcends the insularity of the *Éloge* or of *Lettres créoles,* considers (French) Creole—as spoken in the French Caribbean and the French Indian Ocean territories—to be the *only* real creole language (except Papiamentu, which he acknowledges in a footnote) and dismisses others—such as Sranan, Palenquero, Jamaican, or Saramaccan—as mere "pidgins" or "derivative dialects" (*Poétique,* 110–11). And more recently he has developed this position in considerable detail (*Introduction*). It would be hard to overestimate the continuing hegemony of the imperial French perspective (*la francophonie*), even among Martiniquan intellectuals who do not consciously embrace it and sometimes even fulminate against it (see, for example, Glissant, *Poétique,* 126–28).

Confiant's most recent work may represent the most extreme statement yet of the *créolistes'* effort to subsume much of Caribbean (and southern United States and northeastern Brazilian) culture into their Martiniquan model (*Contes*). "For three centuries several million men of every race (Amerindians, blacks, whites, mulattoes, Hindus, Chinese, and Syro-Lebanese) have spoken the same language, shared the same dreams, experienced the same fears, sung the same songs, and above all told the same tales . . . from the bayous of Louisiana to the Guyano-Brazilian Amazon . . . and encompassing a multitude of Caribbean islands. . . . That sole and identical language is French Creole" (9). This collection of tales joins Chamoiseau's (*Creole Folktales*) in depicting *French* Creole culture as the undisputed culture of reference for Plantation America.

16. We would in no way deny that Caribbean people, no matter how apparently rural, as well as Caribbean societies themselves, have long been in the vanguard of modernity; indeed, this argument was developed with considerable subtlety by Sidney Mintz as much as three decades ago (see, for example, "Caribbean"). But we would strongly contest the notion that Puerto Ricans or Trinidadians or Curaçaoans are any less part of these processes than are Martiniquans.

17. We would exempt from this generalization *Chronique des sept misères,* which, despite its loving evocation of a bygone Fort-de-France, also treats in considerable depth the processes of change involved in *départementalisation.*

18. We have made an analogous argument concerning the cultural politics of Martinique's sister *département,* French Guiana (Price and Price, "Ethnicity"). Our detailed critique there centers on the state's elimination of ethnic

diversity (through educational, cultural, and administrative programs designed to uniformize the population) and the simultaneous celebration of "traditional" cultures in selected, framed settings (particularly the proposed Musée Régional). More recently, Françoise Vergès has argued that *métissage* itself has been packaged as a consumable cultural product (along the lines of the United Colors of Benetton), that it can serve as "an 'artifact' in the Great French Museum of Human Diversity as long as the historical conditions that gave birth to this diversity—colonial wars, slavery, the construction of the French nation—are denied or swept under the rug" ("Métissage," 81). It is partly for these reasons that the celebration of an "authentic" Martinique (or French Guiana) plays so well among readers in the metropole today.

19. Burton rightly notes, largely based on reading current novels and more ephemeral print media, that "there is a certain vogue for 'indianité' in contemporary Martinique" ("Idea," 29).

20. This kind of martial arts dueling-dancing, with drummed accompaniment, is an icon of "traditional" Martinique. See, for example, Katherine Dunham's 1938 ballet *L'Ag'Ya* (discussed in Clark, "Performing") and Zobel, *Laghia*.

21. This novel, like Confiant's other early works written in Creole for an almost-absent audience, deserves to be analyzed seriously as a political project as well.

22. Beverley Ormerod notes that "the title of Patrick Chamoiseau's first novel, *Chronique des sept misères* . . . signals the writer's conscious use of fiction as historical record, stemming from Glissant's position that the novelist is the archivist of the Caribbean past" ("Realism," 446).

23. An interesting foil to the pastifying gaze of Confiant's novel is found in the works of Tony Delsham, editor-in-chief of the *créoliste* magazine *Antilla* and author of a series of French-language paperbacks aimed largely at a popular Martiniquan audience. His latest, *Kout fè* (1994), depicts once proud and successful men caught up in the modernization process, haunted by their resulting loss of masculinity, and reacting with either excessive passivity or violence. These troubled male characters are set off against modernizing women (of the sort who represent Delsham's main readership), who seem far better adapted to changing Martiniquan realities. Unlike those of the *créolistes*, Delsham's novels are situated squarely in the present.

24. Arnold contrasts the *créolistes*' portrayal of Antillean oral literature as the exclusive prerogative of male *conteurs* with that expressed by other Caribbean writers (particularly, but not exclusively, women—and including Walcott), who acknowledge the many mothers, aunts, and grandmothers— "those repositories of oral history, folk medicine, and stories of all sorts"— who provided them with inspiring models in the art of narration ("Erotics," 11, 13). See now also Pineau, *La grande*, 290, as well as Edwidge Danticat's

*éloge* to "the extraordinary female story tellers I grew up with [in Haiti]" (cited in Casey, "Remembering," 525–26).

25. The practice of Martiniquan men's routinely "speaking for" women is paralleled by a remarkable rhetorical device employed by the *créolistes* in *Lettres*—speaking in the first person on behalf of immigrants from India, China, and the Levant (in stereotypic "if I were a . . . " style) and even allowing themselves to ventriloquize memories of childhood by the "white" Nobel Prize–winning poet from Guadeloupe, Saint-John Perse (Chamoiseau and Confiant, *Lettres*, 41–44, 47–48, 49–51, 157–59). It may be worth signaling the contrast between the *créolistes*' somewhat grudging acceptance of Saint-John Perse into their literary canon (following the lead of Glissant [*L'intention*, "Saint-John"] and Yoyo [*Saint-John*] and motivated in part by the nonexclusionist logic of the theory of *créolité*) and the unembarrassed celebration of this poet and his work in a Caribbean context, two decades ago, by Derek Walcott reading across language barriers (Chamoiseau and Confiant, *Lettres*, 160–61; Walcott, "Muse").

26. Given the *créolistes*' agenda, it is not surprising that *Lettres créoles* makes no mention of Martiniquan writers such as Françoise Ega (whose *Lettres à une noire* [1978] has been described as " 'obsessed'—virtually in the psychoanalytic sense—with the question of maternity as it relates metaphorically to the questions of autobiography, the woman writer, and the writing of the female body" [Flannigan-Saint-Aubin, "Reading," 49]) or the prolific Marie-Magdeleine Carbet (whose "response as a woman was inevitably different from male writers" and whose work, e.g., *Rose de ta Grâce* [1970], contains a "strong message of her appropriation of equality as a Martinican, as a *nègre*, and as a woman" [Hurley, "Woman's," 96]). And we would point out that among Ina Césaire's most important works is M*émoires d'isles* (1985), a dialogue between two elderly women about memory and history.

27. Given their readiness to comment on the state of Lebrun's ovaries, we can only commend their restraint in sparing readers a vision of Schwarz-Bart's nipples or pubic hair. Several characters in Confiant's *Eau de café* adopt a masculinist gaze that celebrates essentialized racialist categories, extolling, for example, "les coucounes bombées et crépues des négresses-bleues, les plus sublimes qu'on pût imaginer, les plus affolantes aussi, . . . les coucounes hardies des chabines aux poils jaunes comme la mangue-zéphyrine, la fente mordorée et pudique des mulâtresses qui ne se déchaînait qu'à l'instant de l'extase, la toison chatoyante des câpresses et . . . les poils [coupants] des Indiennes" (85, see also 293). The poetic enthusiasm of this passage defies translation, but we might propose the following approximation: "the bulging, frizzy cunts of jet-black *négresses,* the most sublime imaginable and also the most terrifying, . . . the brazen cunts of *chabines* with hair as yellow as the *zéphyrine* mango, . . . the modest bronze slit of *mulâtresses* which ex-

plodes at the final moment of ecstasy, the glistening fleece of the *câpresses,* the razor-sharp bristles of the *Indiennes.*" As Thomas Spear aptly queried ("Jouissances," 147), specifically addressing the women in his multiethnic audience: "What do you make of Confiant's descriptions of *coucounes?* Do you recognize your own racial place as easily as does the connoisseur?"

28. Our discussion here is based on a single viewing of the film, on 6 April 1995; we have not been able to double-check the details of our description.

29. This phrase is part of an *éloge* addressed near the end of the film either to Régina or to Martinique itself—we don't remember which. In a similar spirit, a coffee-table book on Martinique written by Chamoiseau includes a full-page image of a handsome Creole woman in "traditional dress," captioned in a similar spirit: "Le mélange de la diversité du monde confère ici aux métissages leurs audaces les plus exquises" (*Martinique,* 10).

30. This statement by Guy Deslauriers betrays an implicit, unacknowledged subject position common to the great bulk of *créoliste* expression. Blacks can go unmentioned in the enumeration of Martiniquan diversity precisely because the speakers or writers are of predominantly African ancestry. For people who, a generation ago, might have been celebrating their *négritude,* the celebration of (for example) *indianité* is an add-on; the African heritage is so obvious that it can remain un(re)marked.

31. In the film, some of Béhanzin's lines are in Fon. In a television interview, Chamoiseau excused the actor's poor execution of them by remarking that "it's a difficult language, with tones" (RFO, 28 March 1995).

32. Similarly, a character in Condé's *Traversée de la mangrove* remarks, "You don't cross a mangrove swamp. You get impaled on the palisade of its roots. You get buried and you suffocate in the brackish mud" (202).

33. Note that one of Martinique's nonmetaphorical mangroves, not far from the international airport, remains today a central battleground between ecological conservation groups (notably the ASSAUPAMAR, which the *créolistes* support), desperately poor squatters (some of whom are illegal Haitian immigrants and many of whom are involved in drug dealing), and the advocates of modernization who are inexorably expanding roads, shopping centers, and other infrastructure throughout the area.

34. Maryse Condé's muscular critique of the *créoliste* project argues that, despite the transnational, globalized nature of the world we all live in, the *créolistes* continue to write and think in terms of old-fashioned, neatly separable categories based on race, nationality, and origin ("Chercher," 305). Or as Hal Wylie has remarked about the authors of *Éloge,* "One is tempted to ask the gang of three if, and where, the diaspora fits into their conception of *créolité*" ("Métellus," 252). Condé laments that the French Caribbean literature of our time "fails to take into account these upheavals, these shifts, and these redefinitions of identity" ("Chercher," 308). "Savoring" the realization that the *créolistes* "have all spent years of their lives as '*négropolitains*' or

'*nèg'zagonaux*' [that is, in France]," she notes "how conveniently they forget those experiences and create a vision of Antillean life that would have fit right in with Jamaica in the time of Lady Nugent's [1801–5] visit" (ibid.). Condé goes on to criticize their imprisonment in the binary opposition French/Creole, which, she argues, is a legacy of the colonial obsession to separate conqueror and victim (308–9). And she castigates them for repeatedly "decreeing" orthodoxies for Antillean literature (309–10). She ends by asking rhetorically whether there aren't (shouldn't be) *multiple* versions of Antilleanness, different ways to live and write *créolité* (310).

## Works Cited

Abrahams, Roger D. *The Man-of-Words in the West Indies: Performance and the Emergence of Creole Culture.* Baltimore: Johns Hopkins Univ. Press, 1983.

Appiah, Kwame Anthony. *In My Father's House: Africa in the Philosophy of Culture.* London: Methuen, 1992.

Arnold, A. James. "The Erotics of Colonialism in Contemporary French West Indian Literary Culture." *New West Indian Guide* 68 (1994): 5–22.

———. *A History of Literature in the Caribbean.* Vol. 1. *Hispanic and Francophone Regions.* Amsterdam: John Benjamins, 1994.

Bastide, Roger. *Les religions afro-brésiliennes: Contributions à une sociologie des interpénétrations de civilisations.* Paris: Presses Universitaires de France, 1960.

Benítez-Rojo, Antonio. *The Repeating Island: The Caribbean and the Postmodern Perspective.* Durham: Duke Univ. Press, 1992.

Bernabé, Jean, Patrick Chamoiseau, and Raphaël Confiant. *Éloge de la créolité.* 1989. Paris: Gallimard, 1993.

Bhabha, Homi K. *The Location of Culture.* New York: Routledge, 1994.

Brathwaite, [Edward] Kamau. *History of the Voice.* London: New Beacon, 1984.

———. *Roots.* Ann Arbor: Univ. of Michigan Press, 1993.

Brodber, Erna. *Jane and Louisa Will Soon Come Home.* London: New Beacon Books, 1980.

Burton, Richard. "*Ki Moun Nou Ye?* The Idea of Difference in Contemporary French West Indian Thought." *New West Indian Guide* 67 (1993): 5–32.

Carpentier, Alejo. "Prologo" to *El reino de este mundo.* 1949. Montevideo, Uruguay: ARCA, 1964.

Casey, Ethan. "Remembering Haiti." *Callaloo* 18 (1995): 524–26.

Césaire, Aimé. "An Interview [by René Depestre] with Aimé Césaire." In *Discourse on Colonialism,* 65–79. New York: Monthly Review Press, 1972.

———. "Moi, laminaire." 1982. In *Lyric and Dramatic Poetry 1946–82,* 76–197. Charlottesville: Univ. of Virginia Press, 1990.

Chamoiseau, Patrick. *Antan d'enfance*. Paris: Hatier, 1990.

———. *Au temps de l'antan: Contes du pays Martinique*. Paris: Hatier, 1988.

———. *Chemin-d'école*. Paris: Gallimard, 1994.

———. *Chronique des sept misères*. Paris: Gallimard, 1986.

———. Creole Folktales. New York: New Press, 1994.

———. *Martinique*. Photographs by Michel Renaudeau and Emmanuel Valentin. Paris: Richer-Hoa-Qui, 1994.

———. "Les nègres marrons de Richard Price [review of *Les premiers temps*. Paris: Editions du Seuil, 1994]." Antilla *576* (18 March 1994): 4–5.

———. "Penser créole." Antilla 408 (1990): 32–34.

———. "Une semaine en pays dominé." *Antilla* 619 (10 February 1995): 4–6.

———. *Solibo magnifique*. Paris: Gallimard, 1988.

———. "En témoignage d'une volupté." *Carbet* 10 (1990): 143–52.

———. *Texaco*. Paris: Gallimard, 1992.

Chamoiseau, Patrick, and Raphaël Confiant. *Lettres créoles: Tracées antillaises et continentales de la littérature*. Paris: Hatier, 1991.

Chapelle, David. "Dieu, l'exil, l'amour et la mort: Béhanzin." *France-Antilles,* 30 March 1995, 7.

Clark, Vévé. "Performing the Memory of Difference in Afro-Caribbean Dance: Katherine Dunham's Choreography, 1938–87," In *History and Memory in African-American Culture,* ed. Geneviève Fabre and Robert O'Meally, 188-204. New York: Oxford Univ. Press, 1994.

Condé, Maryse. "Chercher nos vérités." In *Penser la créolité,* ed. Maryse Condé and Madeleine Cottenet-Hage, 305-10. Paris: Karthala, 1995.

———. *Hérémakhonon*. Paris: Union Générale d'Éditions, 1976.

———. *Moi, Tituba, sorcière . . . noire de Salem*. Paris: Mercure de France, 1986.

———. *La parole des femmes*. 1979. Paris: Harmattan, 1993.

———. *Ségou: Les murailles de terre*. Paris: Robert Laffont, 1984.

———. *Traversée de la mangrove*. Paris: Mercure de France, 1989.

Confiant, Raphaël. *Aimé Césaire: Une traversée paradoxale du siècle*. Paris: Stock, 1993.

———. *L'allée des soupirs*. Paris: Grasset, 1994.

———. *Contes créoles des Amériques*. Paris: Stock, 1995.

———. *Eau de café*. Paris: Grasset, 1991.

———. "Les élucubrations de Dame Lebrun." *Antilla* 619 (10 February 1995): 33.

———. *Le gouverneur des dés*. Paris: Stock, 1995.

———. "*Kòd yanm.*" Fort-de-France: Éditions K.D.P., 1986.

———. *Les maîtres de la parole créole*. Paris: Gallimard, 1995.

———. *Mamzelle Libellule*. Paris: Serpent à Plumes, 1994.

———. *Le nègre et l'amiral*. Paris: Grasset, 1988.

————. "Un peu de courage, camarades." *France-Antilles,* 4 February 1995.

————. *Ravines du devant-jour.* Paris: Gallimard, 1993.

————. *La savane des pétrifications.* Paris: Mille et Une Nuits, 1995.

Cooper, Carolyn. *Noises in the Blood: Orality, Gender and the "Vulgar" Body of Jamaican Popular Culture.* London: Macmillan, 1993.

Cottenet-Hage, Madeleine. "Introduction." In *Penser la créolité,* ed. Maryse Condé and Madeleine Cottenet-Hage, 11–20. Paris: Karthala, 1995.

Cottias, Myriam. "Société sans mémoire, société sans histoire: La patrimoine désincarné." *Encyclopedia Universalis,* 1992, 263–65.

Crosta, Suzanne. "Narrative and Discursive Strategies in Maryse Condé's *Traversée de la Mangrove.*" Callaloo 15, no. 1 (1992): 147–55.

Dash, J. Michael. *Édouard Glissant.* Cambridge: Cambridge Univ. Press, 1995.

Davies, Carole Boyce, and Elaine Savory Fido, eds. *Out of the Kumbla: Caribbean Women and Literature.* Trenton: Africa World Press, 1990.

Delsham, Tony. *Kout fè.* Schoelcher, Martinique: Éditions M.G.G., 1994.

E. H.-H. "Le premier éco musée de Martinique." *France-Antilles Magazine,* 28 November–4 December 1992, 44–45.

Edgell, Zee. *Beka Lamb.* London: Heinemann, 1982.

*L'exil de Béhanzin.* Guy Deslauriers, director; Patrick Chamoiseau, screen writer. Produced by Série-Limitée, France 2, 1995.

"Les femmes et les municipales." *France-Antilles,* 12 May 1995, 5.

Fernández Retamar, Roberto. *"Caliban" and Other Essays.* Minneapolis: Univ. of Minnesota Press, 1989.

Flannigan-Saint-Aubin, Arthur. "Reading and Writing the Body of the *négresse* in Françoise Ega's *Lettres à une noire.*" Callaloo 15, no. 1 (1992): 49–65.

France Télécom. *Les pages jaunes, les pages blanches.* Martinique: France Télécom, 1994.

García Canclini, Néstor. *Culturas híbridas: Estrategias para entrar y salir de la modernidad.* Mexico: Consejo Nacional para la Cultura y las Artes, 1990.

Gikandi, Simon. *Writing in Limbo: Modernism and Caribbean Literature.* Ithaca: Cornell Univ. Press, 1992.

Glissant, Édouard. *Caribbean Discourse.* Charlottesville: Univ. Press of Virginia, 1989.

————. *Le discours antillais.* Paris: Seuil, 1981.

————. *L'intention poétique.* Paris: Seuil, 1969.

————. *Introduction à une poétique du divers.* Montreal: Presses de l'Université de Montréal, 1995.

————. *Poétique de la relation.* Paris: Gallimard, 1990.

————. "Saint-John Perse et les Antillais." *La Nouvelle Revue Française* 278 (February 1976): 68–74.

González, José Luis. *"El país de cuatro pisos" y otros ensayos.* San Juan: Huracán, 1980.

*Guide Gallimard: Martinique.* Paris: Gallimard, 1994.

Gyssels, Kathleen. "Littérature et critique post-coloniales: Le marronnage antillais." In *The Empire Writes Back (Again): Vergelijkende literatuurwetenschap en post-koloniale literatuurstudie,* ed. Luc Herman, 91–106. Antwerp: ALW Cahier 15, 1994.

Handler, Richard. "Fieldwork in Quebec, Scholarly Reviews, and Anthropological Dialogues." In *When They Read What We Write: The Politics of Ethnography,* ed. Caroline B. Brettell, 67–74. Westport CT: Bergin and Garvey, 1993.

Harris, Wilson. *Explorations: A Selection of Talks and Articles 1966–1981.* Mandelstrup, Denmark: Dangaroo Press, 1981.

Hodge, Merle. *Crick Crack, Monkey.* London: Heinemann, 1981.

Hurley, E. Anthony. "A Woman's Voice: Perspectives on Marie-Magdeleine Carbet." *Callaloo* 15, no. 1 (1992): 90–97.

INSEE. *Tableaux économiques régionaux· Martinique 95.* Pointe-à-Pitre: INSEE, 1995.

Jackson, Jean. "Is There a Way to Talk about Making Culture without Making Enemies?" *Dialectical Anthropology* 14 (1989): 127–43.

Kwateh, Adams. "Pourquoi le cri d'Annie Lebrun dans 'Pour Césaire'?" *France-Antilles Magazine,* 4–10 February 1995, 40–41.

———. "Raphaël Confiant: 'Je ne suis pas un éternel révolté.'" *France-Antilles Magazine,* 14–30 September 1994, 37–38.

Lamming, George. *The Pleasures of Exile.* 1960. Ann Arbor: Univ. of Michigan Press, 1992.

Laouchez, R. "Patrick Chamoiseau est-il un ayatollah?" *Question* 56 (March 1995): 2.

Lebrun, Annie. *Pour Aimé Césaire.* Paris: Jean-Michel Place, 1994.

Lewis, Gordon K. *Main Currents in Caribbean Thought: The Historical Evolution of Caribbean Society in Its Ideological Aspects, 1492–1900.* Baltimore: Johns Hopkins Univ. Press, 1983.

Linnekin, Jocelyn, and Lin Poyer. *Cultural Identity and Ethnicity in the Pacific.* Honolulu: Univ. of Hawaii Press, 1990.

Lombard, J. "The Kingdom of Dahomey." In *West African Kingdoms in the Nineteenth Century,* ed. Daryll Forde and P. M. Kaberry, 70–92. London: Oxford Univ. Press, 1967.

Mais, Roger. *The Three Novels of Roger Mais ("The Hills Were Joyful Together," "Brother Man," "Black Lightning").* London: Jonathan Cape, 1966.

Marie, Claude-Valentin. "Les populations des Dom-Tom en France." *Ici Là-Bas,* suppl. 7 (Journal nationale pour l'insertion et la promotion des travailleurs d'outre-mer, n.d. [ca. 1986]).

Marshall, Paule. *The Chosen Place, the Timeless People*. New York: Harcourt, Brace and World, 1969.

Miller, Daniel. *Modernity, an Ethnographic Approach: Dualism and Mass Consumption in Trinidad*. Oxford: Berg, 1994.

Mintz, Sidney W. "The Caribbean as a Socio-cultural Area." *Cahiers d'Histoire Mondiale* 9 (1966): 912–37.

Mintz, Sidney W., and Richard Price. *The Birth of African-American Culture*. 1972. Boston: Beacon, 1992.

Naipaul, V. S. *The Middle Passage*. Harmondsworth, England: Penguin, 1969.

Ormerod, Beverley. "Realism Redefined: The Subjective Vision." In *A History of Literature in the Caribbean*, vol. 1, *Hispanic and Francophone Regions*, ed. A. James Arnold, 435–49. Amsterdam: John Benjamins, 1994.

Ortiz, Fernando. *Contrapunteo cubano del tabaco y el azucar*. Havana: Consejo Nacional de Cultura, 1940.

Party, Jean-Marc. "Femmes, les écrivains vous aiment." *France-Antilles Magazine*, 30 October–5 November 1993, 53.

Patterson, Orlando. "Recent Studies on Caribbean Slavery and the Atlantic Slave Trade." *Latin American Research Review* 17 (1982): 251–75.

Pépin, Ernest. *Coulée d'or*. Paris: Gallimard, 1995.

Pineau, Gisèle."Écrire en tant que Noire." In *Penser la créolité*, ed. Maryse Condé and Madeleine Cottenet-Hage, 289–95. Paris: Karthala, 1995.

———. *La grande drive des esprits*. Paris: Serpent à Plumes, 1993.

Price, Richard. *Alabi's World*. Baltimore: Johns Hopkins Univ. Press, 1990.

———. *First-Time: The Historical Vision of an Afro-American People*. Baltimore: Johns Hopkins Univ. Press, 1983.

Price, Richard, and Sally Price. *Afro-American Arts of the Suriname Rain Forest*. Berkeley: Univ. of California Press, 1980.

———. "Ethnicity in a Museum Case: France's Show-Window in the Americas." *Museum Anthropology* 18, no. 2 (1994): 3–15.

———. "Migan." *New West Indian Guide* 68 (1994): 81–91.

Reid, Vic. *New Day*. New York: Knopf, 1949.

Scarboro, Ann Armstrong. "A Shift toward the Inner Voice and *Créolité*." *Callaloo* 15, no. 1 (1992): 12–29.

Schwarz-Bart, Simone. *Pluie et vent sur Télumée-Miracle*. Paris: Seuil, 1972.

Segal, Daniel A. "Living Ancestors: Nationalism and the Past in Postcolonial Trinidad and Tobago." In *Remapping Memory: The Politics of Time-Space*, ed. Jonathan Boyarin, 221–39. Minneapolis: Univ. of Minnesota Press, 1994.

Spear, Thomas C. "Jouissances carnavalesques: Représentations de la sexualité." In *Penser la créolité*, ed. Maryse Condé and Madeleine Cottenet-Hage, 135–52. Paris: Karthala, 1995.

Staszewski, Gérard. "Images et couleurs d'un village d'antan." *France-Antilles Magazine*, 6–12 March 1993, 48–50.

Taylor, Lucien. "Isle of Intellectuals." Doctoral dissertation in preparation, Department of Anthropology, University of California, Berkeley, n.d.

———. "Mediating Martinique: The 'Paradoxical Trajectory' of Raphaël Confiant." In *Cultural Producers in Perilous States: Editing Events, Documenting Change,* ed. George Marcus, 259–330. Chicago: Univ. of Chicago Press, 1997.

Thomas, François. "Guy Deslauriers . . . la passion du cinéma." *France-Antilles Magazine,* 22–28 October 1994, 36–37.

Todorov, Tzvetan. *On Human Diversity.* Cambridge: Harvard Univ. Press, 1993.

Vergès, Françoise. "Métissage, discours masculin et déni de la mère." In *Penser la créolité,* ed. Maryse Condé and Madeleine Cottenet-Hage, 69–83. Paris: Karthala, 1995.

Walcott, Derek. *The Arkansas Testament.* New York: Farrar, Straus and Giroux, 1987.

———. "History in E. K. Brathwaite and Derek Walcott: Panel Discussion." *Common Wealth of Letters Newsletter* (Yale University) 1, no. 1 (1989): 3–14.

———. "The Muse of History." In *Is Massa Day Dead? Black Moods in the Caribbean,* ed. Orde Coombs, 1–27. New York: Anchor, 1974.

———. "What the Twilight Says: An Overture." In *"Dream on Monkey Mountain" and Other Plays,* 3–40. New York; Farrar, Straus and Giroux, 1970.

Walmsley, Anne. *The Caribbean Artists Movement, 1966–1972.* London: New Beacon Books, 1992.

Webb, Barbara J. *Myth and History in Caribbean Fiction: Alejo Carpentier, Wilson Harris, and Edouard Glissant.* Amherst: Univ. of Massachusetts Press, 1992.

Williams, Brackette F. *Stains on My Name, War in My Veins: Guyana and the Politics of Cultural Struggle.* Durham: Duke Univ. Press, 1991.

Wylie, Hal. "Métellus, Diasporism and *Créolité.*" In *Penser la créolité,* ed. Maryse Condé and Madeleine Cottenet-Hage, 251–62. Paris: Karthala, 1995.

Yelvington, Kevin A. *Producing Power: Ethnicity, Gender, and Class in a Caribbean Workplace.* Philadelphia: Temple Univ. Press, 1995.

Yoyo, Émile. *Saint-John Perse et le conteur.* Paris: Bordas, 1971.

Zobel, Joseph. *Laghia de la mort, ou Qui fait pleurer le tam-tam.* Fort-de-France: Imprimerie Bezaudin, 1946.

# 8

# Beautiful Indians, Troublesome Negroes, and Nice White Men: Caribbean Romances and the Invention of Trinidad

*Faith Smith*

"I keep thinking that someone will say it happened differently," Jamaica Kincaid has said, explaining that she reads widely in Caribbean history, trying to find a new version of the past. "I can never believe that the history of the West Indies happened the way it did" ("Jamaica," 223–24). I read the 1988 novel *Ti Marie* by the Trinidadian writer Valerie Belgrave as a similar engagement with the issue of what really happened. Substituting *pleasure* for the stark, conventional versions that seem to deny this aspect, Belgrave's novel is a fascinating contribution to Caribbean writers' ongoing concern—some would say obsession—with history. At a time when the region's women writers are increasingly prominent in this regard, Belgrave's text shifts the more typical desire for revenge to a desire for reconciliation. Self-consciously addressing herself to the post-independence, post–Black Power moment, Belgrave presents a black heroine who vindicates her race and saves the nation by being desirable enough to attract and wed the white hero.

In characterizing what she calls "the typical West Indian novel" as "usually very heavy stuff," Belgrave has asserted: "Now I think that it is time for us to have books that are also for pleasure" (Tanifeani, "Interview," 24). *Ti Marie* is set in Trinidad in the late eighteenth and early nineteenth centuries. It is a romance about slavery. As someone who has found the "heavy stuff" a very compelling version of "what really happened" and who earns a livelihood from it, I must admit I find Belgrave's story—in which a black woman who may or may not be a slave and a politically correct English aristocrat, nephew of a slaveowner, fall in love with each other and get married—somewhat problematic.

But I am interested in examining the series of contradictions that have to be reconciled or ignored in order to write a romance about slavery—to, as Belgrave says, "take a romance and make something serious of it" (Tanifeani, "Interview," 24). One gets a sense that Belgrave is consciously attempting to distinguish herself—as a batik artist making occasional forays into fiction writing—from the "usual" mode of the Caribbean writer. Novel writing for her has been a practical solution to a specific problem: she saw a need for a certain kind of literature, filled the need, and moved on. Belgrave and her text raise interesting issues about academia and elitism, including the perception that certain readings of the past are the property of academics and do not really meet the needs of the average Caribbean reader. Belgrave has addressed critics of her novel, presumably those who see a contradiction between her use of the Mills and Boon–Harlequin Romance format and her public image as an artist whose work incorporates political themes and who participated in Black Power student protests in the early 1970s: "For someone of my radical background, a romantic novel was seen as a backward step. But you have to respect what the masses of people like. . . . You have to be a part of the people in order to lead them. You can't lead from a great distance in front" (Raymond, "Interview"). Further: "Rather than criticise people for liking soap operas, foreign entertainment, and so on, I look and see what it is in this that attracts them. If you like romance or you like to deal with the aristocracy, I'll deal with it. But what I'll do is to bring it down to our level. I'll show you what truly sympathetic white aristocrats would have been like, what a romance we'd really like to read would be like, if it belongs [sic] to us, if it was in our control or circumstances" (Tanifeani, "Interview," 24).

Belgrave's stated aim is to harness popular but usually negative foreign media for national and regional ends ("Combining," 317). She wants to indigenize the historical romance, imbuing it with ennobling images of Caribbean people, particularly women, and promoting racial and national harmony. In doing so she wants to avoid "exploiting the norm" when it comes to presenting historical events: evil whites, the absence of romantic love, and the brutality of slavery. "The essential theme of the book is humanism trying to establish itself even in the time of slavery. . . . The book doesn't deal with the black man trying to find himself. The black people in it already have pride. It assumes that we know that white people were oppressive. But the book [doesn't] chastise white people" (Raymond, "Interview," 16). Belgrave goes on to note that her readers (and I am interpreting "us" and "our" in the quotations above to mean Caribbean readers and, more specifically, the people of Trinidad) already *know* their history: "We are sufficiently familiar with the characters and characteristics of eighteenth-century slavery that we need not rehash them" ("Thoughts," 325). In our postindependence present, Belgrave seems to suggest, we are mature enough to seek out pleasure from our past. I am interested in why she selects this particular historical moment for her story. This is a period on which the region's historians have spoken the "true-true word," contributing some of the foremost discourses on slavery to the international academic community; a period that Caribbean poets, novelists, dramatists, sociologists, and musicians have struggled to define and interpret. It is as if the question—posed in the reggae group Culture's 1977 hit song "Do You Remember the Days of Slavery?"— constitutes a challenge that must be taken on in the process of understanding the present.

Slavery seems to become a founding event, a beginning, when things as we understand them today took shape, when positions became fixed and players assumed their places. The definition of that period thus becomes crucial to how we think of ourselves in the present, as we rush to fill the gap between "that event" and "this memory" (Scott, "Event," 261–84). G. R. Coulthard has noted how prominent are the themes of the Middle Passage and the master and slave relationship in the Caribbean literary canon (*Race*, 40). Taken nationally, Belgrave's venture continues a line of Trinidadian contributions on the subject, a line including C. L. R. James's *The Black Jacobins* (1936), Eric Williams's *Capitalism and Slavery* (1944), and V. S. Naipaul's *The Loss of El Dorado* (1969), and continued recently with *When Gods Were Slaves* (1993) by Sharlow Mohammed.

Many have argued that the terms employed to meet this challenge have been extremely problematic. Presumably this is part of the reason for Jamaica Kincaid's dissatisfaction, in the statement quoted at the outset of this chapter. Derek Walcott has referred disparagingly to the predilection of the region's writers for a "literature of revenge": "In the New World servitude to the muse of history has produced a literature of recrimination and despair, a literature of revenge written by the descendants of slaves or a literature of remorse written by the descendants of masters" (Walcott, "Muse," 2).

Much of the dissatisfaction has been precisely over the question of this descendant of the master. Walcott himself agonizes over his inability to fully condemn or avenge his European or African ancestors, since he is inextricably tied to both: "I who am poisoned with the blood of both, / Where shall I turn, Divided to the vein?" ("Far Cry," 18). An assessment of the historical role and intentions of the Europeans certainly seems to be crucial not only to determining the proper way to handle the past (whether one's attitude should be guilt, despair, or rage) but to determining the very character of slavery itself—its mildness or harshness as an institution.

*Ti Marie's* presentation of a union, sanctioned by marriage, of a black woman and a white man riding off into the sunset responds to needs that previous historical accounts appear to have left unfulfilled. Barry, the fair, blue-eyed Englishman the heroine, Eléna falls in love with, is a liberal par excellence. Newly arrived from England, he has no financial connection to slavery or the slave trade. (Though his uncle is a slaveowner in Barbados, Belgrave makes sure that Barry's own income is "clean"; it is secured by oppressing white people in England rather than black people in Africa and the West Indies.) He applauds when slaves commit arson, and when they are whipped he demands to know why compassion is not shown. He purchases a slave to save him from punishment, renames him, and teaches him to read and write. The two men become the best of friends.

It is interesting that Belgrave should feel the need to redeem this particular player in the West Indian historical drama. As lovers, fathers, and surrogate fathers, in this novel European males are willing and welcome family members, whereas Caribbean historians and writers generally have shown that they embraced and rejected these roles oppressively and at their convenience. James's *Black Jacobins* and Williams's *Capitalism and Slavery* demystify the liberal intentions of the radicals of the French Revolution and the British abolitionist "saints," respectively. In doing so, they show that the slave trade and slavery came to an end because of economic considerations and the agency of the African Caribbean population, whereas metropolitan versions held that European liberalism beneficently bestowed freedom on the slaves.

While James and Williams showed the distinction between liberal and illiberal to be ultimately insignificant, this distinction is crucial to Belgrave's project. Barry's humanism (the state of his heart) is at the crux of whether this story can be a romance. His willingness to ignore his society's—history's—stipulations regarding whom he can love romantically allows for history itself to be rewritten and transformed. Whereas James's and Williams's texts are preoccupied with confronting and overturning European scholarship, Belgrave has a quite different agenda.

Besides being faithful to the requirements of the genre, which presumably requires a handsome white man, why does Belgrave recuperate the white liberal? Is she suggesting that now that Caribbean readers have come to terms with the oppression defining slavery, it is time to teach Europeans to be humane, as a way of welcoming them back into some sort of national fold? Is she saying that James's and Williams's responses to metropolitan historiography are not sufficient to satisfy the needs of her readers? Or is she trying to address other grievances, related to beauty and desirability rather than confrontation?

Oh, to be the white man's wife rather than his wench! This position has proved difficult even for *white* Caribbean heroines (and heiresses to boot): witness Antoinette/Bertha Mason's ignominious relegation to the attic in Charlotte Brontë's *Jane Eyre* and Jean Rhys's *Wide Sargasso Sea*. Clare Savage's contentious relationship with her white father in Michelle Cliff's novel *Abeng* is the paradigmatic example of the relationship between the white man and the politically conscious Caribbean woman, whatever her complexion. The writer who dares to imply that this heroine actually desires the white man should tread with caution. Mayotte Capécia found herself accused by Frantz Fanon of a pathological desire for "lactificaton," and Maryse Condé's Véronica, from her novel *Hérémakhonon*, also received some heat (see Andrade, "The Nigger of the Narcissist," for a useful discussion of both Mayotte Capécia and Maryse Condé's Véronica, particularly in relation to Fanon's diagnosis in *Black Skin, White Masks*). A recent and interesting option—sleeping with him outside the paradigms of rape *or* of marriage, by "holding his tongue in my mouth" and claiming his power without being subsumed by him—is explored by

Kincaid's Lucy Potter in *Lucy*. Time will tell if other writers or protagonists will find this option viable.

Belgrave's decision to redeem the more typical portrayal of sexual
relations in the way she does is worth pursuing here, since it seems to
be tied to the perceived anxieties of her readers. As she has said, historically the black woman would be the white man's "mistress or bed
wench and would fill in the time until he met 'Miss Right' i.e. Miss
White . . . but such a story although typical, would neither be truly
romantic nor ennobling to black readers" ("Fairy," 10). Who loves the
Caribbean woman? How must she look in order to be loved? Since
this is a postindependence, black-conscious romance, it is important
that the heroine should not be white. Belgrave is careful to make Eléna
the darker of a set of twins, and it is important that Barry thinks her
beauty and intellect far outweigh those of the white women in his social circle in England. As every good heroine should, however, Eléna
has a straight nose and long hair. Her Amerindian and European genetic strains ensure that she is, physiognomically speaking, a heroine of
whom her readers can be proud. In addition, she is sensitive, swoons
appropriately, and is chaste. This last is important in a historical romance that places the black woman as the love interest of a white man.
This relationship, usually described in terms of rape or concubinage,
here ends in marriage.

Belgrave is inserting "woman" into a historical space where, as the
Caribbean historian Lucille Mathurin has noted, "there is very little
about the inner lives of slaves . . . [so that] one must probe deeply into
the conventional sources of Caribbean history to find those missing
women, to attempt new interpretations" ("Recollections," 53). More
recently, historians such as Mathurin have documented a wealth of
evidence indicating that black women were being brought before the
court for poisoning, sorcery, running away, and so on. Many of the
authors of contemporary travel narratives could not seem to make
up their minds whether to admire her industry or be horrified at her
total disregard for Victorian sexual and social norms (see Cobham,
"Women").

This woman, however, resisting an oppressive system whenever possible, loud and vulgar to her European onlookers (Charles Kingsley,
visiting Trinidad in 1869, found her "masculine" "ungainly," "loud,"
and "coarse" [*At Last*, 1:51]), does not appear in Belgrave's text. She
is apparently too crude to qualify for the romance, which requires
refinement—in sentiment, behavior, and features. Eléna is black, there-

fore, but carefully so. Historically, European women were scarce in
the Caribbean, a factor usually used to explain the liaisons between
white men and black women that accounted for the creation of a mulatto class. As a very powerful missing referent, however, the white
woman was central to the definition of femininity, with the black
woman occupying the unsavory pole of those dreaded binary oppositions: wife/whore, beautiful/ugly, refined/coarse. While retaining the
conventional hero of the "foreign" romance, Belgrave replaces the
typical heroine but takes care to make her worthy of the role.

We can link this anxiety about physical features to the annual ag-
onizing over national beauty contests in the Caribbean. Who is picked
to represent the nation in the international phase of these contests is
an issue of great importance. The "mixed" beauty is often touted as
the obvious choice. With a liberal helping of Chinese, (East) Indian,
or any of the "white" genes ("European" and "Middle Eastern"), the
winner, who might well be termed black in Europe or North America, supposedly represents the best blend of all the Caribbean offers,
and it is often argued that "Caribbeanness" is betrayed if there is no
such mixture. On the other hand, when it is considered that "high-
brown" and "near-white" qualify as "functionally white," mixture
becomes a celebration less of the best blend of everyone than the privileging of one aspect of the genetic spectrum to the detriment of
others. Stuart Hall's characterization of the African component of
Caribbean culture as "the site of the repressed" resonates loudly when
the results of many of these contests are announced ("Cultural," 229).
For those who would quibble that Belgrave offers us a lighter shade
of black consciousness when her stated intention is to nationalize a
foreign product, it is worth reflecting that precisely by bringing on
board national and regional neuroses, she has successfully indigenized
the genre.

Where the traditional romance and the history books deny love,
marriage, and inheritance to the black woman, then, Belgrave writes
it in. There are interesting parallels between the anxieties and strategies that I am arguing provide a context for understanding *Ti Marie*
and nineteenth-century representations of Trinidad by Trinidadian and
English writers. I want to consider how three writers, in response to an
African Caribbean presence that is unsettling, either "refine" its cruder
propensities with aquiline noses and intellectual high-mindedness or
write it out altogether. Whether he is punished for his failure to marry
the nonwhite mother of his children or desires and weds an Indian

heroine, in these narratives the liberal white male is at the center of a Caribbean family romance.

The 1854 novel of the Trinidadian lawyer Michel Maxwell Philip, *Emmanuel Appadocca,* offers us a protagonist born out of wedlock who avenges himself and his mother by proving himself superior to his wealthy father in morals, ingenuity, and intellect. Written, we are informed in the preface, "at a moment when the feelings of the Author are roused up to a high pitch of indignant excitement, by a statement of the cruel manner in which the slave holders of America deal with their slave-children," the author sets himself the task of imagining what "a high-spirited and sensitive person" would do if he found himself picking cotton on his father's plantation. Clearly then, we are in a scene powerfully staged in the mid-nineteenth century North American context by Frederick Douglass, William Wells Brown, and Harriet Jacobs (see Douglass, *Narrative of the Life of Frederick Douglass* [1845]; William Wells Brown, *Clotel, or The President's Daughter: A Narrative of Slave Life in the United States* [1853]; and Harriet Jacobs, *Incidents in Life of a Slave Girl* [1861]). Like these writers and their central characters, Philip's protagonist smarts at the injustice meted out by an unethical owner-father and bravely expresses outrage at his treatment with the oratorical skills and high ethical principles befitting true vindicators of the race. Like Wells Brown and Douglass, Philip keenly felt all his life the circumstances of his "illegitimate" birth—his mother was a black woman on his white father's plantation (James, "Michel," 254–55).

Though plantation tensions provide the context of the novel, however, Philip's setting is the seventeenth-century period of the buccaneers. The plantation setting seems to be less appealing—less romantic?—for his purposes than swashbuckling on the high seas. Most of the characters, including the protagonist (Appadocca) and his father are ambiguously or never racially marked. Appadocca's "complexion was of a very light olive, it showed a mixture of blood, and proclaimed that the man was connected with some dark race, and in the infinity of grades in the population of Spanish America, he may have been said to be of that which is commonly designated Quadroon" (26). His "high aquiline nose, compressed lips, and set jaws, pointed clearly to a disposition that would undertake the most arduous and hazardous things, and execute them with firmness in spite of perils" (27) and "his black raven locks flowed over his shoulders in wild and unrestrained profusion" (28).

Assuming that Philip does not imply dreadlocks here, the parallels with the main characters in both Wells Brown's *Clotel* and Belgrave's *Ti Marie* are clear: Appadocca looks the part of a hero. And to underline the point that the looks are but the outward sign of a civilized and sensitive spirit, Appadocca is reading when we first meet him: "The young man was standing by a table, on which lay open a richly ornamented volume of 'Bacon's Novum Organum,' with the books of 'Aristotle's Philosophy' by its side. It was evident that he was making his morning meditation on those learned tomes" (28). Philip and his character are the vindicators who, like Frederick Douglass and C. L. R. James, would outread and outdignify the white oppressor.

In sharp contrast to Appadocca, the only character in Philip's novel who is unambiguously marked racially is Jack Jimmy, who, soon after we meet him, "was observed in his crouching position, where it was difficult to distinguish him from the ideal of a rolled up ouranoutan [*sic*]" (38), and later: "The movements of the little negro were as brisk and as rapid as those of a monkey" (82). "Peculiarly comical," Jack Jimmy's "huge large eyes looked like balls inserted into two large holes, bored on an even surface, while what was intended for a nose, was miserably abbreviated and flat, added the culminating point to an ugliness which was almost unique" (39).

This is worthy of anything written by Thomas Carlyle, Anthony Trollope, or J. A. Froude (see Carlyle, "Occasional Discourse on the Nigger Question" [1853]; Trollope, *The West Indies and the Spanish Main* [1860]; Froude, *The English in the West Indies* [1888]). Race vindication notwithstanding, it appears that particular physiognomical types are destined to play fixed roles. As a narrative driven by the punishment of the sins of the white father, Philip's novel seems more in line with the tradition of "the heavy stuff" from which Belgrave distances herself. Both Philip's postemancipation revenge theme and Belgrave's theme of post independence romance stress the physiognomical and intellectual "suitability" of their central characters.

The 1871 travelogue of the English novelist and historian Charles Kingsley, *At Last: A Christmas in the West Indies,* based on his trip to the Caribbean in 1869–70, offers an interesting spin on the relationship of the white man to nonwhite women and to the Caribbean as "home." His text dreams of the restoration of Trinidad's Amerindian population and the union of its destiny with that of English settlers, at a time when most of this population had long been wiped out: "How different might have been the history of Trinidad, if at that early period, while the Indians were still powerful, a little colony of English had joined them, and intermarried with them" (*At Last,* 1:108).

Here Kingsley imagines a different history for Trinidad, one that ties him, as English, not to the African Caribbean colonial subjects he encounters on his trip to Trinidad in 1869, but to "Indians," who become power brokers with the English. They are marriage partners rather than competitors for economic resources, though his scenario does not include English women marrying Indians. He envisions a sharing of power with Indian men, cemented by Indian women as wives. In doing so he conveniently blames their decimation on the wicked Spanish settlers who settled in Trinidad before the English and chooses to assume that in similar circumstances the English would not have been as oppressive as the Spanish. He rewrites the history of a British colony as benign, and with a very different set of colonial relationships than Amerindian genocide, African slavery, and (East) Indian indentured labor might imply. In textually restoring Indians to the contemporary scene in this way in the 1870s—bound familiarly to the English—he removes the historical necessity for African slavery and thus writes the troubling African Caribbeans out of his present.

Kingsley's "Englishness" is undergirded by a strong sense of his nation's greatness. His "Middle Passage" is filled with men-of-war and glorious battles rather than with slave ships. But while this is part of his "national" heritage, he had a much closer personal affiliation to the region. What was in reality a first visit in 1869 seemed more of a homecoming. The numerous references in *At Last* to the seashells in the cabinet of his childhood home, and to family stories of events and fauna, suggest that the Caribbean was something of a psychic resting place for him. His mother was born in Barbados, where her family owned property, and her stories when he was a child bequeathed to him a Caribbean of scientific, contemplative plantation owners taking giddy slaves in hand and restoring order to chaos.

In the thirty years since the abolition of slavery, Caribbean "Negroes" and their flight from the plantations seemed much different from his mother's stories: unredeemable, untrainable, and unfit for the responsibilities of citizenship. In the public trials and debates following the 1865 rebellion in Jamaica, he had taken the ultraconservative, pro-Eyre side, thus jeopardizing his status as a "liberal" (see Hall, *White*). One of Kingsley's biographers notes that when Kingsley was once asked to make a financial contribution to the welfare of formerly enslaved people in the Caribbean he refused, saying that emancipation had "ruined" him, since his family's plantation interests in the Caribbean would have been adversely affected by the abolition of slavery (Martin, *Dust,* 258).

The point here is that race and colonialism were crucial to Kingsley's discourse and to what he thought about himself. Not surprising, then, is his desire to imagine how different Caribbean history would have been without slavery, to rewrite history so that "powerful" Indians replaced lazy, dangerous, and historyless Afro-Caribbean people. Yet powerful "Indians" had presumably been extremely troublesome when they were decimated. A very interesting recasting of national and racial affiliations is suggested by "if at that early period, while the Indians were still powerful, a little colony of English had joined them and intermarried with them," such that the alliance between English and Indian factions brings peace and prosperity and renders African labor unnecessary. In his text, noble Indians are played off against crude Africans to secure a more satisfying Caribbean scenario.

In a poem published in *Macmillan's Magazine* and reprinted in the *Trinidad Chronicle* (1870), Kingsley developed this idea of Indian nobility pitted against African brutishness. In "The Legend of La Brea" an "ancient Spanish Indian" lectures a carefree, thieving "negro hunter" on the environmental and moral evils of hunting for birds near the Pitch Lake. The poem is shot through with the stereotypes of African Caribbean people that permeated the discourses of Carlyle and others: with rolling eyeballs, living an idle existence paid for by the British people, superstitious and cowardly, and fearing only his "sturdy mate's" physical abuse. The poem ends with the "stately, courteous" Indian advising the miscreant to "take care" lest the Pitch Lake boil over as punishment for his theft, to which he responds that as long as the New York market demands bird skins he will continue to hunt as he likes. Thus wicked American capitalists are shown to be cooperating in the destruction of the environment, leading the impressionable and foolish "negro hunter" to further mischief.

Although Kingsley's rendering of the Caribbean here is no less racist or less oblivious to the political aspirations of African Caribbean inhabitants than that of other Victorian writers, it is interesting that whereas someone like Froude sees no future for whites in the region, Kingsley textually inserts English men into the Caribbean scenario, connected to the region as husbands. Faced with a Caribbean situation that interferes with his personal, intellectual, and national sense of well-being, Kingsley thus deploys various strategies of containment in the text in an attempt to wrest control and to give this sense of control to his English readers.

A play written on the occasion of Trinidad's centenary celebrations in 1897, and included in L. O. Innis's *Trinidad and Trinidadians* (1910), makes explicit Kingsley's allusion to romantic liaisons between Indian women and English men. In "Carmelita, the Belle of San Jose," the Indian heroine, Carmelita, dazzles Frank Norton with her exotic beauty. When her father, the noble cacique Oronoko, has his land stolen by the evil Spanish alcalde, the latter is supplanted by a new English governor who recovers the stolen land. Frank wins Carmelita's hand, and Oronoko gives him the land as a wedding present. In the closing scene Frank notes that just as the Spanish have surrendered political power to the English, he surrenders his heart to Carmelita, "as many other English hearts will, when they come under the sway of the lovely Creole girls." The cacique gives his blessing to the marriage and predicts that his descendants will rejoice that the island "has fallen under the strong but gentle and beneficent rule of England."

Here the wise old Indian character distinguishes between evil Spanish and beneficent English conquests and willingly cedes power to a benevolent and vigorous English settler. The latter appears to be a natural successor to Caribbean rule, and marriage strengthens the arrangement. This drama, written to celebrate British rule in Trinidad at the end of the nineteenth century, a time of increasing political agitation by Trinidad's black middle class, reserves a nostalgic space for agreeable Indian men and exotic, available women. Such narrative procedures, as we have seen with Kingsley's text, rewrite the violence of Indian genocide, in which both Spanish and English were implicated, and nostalgically recuperate a decimated population as noble heroes and heroines. They ignore the formidable Amerindian opposition to European colonization throughout the eastern Caribbean in the seventeenth and eighteenth centuries; nostalgia for the Europeans' return is "safe," since they are no longer a threat, and they are a fitting antidote to the troubling presence of black people. Peter Hulme has termed these procedures "colonial disavowal": "An earlier moment of supposed usurpation is projected to act as a screen for the *present* usurpation which can thereby be presented as a rectification of others' crimes . . . to dispossess the dispossessers is merely natural justice" (*Colonial,* 246). (See Renato Rosaldo's critique of "mourning for what one has destroyed": "Evidently, a mood of nostalgia makes racial domination appear innocent and pure" ["Imperialist," 107"]. See also Doris Sommer's discussion in the context of the Latin American novel [*Foundational*, 21–2].)

These nineteenth-century texts suggest that the African presence in the Caribbean causes particular kinds of anxieties for writers of various perspectives. Black people seem to disturb the possibility of certain readings of the region: they are too crude, their claims too material, to fit comfortably into the national and ideological dreams of these writers. Belgrave, in writing a romance "in our control or circumstances," could be said both to refigure this presence positively (black people are shown to be capable of humanizing whites, for example) *and* to perpetuate elements of the nineteenth-century conventions we have just examined. The marital union of liberal whites with dignified and aquiline-nosed black people, aided by wise Amerindians, is at the core of a narrative filled with a majority black population that needs their reasoned direction. The love of Barry and Eléna, born auspiciously in the same year on two different continents, represents the possibilities of a new Trinidad defined by difference (it is not like the rest of the Caribbean), racial mixture, and harmony (everyone can get along if they have the same spirit).

Arguably there is much in this novel that revises our expectations of the genre. The words of love that Barry and Eléna whisper in each other's ears are laced with resolutions to make life better for field slaves. The relationship between "black-skinned" Tessa and the "remarkably handsome African" Fist, one of the many romantic subplots, allows Belgrave to demonstrate the brutality of slave existence. The two are freed from the clutches of evil owners by Eléna and Barry, respectively, and their doomed relationship indicates the tragedy of slavery. As Tessa says, "You ain't see how hard black people life is? Anything could always happen to we, but the chance to love, we lucky to get that. That didn't have nothing to do with no massa and I never could be sorry for that" (163).

Tessa's broken body, at the heart of the central plot, allows Belgrave to use actual events from Trinidad's history and thus to reinforce the terrible conditions under which black people lived. Tortured by Begorrat, a slaveowner who was infamous for his brutality, she reminds us of Luisa Calderon, the young woman whose treatment created such a sensation in England at the turn of the nineteenth century that Trinidad's governor, Sir Thomas Picton, was recalled (see V. S.

Naipaul's discussion of this event in *The Loss of El Dorado*). On the other hand, Tessa's general flightiness and Fist's amiability (Does he *have* to say, "You the boss now, Massa" after being rescued by Barry at their first meeting?) confirm Eléna's and Barry's reasoned and compassionate natures. In this sense, then, Tessa and Fist's love must be sacrificed for the "higher" good.

The fate of another couple in the novel also bears thinking about. Eléna's mother, Yei, mysteriously gives birth to twins at the beginning of the novel. Later we discover that the father is the radical Frenchman, Louis, who lives in the same household. This information paves the way for the marriage between Eléna's twin and her beau (since they now know they are not brother and sister) and, incredibly, between Louis and his long-lost Irish belle. And Yei? Not to worry. As Louis says of the brief coming together that produced the twins: "She once took pity on a broken-hearted young man. It was the Indian way of things. . . . Understand, she had no regrets. To the Amerindians, children were always a blessing and were welcomed. But seeing my distress and the difficulties which I explained to her would affect our livelihood, she made me swear never to tell anyone, never" (69–70). Whew! Thank goodness for strong, silent, wise Amerindian women, who, when impregnated by European men, are understanding enough to know their place! Once again, some relationships are conveniently shelved for the sake of the big picture.

The key to Belgrave's ability to simultaneously portray the brutality of slavery and the possibility of harmony between characters who would seem to be historically pitted against one another is her presentation of the plantation system as being introduced too late in its history to *define* Trinidad. Because the large labor force required by sugar cultivation did not really begin in this territory until the last decades of the eighteenth century, the relationship between African or Amerindian laborers and European (mainly Spanish) masters was considered relatively mild compared with that in territories where the plantation system was more entrenched and brutal—Barbados, Martinique, and Jamaica, for instance.

Beginning in the 1780s the Spanish government invited Roman Catholic planters (mainly French Creole) from other territories to settle in Trinidad and foster its transformation into a profitable sugar-producing territory. Incoming planters were offered land based on how many slaves they brought into Trinidad with them, and by the final years of the eighteenth century African slave labor had become the foundation of a "new" Trinidad. That some of the immigrant planters from neighboring territories were of African descent added to the perception that Trinidad was a place where racial oppression was less entrenched than in older colonies, since these planters had faced discrimination in their former territories. As the novel's preface states: "Trinidad and Tobago prides itself on being an exceptionally cosmopolitan and racially harmonious nation . . . even in the dawn of its modern-day period (the late eighteenth century), it was a haven of liberalism and racial and cultural tolerance. I have set my fairy-tale of the beautiful coloured girl and her Georgian beau, a young Corinthian, at this early period in the island's history, a period when its liberalism was being sadly shaken" (vii).

Britain's assuming control of the colony soon after its transformation to full-scale sugar production seemed to confirm this impression that the denial of rights associated with slavery was something foreign to Trinidad, brought in by others from outside. Trinidad became absorbed into the British Empire as a Crown colony rather than one with a representative assembly, and this meant—theoretically—that there was no entity corresponding to the European planter elite that wielded political power in other territories and were perceived as thwarting any metropolitan efforts to improve the conditions of the enslaved population. It was supposedly, then, something of a model British colony where measures aimed at ameliorating the excesses of slavery could be enforced with less opposition than elsewhere.

*Ti Marie* opens in this setting of a territory on the eve of large-scale sugar production and slavery. Don Diego, a struggling Spanish landowner who wonders how he will provide for his family with his small-scale cocoa cultivation, tells his son that "in a companionship of misery, there's no room for discrimination" (5), and Louis believes passionately in the liberal ideals of the French Revolution. Yei, daughter of an Amerindian mother and a "strapping Mandingo," turns up one day, decides to stay and is absorbed into the household as housekeeper-cum-physician.

Eléna, then, lives her childhood in the belief that the world is just like Don Diego's household: the small band of slaves is happy and well cared for, the two European men at the center of the arrangement are either openly liberal (Louis) or too poor to be oppressive (Don Diego), and she and her mother and sister are not really slaves, since they have been a part of the family too long for such distinctions to be important. Her increasing awareness of the harsh conditions of the growing slave population seems to parallel the transformation of Trinidad from a state of innocence where everyone is so poverty stricken that they are more or less equal to a slave colony characterized by oppression and brutality.

The distinction between the humane and inhumane treatment of slaves is very important. When Eléna witnesses scenes of brutality, her disgust and horror give the impression that such harshness is an aberration, since *she* treats Don Diego's slaves with love and kindness. The sin resides more in the brutality than in the institution itself.

Historians do not seem to agree that French Creole planters treated their slaves like "treasured children" or that slavery in this territory was milder than anywhere else (see, for instance, Brereton, *History*, 26). In addition, the emphasis on differences from territory to territory ignores the fact that slavery was a way of life in the Caribbean—indeed in the Americas—generally. Decisions about who was free and who was not were based on an elaborate and centuries-old network of law and custom. Someone technically "free" in one territory could be kidnapped and sold as a slave to another territory, and so on. In short, the Caribbean was a place where slavery was "not to be avoided" (see Goveia, *Slave*, 155). Elsa Goveia's work on eighteenth-century slave society describes the 1827 judgment handed down on the status of Grace, a man who had secured his freedom in England and then returned to the Caribbean territory where he had originally been enslaved. He was promptly sold into slavery again. The judgment was that he could not expect freedom, since "he had gone back to a place where slavery awaited him and where experience had taught him that slavery was not to be avoided." (Goveia's reference for the judgment is Cutterall, *Judicial*, 5–8.)

That Trinidad had not been steeped in the system for centuries, then, something Belgrave exploits here, does not really matter, unless of course we are not perturbed by the "heavy stuff." Don Diego's household, which exists before full-blown slavery and remains largely isolated from its more oppressive aspects, becomes a paradigm for right-thinking people, a place that could have existed given Trinidad's relatively short experience of slavery. The romance requires this haven where anything is possible and where the exception is the rule. Don Diego's home—and Trinidad—represents what could have been and what can be.

As I have noted, Belgrave claims her readers already know the "heavy stuff." They want something else. The market certainly seems to bear this out, both in the Caribbean and internationally. After the publication of *Ti Marie* in 1988, Heinemann Press, heartened by the novel's impressive sales, launched a Caribbean Caresses romance series, for which Belgrave contributed *Sun Valley Romance* (1993). The heroine, Giselle, has "Cleopatra braids . . . hundreds of small plaits that fell to her shoulders and gave her an Egyptian look," "rich brown skin," and "high cheek bones [that] must have come down from a forgotten Amerindian ancestor" (28–29).

Her beau, Gary, a black architect and civil engineer with a diploma in business administration, wins her love by choosing her Cleopatra beauty over a potential rival from Europe ("tall, attractively tanned, very very blonde" [43]) and by using his family fortune to stop environmentally unsafe mining in Giselle's district. By, as he says: "understand[ing] the pitfalls and casualties of unlimited power, and the human responsibilities that so much power demands" (137), he combines the best of all possible worlds, and his physical description bears this out:

> He had unconsciously spoken in the vernacular and, suddenly, all reservations lifted from her heart. Hearing him speak polished English in that beautiful voice was intriguing, but knowing that he could occasionally master Trinidadian was infinitely reassuring. It made him seem more real and stirred her mind and her body with untold possibilities. . . . His skin was a true brown colour and not a yellow brown. His face was beautifully sculpted with a high intelligent forehead and a long aristocratic nose. (23, 26–27)

The happy couple have a Divali engagement and a Christmas wedding. In presenting a black couple in contemporary Trinidad, Belgrave follows precise physiognomical and ethnic specifications. The Arabesque series published by Kensington Publishing Corporation in New Jersey, the phenomenal success of Terry McMillan's *Waiting to Exhale* (1992), and the London-based X Press series (including Anton Marks's *Dancehall* [1996]: "It was level vibes until [Dancehall deejay Simba Ranking] made the mistake of dealing with the wrong woman") indicate the growing market for romance novels featuring all-black couples.

My reading of *Ti Marie* has tried to show how catering to this market is perhaps more complex and certainly more contradictory than we may think—how marrying Massa rather than killing him, for example, is deemed as ideologically satisfying for contemporary readers as two black lovers on a book cover. As an elitist reader-critic I would have preferred Belgrave to try to find a "pleasurable" way to demystify the romance itself, to show how slavery proved the lie of the romance, that definitions of womanhood and liberalism are found wanting when they are placed in the context of the ideological requirements of those who owned slaves and tolerated slavery.

Where is the pleasure to be found in such a version, however? Can the textbook accounts of Caribbean history bring pleasure? Should they? Given the usual route for West Indian literature—recognition by a local and foreign middle-class readership, canonization, and a place on the examination syllabus—is not the denial of pleasure inevitable? I am struck both by the continuing desire to redefine the period of slavery and by the variety of options available in this redefinition. In offering us a recuperation of the Harlequin Romance that claims the genre for Caribbean readers, it seems to me that Belgrave vastly complicates our present "truths" regarding the textual production of "Caribbean women writers" or even "Third World feminism."

## Notes

I have benefited from various discussions of the novel, including Carolyn Cooper, "Perverse Romance"; Steve Harney, "Men Goh Respect All o' We"; Selwyn Cudjoe, "Women Writers on the Right Path"; and Paula Morgan, "Like Bush Fire in My Arms." I am also indebted to the enthusiasm of audiences before whom I delivered versions of this essay: at the African Literature Association meeting in Guadeloupe, 1993; the Women's Studies Graduate Research Conference at Duke University, 1993; and the Caribbean Studies Association, Mérida, Mexico, 1994.

## Works Cited

Andrade, Susan. "The Nigger of the Narcissist: History, Sexuality and Intertextuality in Maryse Condé's *Heremakhonon.*" *Callaloo* 16, no. 1 (1993): 213–26.

Belgrave, Valerie. "A Fairy Tale of Humanist Triumph." *Trinidad and Tobago Review,* July 1989, 10–11.

———. "On Combining Batik and Novel Writing." In *Caribbean Women Writers: Essays from the First International Conference,* ed. Selwyn Cudjoe, 317–24. Wellesley MA: Calaloux, 1990.

———. *Sun Valley Romance.* London: Heinemann, 1993.

———. "Thoughts on the Choice of Theme and Approach in the Writing of *Ti Marie.*" In *Caribbean Women Writers: Essays from the First International Conference,* ed. Selwyn Cudjoe, 325. Wellesley MA: Calaloux, 1990.

———. *Ti Marie.* London: Heinemann, 1988.

Brereton, Bridget. *A History of Modern Trinidad, 1783–1962.* London: Heinemann, 1981.

Carlyle, Thomas. "Occasional Discourse on the Nigger Question." 1853. In *English and Other Critical Essays.* New York: E. P. Dutton, 1915.

Chitty, Susan. *"The Beast and the Monk": A Life of Charles Kingsley.* New York: Mason/Charter, 1975.

Cobham, Rhonda. "Women in Jamaican Literature, 1900–1950." In *Out of the Kumbla: Caribbean Women and Literature,* ed. Carole Boyce Davies and Elaine Savory Fido, 195–222. Trenton NJ: Africa World Press, 1990.

Condé, Maryse. *Heremakhonon.* Trans. Richard Philcox. Washington DC: Three Continents Press, 1982.

Cooper, Carolyn. "Perverse Romance." *Third World Quarterly* 11, no. 4 (1989): 289–93.

Coulthard, G. R. *Race and Colour in Caribbean Literature.* Oxford: Oxford Univ. Press, 1962.

Cudjoe, Selwyn, ed. *Caribbean Women Writers: Essays from the First International Conference.* Wellesley MA: Calaloux, 1990.

———. "Women Writers on the Right Path." *Trinidad Guardian,* 12 May 1989, 20.

Cutterall, Helen T., ed. *Judicial Cases concerning American Slavery and the Negro.* Vol. 1. Washington DC: Carnegie Institution of Washington, 1926.

Fanon, Frantz. *Black Skin, White Masks.* Trans. Charles Markham. New York: Grove Press, 1982.

Froude, J. A. *The English in the West Indies.* London: Longmans, Green and Co., 1888.

Goveia, Elsa. *Slave Society in the British Leeward Islands at the End of the Eighteenth Century.* New Haven: Yale Univ. Press, 1965.

Hall, Catherine. *White, Male and Middle Class.* Cambridge: Polity Press, 1992.

Hall, Stuart. "Cultural Identity and Cinematic Representation." *Ex-Iles: Essays on Caribbean Cinema,* ed. Mbye Cham, 220–36. Trenton NJ: Africa World Press, 1992.

Harney, Steve. "Men Goh Respect All o' We: Valerie Belgrave's *Ti Marie* and the Invention of Trinidad." *World Literature Written in English* 30, no. 2 (1990): 110–19.

Hulme, Peter. *Colonial Encounters.* London: Methuen, 1986.

Innes, C. L. Review of *Ti Marie, Wasafiri* 11 (spring 1990): 38–39.

Innis, L. O. *Trinidad and Trinidadians,* Port-of-Spain: Mirror Printing Works, 1910.

James, C. L. R. *The Black Jacobins,* 1936. New York: Vintage 1962.

———. "Michel Maxwell Philip: 1829–1888." 1931. In *From Trinidad: An Anthology of Early West Indian Writing,* ed. Reinhard Sander, 253–69. New York: Africana, 1978.

Kincaid, Jamaica. "Jamaica Kincaid and the Modernist Project: An Interview." In *Caribbean Women Writers: Essays from the First International Conference*, ed. Selwyn Cudjoe, 215. Wellesley MA: Calaloux, 1990.

Kingsley, Charles. *At Last: A Christmas in the West Indies*. 2 vols. London: Macmillan, 1871.

Marks, Anton. *Dancehall*. London: X Press, 1996.

Martin, Robert. *The Dust of Combat: A Life of Charles Kingsley*. London: Faber and Faber, 1959.

Mathurin, Lucille. "Recollections of a Journey into a Rebel Past." In *Caribbean Women Writers: Essays from the First International Conference*, ed. Selwyn Cudjoe, 51–60. Wellesley MA: Calaloux, 1990.

McMillan, Terry. *Waiting to Exhale*. New York: Washington Square Press, 1992.

Mohammed, Sharlow. *When Gods Were Slaves*. Longdenville, Trinidad: Sharlow Mohammed, 1993.

Morgan, Paula. "Like Bush Fire in My Arms: Interrogating the World of Caribbean Romance." Paper presented at the Caribbean Women Writers Conference, Miami, 1996.

Naipaul, V. S. *The Loss of El Dorado*. New York: Alfred Knopf, 1969.

Philip, Maxwell. *Emmanuel Appadocca, or Blighted Life: A Tale of the Boucaneers*. 2 vols. London: Charles J. Skeet, 1854.

Prince, Mary. *The History of Mary Prince, a West Indian Slave, Related by Herself*. 1831. London: Pandora, 1987.

Raymond, Judy. Interview with Valerie Belgrave. *Trinidad Sunday Express*, 21 July 1991, 16–17.

Rosaldo, Renato. "Imperialist Nostalgia." *Representations* 26 (spring 1989): 107-22.

Scott, David. "That Event, This Memory: Notes on the Anthropology of African Diasporas in the New World." *Diaspora* 1 (winter 1991): 261–84.

Sommer, Doris. *Foundational Fictions: The National Romances of Latin America*. Berkeley: Univ. of California Press, 1991.

Tanifeani, William. "Interview with Valerie Belgrave: Novelist, Visual Artist." *Wasifiri* 11 (spring 1990): 24–25.

Thomas, J. J. *Froudacity: West Indian Fables Explained*. 1889. London: New Beacon Press, 1969.

Trollope, Anthony. *The West Indies and the Spanish Main*. New York: Harper, 1860.

Walcott, Derek. "A Far Cry from Africa." In *Collected Poems 1948–1984*, 17–18. London: Faber and Faber, 1992.

———. "The Muse of History." In *Is Massa Day Dead? Black Moods in the Caribbean*, ed. Orde Coombs, 1–27. New York: Anchor, 1974.

# 9

# Homing Instincts: Immigrant Nostalgia and Gender Politics in *Brown Girl, Brownstones*

## Supriya Nair

Because the majority of women are "miracle workers," labouring long hours both inside and outside the home, creating "something from nothing," making incredible sacrifices for their children and tolerating the vagaries of their men, yet are capable of "raising their voice up" when aroused, the general belief is that Caribbean women are "strong," "powerful," "matriarchic," etc. The corollary is, at what price?

Olive Senior, *Working Miracles*

Black working-class women, in particular, have a long history of being perceived as overpowering earth mothers whose sturdy shoulders have assumed the burdens of not just their own families, but those of their employers as well. The subsequent tensions with their menfolk, their "castrating" potential, and the hostility and fear they evoke have been recorded in Caribbean popular culture, calypsos being one example. As Olive Senior notes in her landmark study of women in the Caribbean,[1] these narratives have coexisted with images of working-class women who stoically endure the slings and arrows of outrageous fortune, working at traditionally unpaid roles such as mother and wife while simultaneously doing wage labor in the so-called public sphere. Traditionally, the domestic woman in feminist theory is a designation that marks the gender blindness of conventional Marxist paradigms. It draws attention to the invisible sphere of production within the home. But the domestic woman this chapter focuses on participates in a marketable domesticity: she works unpaid within her home and as a waged domestic laborer in the homes of others. For, as Senior states, domestic labor constituted over 50 percent of female employment in private homes and in the hotel industry in Jamaica for several decades (Senior, *Working,* 119).

Indeed, the limited terrain of the domestic does not quite capture the traveling potential of this category. Given the migratory labor of the islands, the domestic woman of the home and the nation is often necessarily a transnational subject.

The domestic employment category in the Caribbean radically redefines the binaries of the home/market, the domestic/national, and the national/transnational spheres. Black domestic labor in the Caribbean travels well past the confines of home and even beyond the geographical borders of the nation. Many women who migrated from their home countries in the archipelago to metropolitan centers such as New York found employment in a range of domestic services, especially with the huge expansion of the service sector in the 1970s (Kasinitz, *Caribbean,* 97).[2] The transnational system of stratified reproduction enabled the metropolis to handle the internal pressures caused when many female baby boomers joined the labor force. In fact, some immigrants were encouraged to enter domestic occupations working for white middle-class households with the promise of green cards. Rather than radically revise or reduce the gender divide of home-bound work as more women visibly entered the market, metropolitan domestic services "crossed class, race, and national lines" to use West Indian migrant women instead (Colen, "Like," 83).[3] The legacy of the mammy not only was an enduring one, it had global implications that may have prompted the novelist Paule Marshall to depict one of her characters, Carrington, the maid in *The Chosen Place, the Timeless People,* as "the mother figure who suckles the world" (Marshall, "Re-creating," 23). Unlike the middle-class domestic woman of nineteenth-century England, the domestic lower-class woman in the West Indies was likely to operate directly both at home and in the public, even global, economy. She was also marked by her work such that she represented a national type, a class of labor, and a gendered subject all at the same time, as Marshall's loaded allegory implies.

The micropolitics of domestic labor and of women's equality, usually subsumed within a macropolitical nationalist rhetoric, reconfigures the questions raised about the transnational domestic woman's relationship to the nation. If a good many allegorical representations of the nation were imaged through the gendered *Heimlich,* the pleasantly "familiar" space of home that was inextricably bound in the private body of a wife-mother who remained unsoiled by excessive mobility or market transactions, how does the migrant woman who leaves home and nation in search of paid employment disrupt and estrange this familiar discourse? She is no less unsettling to the equally gendered discourse of diaspora that etymologically implies the scattering of seed, rooting women while making travel the privileged terrain of the errant male. Finally, in the nostalgic narrative of return that forms the final frontier of diasporic migration, how does the absent woman's divorce from an affiliation with the metaphorical motherland constitute a challenge not to maternal bonds, but to patriarchal fantasies?

Paule Marshall herself is a product of a unique multilayered history of diasporic displacements. Like others of their colonial generation from Barbados, her parents found it almost impossible to gain profitable employment on their impoverished native island. An entrenched white settler class and an emerging national bourgeoisie maintained a stranglehold over the emancipated but virtually landless Afro-Caribbean labor. Migration outward has long been a survival strategy, an alternative channel of employment on these islands. Deprived of land, material resources, educational opportunities, and steady jobs in the politically unstable, economically stagnant, and demographically cramped island societies, thousands of native islanders left in search of what George Lamming called "a better break" (*Emigrants*, 33). Many sought it in the symbolic city of the American dream, New York, extending an additional leg of the African diaspora in its history of dislocation and relocation. Marshall's parents came to New York in one of the immigrant influxes after World War I, settling down by World War II in a Brooklyn neighborhood that forms the setting of her first novel *Brown Girl, Brownstones* (1959).

In an essay explaining the creative force of the domestic on her own writing, Marshall outlines the working schedule of her mother's group in the metropolis. Armed with an apron and an old pair of shoes, women like her mother would take the train from Brooklyn to Flatbush, haggling with housewives there for a day's work of housecleaning ("Making," 4). Acknowledging the impact these women had on the form and content of her fiction, Marshall also pays tribute in *Brown Girl* to their strategies for economic survival. Daily routines of "scrubbing floor" in the middle and late 1930s partially supported the household, and it is this story of domestic labor and struggle that Marshall's first novel portrays in the figure of Silla Boyce, mother of ten-year-old Selina, the "brown girl" of the narrative. The novel is dedicated to Marshall's mother, in additional homage to the formative impact of the domestic in the author's work.

But Selina's father, Deighton Boyce, might initially seem to be the novel's primary sympathetic character, whose passionate desire to earn enough money to return to Barbados is opposed to Silla's equally passionate need to save enough to "buy house" in Brooklyn. It is curious that Deighton's longing to return home to the island that still claims his primary loyalty is largely interpreted as his expression of the humanism of the Caribbean, while Silla's refusal to go back and instead to claim property for herself in New York is largely read as her cooptation by materialistic American values. (While critics such as Joyce Pettis, Dorothy Hamer Denniston, and Laura Niesen De Abruna are sympathetic to Silla, they nevertheless subscribe to a binary politics of locality in the materialism/humanism divide.) But how antimaterialistic is Deighton's aspiration to be the man who made good not just to the home folks but also to the still struggling Bajan American community? Challenging the legitimacy of Silla's dream, he reveals his own fantasies to an adoring Selina:

> Even your mother can come, but she gon have to watch that mouth. I gon be firm with she 'cause it'll be my house and my land and I ain gon stand for no foolishness. And if they [Silla and Ina, Selina's older sister] don wanna come, I gon make you mistress of the house. The servants gon have to take orders from you. When you want your fancy clothes I gon put you 'pon a plane to New York to do your shopping. And when these Bajan here see you, they gon say, "Wha'lah, wha'lah, look Deighton Selina! I hear that man living like a lord home." (87)

Deighton's desire to go home is just as materialistic as Silla's desire to stay in Brooklyn. If Silla eventually buys into the dog-eat-dog axiomatics of metropolitan capitalism, Deighton's credo of spectacular one-upmanship is not far behind in principle. His lifestyle in Brooklyn is lavish beyond his means as a factory worker, much to Silla's disapproval, and his love for silk shirts and expensive musical instruments is not likely to change, one assumes, regardless of where he ultimately settles. In keeping with a particular history of black macho style, Deighton's finicky attention to his appearance and his zest for fleshly pleasures could be coded as part of a subculture of resistance (Mercer, "Black Masculinity," 137). Nevertheless, it is a very material and materialistic resistance to capital; one that operates in the margins of global capital but does not necessarily exclude the paraphernalia of materialism. In the culturally coded values assigned to a return to the motherland, however, his decision apparently gains a moral ascendancy lacking in Silla's lack of enthusiasm for the land of her birth. The national economic structures are directly projected onto the returning immigrant, suggesting that distancing oneself from the States must necessarily involve rejecting American wealth. Returning to the economically impoverished island nation is proportionally translated into the higher moral ground of placing nation over personal privilege. But the point of return was rarely to disown the imperatives that made one leave in the first place. The immigrant dream was to return not to the same conditions, but to a materially advanced position made possible by the departure. Ironically, Deighton's daydream is the immigrant dream of ultimate privilege, the ease of transnational travel without the pain of exile. Thus Selina would be comfortably rooted in native soil but also able to seek the benefits of the metropolis when she—or more correctly, he—so desires.

Deighton's plans are not unusual in first-generation immigrant ideologies. Immigrant communities from the former British colonies such as the West Indies and India often perceived their stay in the United States as a sojourn, with schemes of retirement in their home countries, with which they refused to sever all ties. This was especially important to the earlier groups of black West Indian immigrants who settled in the United States before the civil rights movement. In holding up the dream of an ultimate return to where one came from, to where one "really" belonged, the foundational ties formed a buffer against the blows of discrimination. Imagining a temporary exile made the stress of migration itself bearable, even if nothing had radically changed at home that might warrant a return. The "birds of passage" philosophy lightened the weight of daily struggle, since home could always be located elsewhere, and relief therefore envisioned as just around the corner. "The self image of those who chose this option was tied to their former status in their homeland, or to their anticipated improved status upon return," concludes Kasinitz (35).

Deighton's "self-image" is explicitly tied not just to his anticipated return but also to his romanticized nostalgia for Barbados. His memories of growing up with the "boys" are articulated in opposition to

Silla's perceived lower-class status: "'Pon a Sat'day I would walk 'bout town like I was a full-full man. All up Broad Street and Swan Street like I did own the damn place" (10). But enmeshed in Deighton's fond flashbacks of imaginary proprietorship and of playful games on the beaches is the uneasy sense of himself as a performer whose games came with a price, and a rather cheap one at that. He recollects, for instance, that one of the games on the beach included diving for coins tossed in the water by visiting American tourists, but he represses the discomfort raised by this memory, just as he quells his guilt over his mother's "quiet willingness to suffer" (26). It is Selina, the recipient of these confidences, who interrupts the smooth gloss of these fancies with intrusive thoughts of her mother's contrasting routine with her companions in Brooklyn: "She could never think of the mother alone. It was always the mother and the others, for they were alike—those watchful, wrathful women whose eyes seared and searched and laid bare, whose tongues lashed the world in unremitting distrust" (10–11). The pointed contrast between Deighton's "spreeing" and Silla's laboring is not just class-informed, as Deighton makes it out to be. Instead, it portrays a specific gendered divide that is experienced here in the modality of class. Contrary to the situation with the affluent middle classes, it is not uncommon in depressed national economies for the lower-class female to enter the labor market, however informally, along with or even earlier than the male. The contrast here humanizes not Deighton but Silla, whose bitterness is a direct consequence of the drudgery of her daily work.

What constitutes the flesh of national experience, or the memory thereof, is distinctly gendered in the novel. Perhaps because of this cleavage, the domestic woman's remembrance diverges from the consoling, commemorating reveries of the *Heimlich*. The *Heimlich* is precisely what terrifies her and alienates her from home. Silla's past involves even more drudgery than her present, and what she remembers about her childhood in Bimshire is working in the canefields and selling fruit. Selina's response is mixed as she hears her mother's side of the story: "The image of her father swaggering through the town as a boy and bounding on the waves in some rough game slanted across that of the small girl hurrying from the dawn ghosts with the basket on her head. It seemed to Selina that her father carried those gay days in his irresponsible smile, while the mother's formidable aspect was the culmination of all that she had suffered" (46). Interpellating "the mother" distances Selina from a depersonalized Silla, because she is far closer to her father, who takes the possessive here, but it also conveys Marshall's sense of the anonymous generality of the working-class black women who perform domestic labor on a mass scale. As Marshall says elsewhere, women like her mother "suffered a triple invisibility, being black, female and foreigners. They really didn't count in American society except as a source of cheap labor" ("Making," 7). The definite article preceding the noun underlines the contiguity of a class formation within a traditionally gendered occupation. Silla the Mother denotes not entitlement but sacrifice, not privilege but privation. The prototype of warm, fuzzy individualized motherhood is crushed by the weight of a universal maternity whose aspect is considerably more grim and less loving. Silla might inherit the mantle of the mammy, but she refuses the mythical persona of service with a broad smile.

The rupture between what is remembered and what is forgotten or repressed in the narrative of national memory locates Deighton's loyalty to his motherland within the discourse of "eroticized nationalism." His love and desire for his country flourish in the selective reminiscences of nurtured youth and "imagined community," to borrow these now familiar concepts from Benedict Anderson. On the other hand, as Elleke Boehmer reminds us, "this same motherland may not signify 'home' and 'source' to women. . . . the lap of the Mother Nation may not be as soft and capacious for women as it is for men" ("Stories," 5–6). The male homosocial bonds that secure Deighton's anchorage in the originary motherland fail to attach the domestic women in the novel in the same way. Instead, their indenture to the adoptive country is as pragmatic as is their connection to the native site. Silla offers no patriotic gratitude to any one of the nations she has ties to: her suspicion of John Bull is as deep as her disillusion with Bimshire, where it's "a terrible thing to know that you gon be poor all yuh life, no matter how hard you work" (70). But giving credit where she thinks it is due, she believes that some headway can be made in New York in spite of "the discrimination and thing." The unabashedly acquisitive work ethic positions the woman in a nonaltruistic relationship with her nation, since her rhetoric is not of a giving loyalty that piously asks what she can do for her country, but calculatedly measures what her country can do for her. The unspoken working contract of the mother to the nation is seriously disturbed when she refuses to accept an ethical duty to correspond with Deighton's erotic desire.

Silla's acknowledgment of the possibility of social mobility in the metropolis is another familiar paradigm of immigrant desire. It is, after all, the stuff the dream is made of; it motivates migration and sweetens exile. But in her case she accepts, however grudgingly, the degradation of her work in the hope of gradually moving up, as indeed she does in the course of the novel. Breaking the cycle of stratified reproduction, a system of domestic labor that reproduces itself through structured inequalities, is itself an achievement. Deighton, on the other hand, reacts to the discrimination he faces by dreaming large dreams of success. Leaving behind a trail of incomplete ventures and hazy plans, he announces grandly that he is an all-or-nothing kind of person because that is "the way a man does do things" (83). Unable to look fully in the eye of a dream that has gone sour, he continues to be optimistic in spite of Silla's increasing frustration with his approach to life. She, along with the rest of the community, seems blind to the imperative behind Deighton's rationalizations, because he implicitly shares their own sense that his lack of success signals his loss of manhood, especially given that other men in the community share Silla's work ethic. Like Suggie's, Deighton's excesses contradict the thrifty economizing of the Bajans. Instead, Silla comes to stand for the idealized immigrant whose focus is to "make it" in the metropolis. But while Silla practices a domesticated economy of savings and thrift, it is not directed toward her nation (although immigrant money sent home has an important economic impact).

Not surprisingly, Deighton is utterly defeated when Silla explodes his sustaining dream by selling his small piece of land in Barbados without his knowledge in order to make money to "buy house" in Brooklyn. Denied his last fantasy of return, Deighton takes revenge by frittering away the money, sustains a critical accident at work, turns to Father Peace, "the smiling patriarch," and his religious cult, and is finally sent back to Barbados after his enraged and embittered wife reports him to the immigration authorities for illegal entry into the States. Father Peace's patriarchal message seems appropriate to Deighton's state of mind after he loses his property: "The mother of creation is the mother of defilement! The word *mother* is a filthy word!" (168; emphasis in original). The castrating potential of Silla as the wife-mother is posed against a seemingly different phantasmatic mother in Barbados. Selina imagines the scenario that led to her father's leap into the sea as the ship neared Barbados and his subsequent death by drowning: "*When he saw the island, he emitted a low frightened cry. . . . For that low mound, resting on the sea like a woman's breast when she is supine, was Barbados. Time fled as the mist fled and he was a boy again, diving for the coins the tourists tossed into the sea*" (190; emphasis in original). Like the slaves who leaped off the ships to their deaths years ago, Deighton's jump enacts his social death, to borrow Orlando Patterson's apt term. The whorl of images brilliantly captures the slave-cruise-immigrant ships that continue to chart the cultural genealogy of the Caribbean. Although his death by delusion in the amniotic fluid of the sea and the maternal "breast" of the island ironically and fatally repeats his childhood leap for tourist money, Deighton's regression is not entirely a result of the force of the past on him. As Suggie shrewdly points out later, Deighton chooses suicide rather than face the humiliation of returning penniless to the island (208).

The battle between the parents over the land takes place with World War II as a backdrop, and as tensions between them escalate, leading to Deighton's death as he is deported to Barbados, the statement "the goddam war's over" at the conclusion of this episode signals the end of the domestic struggle as well. The private argument over land and property is ultimately tied to an embattled public discourse of patriotism and national loyalty. Like the big war, this story of love for the nation has no real happy ending. Lest one get carried away by the iconic sacrifice of a man's body at the altar of the motherland, Marshall speaks of how the big war abroad has devastating effects on the battles at home. Angrily disowning any sense of kinship with her roomers or with the larger black community, Florrie articulates an individualistic philosophy based on the meaning of her loss, not of the country's or the community's gain: "Sorry? . . . I sorry for all the long years I din have nothing and my children din have and now I got little something I too fat and old to enjoy it and my only son dead in these people bloody war and he can't enjoy it. That's what I sorry for!" (224). The subplot of a woman's individual loss overwhelms, however momentarily, the larger narrative of fraternity and sisterhood, not to glorify the individual but to offer a sober corrective to celebratory scenarios of national collectivity.

To accuse Silla of being Hitler in the domestic scenario, as Selina does, is to demonize the mother's politics of location. However uncharitable her motives may be, in enforcing his deportation Silla only exposes the fantastic nature of Deighton's campaign to return. Clearly the homecoming occurs too soon for him, for he is ultimately unable to complete his dream even as he nears the shores of the island. He literally jettisons it. Like most dreams, homecoming is usually most fulfilling in its spectral state. Although the significance of land is equally clear to Deighton and Silla, the crucial difference lies in its location. Whereas Deighton plans to use New York as a step upward and then back to Barbados, Silla's social ladder stays firmly secured in New York. Interestingly, Marshall's autobiographical tribute to her grandmother mentions that it is the father who refuses to make visits back to the Caribbean—"('Blowing out good money on foolishness,' he had said of the trip)"—whereas the mother retains her connections to family and keeps the children in touch with "back home" ("Da-Duh," 99). In the novel, however, Silla is unbending in her refusal to return, while Selina maintains her curiosity about Bimshire through her father's expressed desires to go back. The reversal not just of biographical reality but also of the general expectations of women who long to return while men are the pragmatic migrants is worth emphasizing in the novel.[4] The motives behind the nostalgic yearning of the male parent and the female's intransigent lack of sentiment are politically gendered. Ascribing materialism to the unsentimental female who seemingly caves in to American consumer values and attributing spiritual wholeness to the sentimental male who turns his back on the foreign metropolis neglects the variable histories of nationalist desires. It also reinscribes a clichéd split between a spiritual Third World and a materialistic First World. Considering that Deighton himself has explicit materialistic fantasies about success back home, the tendency to articulate his intention to return to authentic native space as a more conscientious and dutiful one needs further exploration.

In a short story titled "Barbados," which came "practically ready-made" to Marshall during her visit to the island in 1958 when she was revising *Brown Girl,* Marshall draws upon the taciturn, withdrawn landlord who leased her a room in his house. The house in the story is also modeled on the one she stayed at: "Large, white, with tall columns at the front, it was a plantation house for a black man 'playing white.' My aging landlord had built it with money he had accumulated while in the States" (51). Mr. Watford's isolated existence seems a continuation of his "fifty-year exile" in the States, where he calculatedly accumulates money and property with the intention of returning to Barbados. Considering that Marshall wrote this story while working on the novel, Deighton's possible extension into the resentful seclusion of Mr. Watford, who still seethes with memories of a servile and poverty-stricken childhood, is not improbable. The portrayal is not entirely unsympathetic because, as in the case of Deighton's insecurities, Mr. Watford's coldness is partly attributed to his larger cultural environment. He is the only one of ten children to grow up and escape, and the dire poverty of his childhood and the burdened figure of his mother haunt him late into his life. "Gladly had he fled the island," the narrator asserts (56). The story's conclusion does not bode well for prospects of a romantic return of the prodigal son. But what of the daughter? The story of Mr. Watford does not allow for an idealized narrative of redemption, either moral or political. The return only continues his barren isolation, refusing to articulate inevitable nationalist commitments to Barbados. The Bajan American's pursuit of savings and property is not any more alienated than the returned exile's relationship to the island. But in the novel, Selina's decision to leave for Barbados in the face of her mother's opposition bears none of the foreboding that characterizes Watford. She joins a number of other female characters in Marshall's fiction who decide to return to an originary space, either the Caribbean, as Avey Johnson does in *Praisesong for the Widow,* or to an even earlier site of antiquity, Africa, as does Reena in a short story of the same title, or Merle Kimbona in *The Chosen Place, the Timeless People.* As Reena explains,

> Oh, I know I should remain and fight not only for integration (even though, frankly, I question whether I want to be integrated into America as it stands now, with its complacency and materialism, its soullessness) but to help change the country into something better, sounder—if that is still possible. But I have to go to Africa. (90)

Being a displaced black woman in the United States before the civil rights movement and the modern feminist movement may be a key issue in the politics of return, but here too Marshall seems to underline a subtext of spiritual satisfaction that outweighs the material fulfillment of the adoptive country. Ironically, the motive that prompted migration is turned inside out in this trajectory, since material success is now seen as an empty project, and the promise of emotional regeneration fuels a reverse migration or initiates, as in Reena's case, a journey to a foundational site, however imagined. For Marshall and her characters, the magnetic pull of several charged fields must make the issue of what identity one ultimately claims—Bajan American, Afro-Caribbean, Anglo-American, or African—even more confusing as multiple diasporas and cultures swirl around the migrant subject. But the physical departure to an unknown land, even if it occupies the psychic comfort zone of the origin, is a move that must have material pressures as well. In other words, even if Reena and Selina pose their quests as largely spiritual ones, despite or perhaps because of the apparently materialistic sites they renounce, such departures are impelled by tangible social effects that may be different from those that directed their parents' migration. The daughter's presumed completion of her father's desire for the homeland is not as uncomplicated as it seems.

For instance, in spite of Selina's tribute to her mother's influence, in which she admits that she is more Silla's daughter than Deighton's, her departure from the United States may be triggered by a rejection of one part of her mother's heritage. Her encounter with Margaret's mother, who blithely lumps her with her own cleaning maid from the West Indies as she simultaneously praises Selina for rising above her national "type," could very well have been the last straw. As she flees from the humiliating scene, Selina faces her own invisibility, her own indistinguishable identity for women like Margaret's mother: "She was one with them: the mother and the Bajan women, who had lived each day what she had come to know. How had the mother endured, she who had not chosen death by water?" (292–93). Although unlike her father Selina does not choose death, she rejects her mother's option to "endure" as well. However objectionable Silla's complicity in the dog-eat-dog world that Selina rejects, she cannot deny that her mobility is made at least partly possible by her mother's refusal to leave.

Ann Morris and Margaret Dunn argue that the return to the land of one's mothers is a ritual of bonding with one's own mother. Citing the fiction of Jean Rhys, Paule Marshall, Jamaica Kincaid, and Michelle Cliff, all of whom portray complex mother-daughter relationships in their works, they argue that "all four writers suggest that a woman who plumbs and values her connection to the 'mother's land' itself may, even in the absence of a crucial developmental bond with her own or a surrogate mother, thereby find the means of achieving self-realisation" (Morris and Dunn, "Bloodstream," 221). In this trajectory from biology to culture the island home functions as surrogate mother, even performing a healing function when a character's relationship to the biological mother is under stress. And yet Kincaid, for example, expresses disillusion with her home island after her return many years later. She confesses, "I was shocked that it had changed for the worse. All the things I had thought made it a bad place were gone —but it was worse. . . . It turns out that we're not interested in the Caribbean Sea—we're interested in New York" ("Jamaica," 225; my emphasis). What is striking about Kincaid's remarks is her use of a complicit "we" rather than "they" and her observation that the Caribbean Sea is "now so much money." In spite of her sense of betrayal, it is also noteworthy that she refuses to posit a past golden age to substitute for a bleak future. Even if Antiguans were to return, they would still be squatters on their national land, since the neocolonial structures of the island's economy have ensured that native Antiguans own less land than the foreigners, who have bought up prime beachfront property. A large number of West Indians therefore confront the bizarre prospect of a nationalism that is not tied to landownership (Bryce-Laporte, "Black," 38). In such a situation, the value of claiming an affirmative and essential bond with the "mother's land" assumes ironic dimensions. Instead, the ceaseless cycle of out-migration from the Caribbean destabilizes the notion of any primal home space. The green card has a more naturalized reality than the birth certificate. It is the "alien" identity card that one does not leave home without.

Although the search for ancestry leading to a physical return to an identifiable motherland is understandable in the context of diaspora history, the consequences of the search cannot always be assumed to bear the fulfillment of reconnection. Nor do historical and fictional mothers always provide an easy bridge from nation to woman. In an account of a recent heritage quest trip to Ghana, a young African American woman confesses, like Kincaid, to a predominant feeling of anticlimax. Marked as a foreigner by her American accent, as a tourist by her camera and other travel gear, and as "not black" by her light skin, Chastity Pratt confronts estrangement rather than a sense of complete homecoming. Battling with her ambivalence, she remembers her mother's skepticism about the trip: " 'Girl,' she said, 'they barely want us here. What makes you think they want you over there?'" ("American"). Marshall's novel stops short of Selina's actual return, leaving the possibilities perhaps deliberately hazy. It is more than likely that a second-generation immigrant may not share her parent's experience of invented origins, however romantically childhood memories of "back home" are invoked. It is also quite probable that Selina might find herself a living testimony to the demographic, deterritorialized flows of her age and the diasporic history of her nation.

## Notes

I thank Belinda Edmondson, David Chioni Moore, and Henry Schwarz for the collegial community they provide. I am grateful to Lorand Matory, who generously shared his course materials with me.

1. Although the "Caribbean" embraces a wide range of geographic, linguistic, colonial, ethnic, and racial populations, my focus on Marshall's novel limits the use of the territory to former British colonies (the anglophone West Indies) with a majority black population. However, claiming ancestry in the Caribbean is a messy affair precisely because of the shakiness of categories. Statistics in immigration data are therefore not entirely reliable. The debate the novel raises about the affiliation between Barbadians and African Americans is also complicated by diverse histories and definitions of the relation between ethnicity and race. In the case of Barbadian immigrant-identified communities, it is interesting that ethnicity and national identity slide into one another. Additionally, the reluctance to embrace a larger racial consciousness could be related to stereotypes of the locals as lazy, indifferent, and lawless and of immigrants as hardworking, disciplined, and law-abiding.

2. Listing the major occupations by gender, Kasinitz reports the employment of West Indian women age sixteen and over in 1979 as nursing aide, secretary, nurse, servant, cleaner, maid or housekeeper, and welfare service. Men's employment included machine operator, guard, janitor, taxi driver, houseman, auto mechanic, and so on (*Caribbean*, 104).

3. By "stratified reproduction," Colen means a structured and hierarchized system of physical and social reproductive tasks categorized by inequalities based on class, gender, ethnicity, migrant status, and so on ("Like," 78).

4. Pettis argues that in a couple of Marshall's works, including this novel, "women [are] more receptive than men to the metaphorical journeys necessary to attain spiritual wholeness" (*Wholeness*, 94). Although this argument works with Selina, it does not account for Silla's lack of interest in homecoming.

## Works Cited

Anderson, Benedict. *Imagined Communities: Reflections on the Origin and Spread of Nationalism*. London: Verso, 1983.

Boehmer, Elleke. "Stories of Women and Mothers: Gender and Nationalism in the Early Fiction of Flora Nwapa." In *Motherlands: Black Women's Writing from Africa, the Caribbean and South Asia,* ed. Susheila Nasta, 3–23. New Brunswick: Rutgers Univ. Press, 1992.

Bryce-Laporte, Roy Simon. "Black Immigrants: The Experience of Invisibility and Inequality." *Journal of Black Studies* 3, no. 1 (1972): 29–56.

Colen, Shellee. "'Like a Mother to Them': Stratified Reproduction and West Indian Childcare Workers and Employers in New York." In *Conceiving the New World Order: The Global Politics of Reproduction,* ed. Faye D. Ginsburg and Rayna Rapp, 78–102. Berkeley: Univ. of California Press, 1995.

Denniston, Dorothy Hamer. *The Fiction of Paule Marshall: Reconstructions of History, Culture, and Gender.* Knoxville: Univ. of Tennessee Press, 1983.

Kasinitz, Philip. *Caribbean New York: Black Immigrants and the Politics of Race.* Ithaca: Cornell Univ. Press, 1992.

Lamming, George. *The Emigrants.* 1954. Ann Arbor: Univ. of Michigan Press, 1994.

Marshall, Paule. "Barbados." In *"Reena" and Other Stories,* 51-67.

———. *Brown Girl, Brownstones.* 1959. New York: Feminist Press, 1981.

———. "The Making of a Writer: From the Poets in the Kitchen." In *"Reena" and Other Stories,* 3–12.

———. "'Re-creating Ourselves All over the World.' A Conversation with Paule Marshall." Interview by Molara Ogundipe-Leslie. In *Moving beyond Boundaries: Black Women's Diasporas,* vol. 2, ed. Carole Boyce Davies. New York: New York Univ. Press, 1995.

———. "Reena." In *"Reena" and Other Stories,* 71–91.

———. *"Reena" and Other Stories.* New York: Feminist Press, 1983.

———. "To Da-Duh, in Memoriam." In *"Reena" and Other Stories,* 95–106.

Mercer, Kobena. "Black Masculinity and the Sexual Politics of Race." In *Welcome to the Jungle: New Positions in Black Cultural Studies,* 131–70. New York: Routledge, 1994.

———. *Welcome to the Jungle: New Positions in Black Cultural Studies.* New York: Routledge, 1994.

Morris, Ann R., and Margaret M. Dunn. "'The Bloodstream of Our Inheritance': Female Identity and the Caribbean Mothers'-Land." In *Motherlands: Black Women's Writing from Africa, the Caribbean and South Asia,* ed. Susheila Nasta, 219–37. New Brunswick: Rutgers Univ. Press, 1992.

Niesen De Abruna, Laura. "Twentieth-Century Women Writers from the English-Speaking Caribbean." In *Caribbean Women Writers: Essays from the First International Conference,* ed. Selwyn R. Cudjoe, 86–97. Wellesley MA: Calaloux, 1990.

Patterson, Orlando. *Slavery and Social Death: A Comparative Study.* Cambridge: Harvard Univ. Press, 1982.

Pettis, Joyce. *Toward Wholeness in Paule Marshall's Fiction.* Charlottesville: Univ. Press of Virginia, 1995.

Pratt, Chastity. "An American Face in an African Mirror." *New Orleans Times-Picayune,* 16 February 1997, D1.

Senior, Olive. *Working Miracles: Women's Lives in the English-Speaking Caribbean.* London: James Currey, 1991.

# 10

# Derek Walcott: Liminal Spaces/ Substantive Histories

*Tejumola Olaniyan*

Derek Walcott's unimpeachable career-long insistence is that though the Caribbean, with its origins in genocide, slavery, colonialism, and enduring racial antagonism, is a particularly alluring ground for all kinds of originary and substantivist claims —whether by the dominant or by the dominated and their offspring— the most productive stance is to envision the region as a liminal space not beholden or accountable to either side. The aesthetics proper to this space Walcott calls, in a seminal essay titled "What the Twilight Says," "mulatto" (9), neither purely black nor purely white; a hybrid aesthetics free to speak in Creole, English, *or both*, or appropriate forms from the diverse cultural traditions that make up the Caribbean —European, African or Asian. He insists that "the future of West Indian militancy lies in art" ("Twilight," 18) and that no effective voice for this art exists outside of conscious hybridity, of a willed invention of an enabling liminal, interstitial space away from the "grand narratives" of *both* the Eurocentric discourse in the Caribbean that privileges "mainstream" Euro-American artistic conventions and the militant Afrocentric discourse that insists on only artistic forms with verifiable Afro origins. This is the defining tension of Walcott's cultural practice, the tension between supposedly uncharted terrains and supposedly well-worn paths.

Walcott's ideal Caribbean play, for instance, will be a composite of treated but still earthy Creole, dance and music, the unapologetic coarseness of carnival forms, the "lyricism and savagery of Lorca," the "rawness and crudity of Elizabethan or Greek staging," the physicality and volubility of a cinema audience, and the profound, expressive subtlety of Japanese art ("National"). If this appears too well said, it is partly because the level of social antagonism Walcott is responding to demands such a gargantuan act of (rhetorical) taming and partly because it is more polemic than practical. It is a heroic act of willing into existence an envisioned ideal, but it is also one of the most enduring romantic[1] representations of the Caribbean to be found in Walcott's essays and interviews.

Walcott's conception of a liminal space unencumbered by the divisive and fractious realities of Caribbean history is anchored by two related propositions in his cultural theory: mimicry as the origin of traditions, and history as myth. These, he believes, authorize a radical revisionist attitude toward the existing in relation to the imagined.

## Mimicry as Tradition

Walcott started out, he said of his colonial education in the 1940s and 1950s, a natural assimilator of the Western tradition. This tradition was what was made formally available everywhere, so he fell "madly in love with English" ("Twilight," 11). This, of course, was not unique; it was a socially generic problem encountered by every native colonial, thanks to a Eurocentric education. He became a "good Friday" "parroting [the] master's style and voice" ("Crusoe's," 93) because his "sense of inheritance was stronger" since "it came from estrangement" ("Twilight," 31). Note that Walcott never gave up this formulation or substantially revised it, although in the history of literary nationalism in the formerly colonized world, it is more typical of the period *before* nationalist struggles and subsequent independence and decolonization. In the latter period, estrangement still remained, but the "sense of inheritance" was often conceived as delusive and dominative because the "inheritance" itself was imposed. "Bad Fridays" and struggles for literary independence were the consequence. This is certainly the sense of relationship to the West to be found in writers such as George Lamming, E. K. Brathwaite, Erna Brodber, Nourbese Phillips, Trevor Rhone, Maryse Condé, and Michelle Cliff.

The distinction between "good" Friday and "bad" Friday helps us specify the precise character of Walcott's relation to the Western tradition that he has made so intimate a part of himself. This relation can be seen as *assenting modification* rather than *dissenting criticism*. The Western tradition is for him not an oppressive tradition to be replaced or subverted, but the example or model to copy, creatively copy, to write the peculiarities of Caribbean experience. The great classics of the West are not antagonists of the erstwhile colonized, but pathfinders and senior colleagues in the same grand project of cultural enrichment of our "common humanity."

To the challenge of the Black Power–influenced poets against this hegemonic Western tradition, Walcott argued in his essay "The Muse of History" that "those who break a tradition first hold it in awe" and that "by openly fighting tradition, we perpetuate it." For him, "revolutionary literature is filial impulse" and "maturity is the assimilation of the features of every ancestor." He derided the poets for racializing literature and culture in seeing the "'classic style' as stasis . . . rejecting it as the language of the master." For their attempts at integrating concepts from African languages, cultural traditions and cosmological systems, and West Indian Creole, Walcott has only scorn, insisting that Calibanism—the imitation of the master's language by the servant—is a more desirable course ("Muse," 3–4).

For a minority tradition subordinate to the hegemonic, there is a fascinating theory of tradition and its development implicit in these contentious formulations. For Walcott, mastery is *the* true and original resistance, not, as commonly believed, revolutionary overthrow or rejection, which is always ephemeral and deceptive. And the path toward mastery is nothing other than a patient, bold, and creative imitation of the status quo, the available tradition. This is the outline of Walcott's "mimicry" theory of tradition, which achieves its unabridged formulation in Walcott's essay "The Caribbean: Culture or Mimicry," first published in 1974.

In the essay Walcott suggests that powerlessness and imperial subordination prod the former colonial world to search for alternatives: either "violent, the total rejection through revolution," or "cunning, or conservative, by which I mean the open assimilation of what is considered from the metropolitan center to be most useful" (52). Walcott chooses the latter as the more desirable and effective. For him, what the New World person—European, African, or Asian in origin—carried over from the Old World, "apart from a few desultorily performed customs, is language." And that language, fortunately or not, is that of the master. "When language itself is condemned as mimicry, then the condition is hopeless." And to suggest the other direction—for instance, Africa—as a model is unnatural and a quest for a "return." But this is "impossible, for we cannot return to what we have never been. The truth in all this is, of course, the amnesia of the American, particularly of the African" (53). Why "particularly the African," we might ask? Walcott resolutely refuses to explore his special qualification of the condition of the African in the New World, an exploration that potentially complicates his contention for revealing the inequality of the degree of amnesia and linguistic alienation among the different "races." The impossibility of return and the need to make the best of available reality, like Crusoe, authorize the American or New World person as an "ape." Walcott's spectacular performance here is the profound rewriting of the common negative connotations of imitation or mimicry, adroitly deploying the word "ape" as both noun and verb with persuasive eloquence. In the imitation of an ape, Walcott argues, "there is something more ancient than the first human effort." In fact, there could be no absolute distinction between originality and mimicry because "there is no scientific distinction possible between the last ape and the first man, there is no memory or history of the moment when man stopped imitating the ape, his ancestor, and became human. Therefore, everything is mere repetition" (53–54). In the passage from the Old World to the New, "there was no line in the sand which said, this is new, this is the frontier, the boundary of endeavor, and henceforth everything can only be mimicry." If there was such a line at all, it could only have demarcated an ambiguity: the simultaneous loss of the old and the gain of the new, "both surrender and claim," both subjection and subjectivity. "The issue is the claim" (54), Walcott asserts without ambiguity. He concludes his classic reversal by insisting that "mimicry is an act of imagination . . . it is design" (55).[2]

In the circumstances of the New World, Walcott contends, imitation is survival and adaptability, the opposite of suicide. And the result of this superior strength of imitation is all around us. The New World American Adam, a mimic in the Garden of Eden a second time around, survived, while the original, the Indian, perished. The Indians broke, Walcott presses on controversially: "They were resilient for a while but were broken. . . . We can praise them for not imitating, but even imitation decimated them . . . humiliated them. . . . What have we been offered here as alternative but suicide. I do not know if apes commit suicide—their mimicry is not that far advanced—but men do, and it appears too, certain cultures" (56).[3]

Mimicry is thus, for the Caribbean, not only survival but creativity, a creativity that alters the hegemonic tradition not by displacing that tradition but precisely by taking a place surely and boldly beside it. The hegemonic tradition is thereby subverted not by rejecting it but by transforming it through imitation to produce greater or equal value. "The speeches of Caliban are equal in their elemental power to those of his tutor," Walcott exhorts ("Muse," 3–4). This is not relativism, for mimicry occupies no ground other than that of the hegemonic.[4] What mimicry does is throw the established canons of evaluation and hierarchy into disarray, for the dividing line between the hegemonic and the subordinated has become blurred even though there is no complete blending.

For all of its much vaunted intimation of historical pragmatism, Walcott's theory of tradition is a deeply romantic one. It consistently suppresses the agon of history and turns tradition into a melodrama, a family romance in which each member, each new change or difference, finds its niche, with minimal or no disruption, within a single structure, capacious enough to accommodate all kinds of discords and differences *harmoniously*. Armed with this theory, it would be very difficult indeed to account in any coherent way for the difference of the tradition of the avant-garde within the West, or that of most post-colonial literatures. "Revolutionary literature is a filial impulse," Walcott argues. In using organic biological imagery—"filial"—to explain social relations of literary production, he transforms history into genetic destiny; he transmutes what is thoroughly a secular, "affiliative" performance into a sacred, "filiative" behavior (see Said, "Secular Criticism," in *World*, 20).

Walcott's overenthusiasm for mimicry in reading the historical predicament of the Indian on the American continent as a case of fated decline of authenticity, a rout of those who refused to imitate by the (innovators) imitators, reads like an apologia for genocide. History is turned to predestination. This is an imperial enterprise, and it is not without violence. The Indian civilization is swept out of focus, and Walcott's victors, the imitators (invaders from the Old World), become Adams in a *virgin* land lying supine waiting to be had. The land is the trophy of conquest. This paradigm is old and classic: Africa, we remember too well, was a virgin and unhistorical land before the arrival of the first white conquerors. Walcott's construct of Adam is patriarchal and colonialist.

The suppression of historical agon marks a point of difference between Walcott and Wilson Harris, otherwise fellow travelers on the same path of seeking nonessentialist, liberating notions of history and tradition for the Caribbean. Harris not only privileges and affirms the agon of history but is also, as a revealing extension of this project, engaged in registering the subjectivity of the Arawak Indian in defiance of the genocide that Walcott assumes was total. The registration is part of Harris's larger attempt to deconstruct the "impoverished dialogue with the past which one sees . . . in the dismissive attitude toward pre-Columbian and Amerindian cultures" (*Womb*, 124). The obsession with history, Harris argues, "need not be . . . a disabling factor or feature: in fact it may constitute a most fruitful obsession: an obsession with *an art of compassion,* a continuous salvage of vessels of sensibility between man and man, man and nature —a salvage which seeks never to block its own agencies of vision by idolatrous fixations" ("Interior," 12; see also "Making," 88–96). In other words, given imagination and creativity, attention to history and its constitutive power relations need not lead to what Walcott fears: the "idolatrous fixations" of both Eurocentrism and Afrocentrism. Homi K. Bhabha's more recent articulation of the discourse of mimicry as a mode of colonial discourse stricken with ambivalence bears especially close resemblance to Walcott's (see Bhabha, "Mimicry"). In the conflict-ridden transactions between the colonizer and the colonized, especially in the tension between the quest for stable identities for orderly government and the counterpressure of rapid change and difference typical of colonial contexts, Bhabha writes, "mimicry represents an *ironic* compromise." And like all compromises, mimicry is unsettling and ambivalent; it is the desire not for an absolute identification but for a "reformed, recognizable Other, *as a subject of a difference that is almost the same, but not quite*" (86). Almost the same, but not quite: this is the disorientation of hegemony Walcott invests with the ideal resistance when he waxes poetic and says that "the speeches of Caliban are equal in their elemental power to those of his tutor." If so, the tutor holds no further claims of superiority. Mimicry is thus "at once resemblance and menace," and its effect on the authority of colonial discourse, Bhabha argues, is "profound and disturbing" (86). Mimicry is menacing because it sees through and unravels the fiction of essential superiority claimed by the dominant. This is what Bhabha calls mimicry's "*double* vision which in disclosing the ambivalence of colonial discourse also disrupts its authority" (88).

But there is one profound difference between Walcott and Bhabha on mimicry. The latter is far more equivocal. Bhabha's mimics are not engaged in acts of conscious resistance—they are not agents of deliberate subversion or liberation, and both the condition of their production and their mimicry are spectrally overdetermined by the contradictions of the colonial context. The menace these mimics carry, because they do so unconsciously, can only result in endless compromises—there is no possibility of a new order on the horizon. It is a pure process without an agent.[5] On the other hand, Walcott's mimics are conscious agents with a dire if incoherent sense of need, Adams impelled to conscious invention by the vulgar needs of survival. Perhaps the dramatist is the more naive than the postcolonial/postmodern theorist in imagining a process and agency with a subject, but it took the theorist another essay at a later date to catch up with the dramatist's naïveté (see Bhabha, "Signs"). This move, however, was on the condition that "mimicry" is superseded by "hybridity," defined by Bhabha as "a problematic of colonial representation and individuation that reverses the effects of the colonialist disavowal, so that other 'denied' knowledges enter upon the dominant discourse and estrange the basis of its authority—its rules of recognition" (114). In mimicry, ambivalence merely results in ironic compromises; but in hybridity, because of the entrance of denied knowledges, ambivalence actually "enables a form of subversion, founded on the undecidability that turns the discursive conditions of dominance into the grounds of intervention" (112).

But hybridity is not intrinsically antihierarchy, and its subversive potential cannot in any way be taken for granted. The entrance of denied knowledges alone, without articulation to specific ends, is not a guarantee of subversion, since hegemony conserves itself precisely by admitting and taming querulous denied knowledges.

If Walcott's mimicry theory of tradition has any validity at all, the weight of the autobiographical must not be overlooked in its evaluation, for whatever it is worth. Here is a writer from one of the former colonies whom metropolitan critics have more or less unanimously proclaimed as one of the few living poets whose work most powerfully evokes the classics of the Great Tradition of English Literature. The Nobel Prize for literature he received in 1992 is the crowning glory. The career of Walcott certainly exemplifies the truth and practicality of his conception of building a resilient and resistant postcolonial literary tradition through creative mimicry. But his personal experience alone will not be adequate to validate the theory, otherwise we would have enthroned crass and defeatist relativism, the kind that mimicry rejected by proposing to share, and considering as shared, the domains of the hegemonic. This is of course not to say that personal experience is a subjectivist illusion that has no place in how we objectively understand our world and our place in it. Experiences, after all, are socially constructed and open to—actually call for—epistemological interrogation. And to emphasize the cognitive character of experiences, in Satya P. Mohanty's useful explanation, is "to argue that they can be susceptible to *varying degrees* of socially constructed truth or error, and can serve as sources of objective knowledge or socially produced mystification" ("Epistemic," 50–51). This is to suggest that the most productive path to evaluate Walcott's theory —to which his personal experience contributed so much—is to historicize it and its condition of possibility. This path takes us through the second and related conceptual armature of his cultural theory: his notion of history and its usefulness to the Caribbean writer.

### History as Myth

> The desolation of poverty that exists in the Caribbean can be very depressing. The only way that one can look at it and draw anything of value from it is to have a fantastic depth of strength and belief, not in the past but in the immediate future. And I think that whenever I come back here, however desolate and however despairing I see the conditions around me to be, I know I have to draw on terrible reserves of conviction. To abandon that conviction is to betray your origins; it's to feel superior to your family, to your past. And I'm not capable of that.
>
> Derek Walcott, "The Art of Poetry"

In "The Muse of History," Walcott distinguishes two ideas of history: history as "time" and as "myth." The former is history that arraigns and judges, and its consciousness assumes a nonnegotiable polarity between Prospero and Caliban. Always backward looking, the "rational madness of history seen as sequential time" could do little else but "contemplate only the shipwreck." This, says Walcott, is the idea of history that subtends both the Eurocentric and Afrocentric discourses. For history as "myth," history is fiction, "subject to a fitful muse, memory," and this "careless" guardian of the past admits breaks, bridges, continuities, and amnesia: imagination is its only god. It refuses to submit to the paralyzing grip of historical time, and instead offers elation at the "elemental privilege of naming the new world." Rather than debilitating nostalgic quests, its "vision of man in the New World is Adamic . . . a world without monuments and ruins" ("Muse," 2, 6, 7, 2, 2, 5, 2–3, in order of citation). "We make too much of that long groan that underlines the past"; thus Walcott returned again in 1992 to his choice critique in his Nobel Prize acceptance speech ("Antilles," 28).

What Walcott has brilliantly done is give a poetical theory of history, at the expense of a historical theory of poetry; a poeticized history that needs the banishment of historicized poetry for validation. Walcott conceived his vision of history as deeply embattled by the proponents of the idea of history as time. Given the highly polemic tone of Walcott's formulations, it is amazing that he did *not* specifically identify his opponents but simply took the liberty of representing their claims. If we place Walcott's denunciation in its historical context, it is not difficult at all to identify his target. "The Muse of History" was written between the late 1960s and 1974, when it was published—the height, we must remember, of the Black Power movement in the Caribbean (see Coombs, *Massa;* Pantin, *Black;* and Rodney, *Groundings*). The literary tradition that Walcott made the center from which he feels and seeks other sources for inspiration is the Western tradition. It was precisely this tradition that poets influenced by Black Power made a target of attack in their quest for a "black aesthetic." In the words of Edward Brathwaite, a leading poet and proponent of a black Caribbean aesthetic, the search is for "a possible alternative to the European cultural tradition which has been imposed upon us and which we have more or less accepted and absorbed, for obvious historical reasons, as the only way of going about our business" ("Jazz"). This, for Walcott, is the identity of the poets enslaved to "historical truth," the defenders of the idea of history as time.

The correlation between Walcott's history as myth and his notion of tradition as mimicry is this: the former made possible the latter. Mimicry as a program for the "native" across the time-space of colonial/postcolonial demands the bracketing, or at least an abbreviation, of history. Walcott thinks it is mainly *history as the bygone past* that determines our actions and transactions today, rather than *history as the present:* social life as currently lived and whatever connections it is seen to have with the past. I insist that it is *not* so much a preoccupation with the past that gave rise to Black Power and "black aesthetic" movements as concern with the inequities of the moment. There can be no absolute separation between the past and the present, for it is most often the pressures of the present that drive us to history for crutches.

Because Walcott usually takes history to mean exclusively the past, he often gains undue polemical and critical capital by his idea of history as myth that ever so subtly invokes our common anodyne clichés and tools of superficial gloss: "That's history"; "The future is what matters"; and so on. Thus, in Walcott's construct of Adam the Caribbean is a passive, obliging tabula rasa, waiting for the inscription of the great poet (with his phallic pen) who towers far above the nitty-gritty of past and present Caribbean politics and history and global unequal relations. Yet the writer's corpus is unthinkable outside these sociological factors. There is just no such thing as absolute separation between history as myth (by which he really means history as *culture*) and history as time (meaning history as *politics*). Liminality is never an absolute identity, and substantive history, theoretically discredited as epistemology, is still the stuff of social and transnational relations. The profoundly fascinating point here, which underscores more than anything else the shrewd earthiness of Walcott's genius, is that his literary works, specifically the drama rather than the poetry, most often subvert the absolutist polemical critical claims that distinguish the essays. Very few critics have noticed this productive disjunction, which I will now briefly explore.

### Disciplined, the Extragavance of Theory

An excellent example to examine is the play *Pantomime,* first produced in 1978 and published in 1980. Described in the blurb as a variation on the master-servant relationship, the play's immediate pretext is Daniel Defoe's *Robinson Crusoe* (the 1994 edition is cited in the text). But unlike what happens in conventional adaptations, here there are very few recognizable details from Defoe's text. Gone are those tiresome trivia of Crusoe's mercantilist and imperialist adventures among primitive Africans and barbaric Arabs, or indeed the literal particulars of Crusoe's shipwreck on a lonely island and his relations with the Carib he calls Friday. What we get in *Pantomime* is a distillation of Defoe's text exclusively into the problematic of social relations in a postcolonial context in which the contemporary relations between a white master and a black servant ceaselessly and metonymically recall the background of vastly unequal histories between them. In other words, Defoe's text is merely a pretext, though a powerfully symbolic one, for Walcott's exploration of contemporary unequal race and class relations and the histories that underwrite them.

Note that the obviously insubstantial link between *Robinson Crusoe* and *Pantomime,* the old and the recent, the Western colonial and the Caribbean postcolonial, has a special significance in the universe of Walcott's cultural theorizing if not his artistic practice. The history that *Robinson Crusoe* tells and its trajectories in the present is a history that has not been kind to the formerly enslaved and colonized, to put things mildly. That is why, for Walcott, the postcolonial needs a special lens to view that history, a lens that would not be obsessed with chronology, linearity, objectivity, actuality, and other such crippling fixations, but that would enable the disempowered to soar and imagine a new way and order. As I have demonstrated, this lens, according to Walcott, is history as myth, a lens that comes bundled with "fantastic depth of strength and belief" and "terrible reserves of conviction," as he says in the epigraph to the preceding section.

Through history as myth, Walcott authorizes himself to plunder the imperial archive and ride roughshod over its hallowed truths. The temporal setting of Walcott's own "Robinson Crusoe" drama is postcolonial Tobago. The unchallenged imperialist reign of Britain has been replaced by independent sovereign nations but also neocolonial relations; the sun has set on empire, but the shadows still linger.

Harry Trewe, retired English actor and now proprietor of the Castaway Guest House, suggests to his black handyman, veteran calypsonian Jackson Phillip, that to entertain guests they stage a satiric pantomime Harry has written on the Robinson Crusoe story. The crucial satiric element is an inversion of roles (and, symbolically, also of history) in which the white Harry plays Friday and the black Jackson plays Robinson Crusoe. Jackson is initially suspicious and reluctant to go along, but Harry assures him that he as a liberal white man has no problems with such a playful inversion. The inversion is a theatricalization of Walcott's advocacy of history as myth, malleable and subject to every kind of twists and bends by the creative imagination. So, with a willed amnesia toward the acrimonious history of the Caribbean that brings them together, both Harry and Jackson, metaphorically if not literally offspring of planter and slave, come together to create, as Walcott recommends in the essay, "The Muse of History," the liminal and "truly tough aesthetic of the New World [which] neither explains nor forgives history . . . [and which] refuses to recognize it as a creative or culpable force" (2).

Rehearsals start in earnest, but in no time Harry begins to regret he ever came up with such an idea. Jackson as Robinson Crusoe plays his part with consummate artistry in the spirit of improvisation, refusing to follow Harry's script but relentlessly rewriting, revisioning, and generally radically extending it, and thus history. To Harry's dismay, Jackson begins to pick apart the whole epistemological and metaphysical edifice that had given meaning and stability to the story's master-slave dialectic (see also Jeyifo, "Eurocentric"). For instance, Jackson renames Friday as Thursday and also renames many other common props of daily survival such as cup and table. His own black Crusoe is an inventor, more humble and more attuned to the rhythms of survival in the new environment where he is shipwrecked than the soppy, egotistical lament of the original.

Daniel Defoe gives us the unforgettable image of submission in Friday's placing Crusoe's foot on his head (147). Walcott's own Friday/Thursday relentlessly deconstructs received reality and its supporting discourse of positivist history (125–28). Jackson's revisions are simply too much for the self-described liberal white man, Harry. Liberalism is friendly and solicitous only as long as its dominance is secure; once threatened, liberalism's real ugly impulse to dominate asserts itself. Harry promptly stops the pantomime and commands that things return to "normal" (124). "I've had enough of this farce," he declares (124). When Jackson protests that such a return to the status quo is atavistic and "not history . . . not the world," Harry shoots back revealingly that he does not "give an Eskimo's fart about the world" (127). He henceforth fully asserts himself as Jackson's master and employer.

For ideological reasons that are not too far-fetched, Defoe constructs the relationship between Crusoe and Friday based on harmony in hierarchy, a kind of harmony constituted by fully realized identities of master and servant that—and we better believe this—are not in conflict at all (147–54). To achieve this extremely seductive unanimity in inequality, the weapon Defoe uses is suppression of historical agon, the constitutive element of all extant social relations. This is a great achievement indeed, but one that Walcott, a postcolonial writing in the shadows of an empire that is only formally over, would have no use for, and that he would sharply rewrite. And so Walcott, for reasons that are equally not far-fetched, makes stoking the fire of historical agon the principle of relations between his own Crusoe and Friday/Thursday. Here the submerged history of empire and slavery and colonialism and hypocritical liberalism, and all their attendant psychic traumas, are excavated for a serious assessment (112–13).

It is to further foreground the centrality of historical agon that Walcott chooses the genre of drama for his revisionist project. In place of the first-person "I" of Defoe's narrative fiction, an eye that more immediately censors what we see and is thus particularly amenable to tyrannical uses, Walcott substitutes dramatic dialogic exchange, a form that is not only constituted by irreducible conflict but also demands verisimilitude for each side of a conflict, irrespective of the validity of its foundational arguments. This is why drama is a more potentially democratic art form than narrative fiction or even poetry. And indeed, Walcott has revisited the Crusoe theme in many of his poems and essays, but the result in privileging historical agon does not even begin to match the achievement in the drama.

The play's attack on Eurocentrism is clear and unmistakable, as we have seen. But there is also a similar assault on Afrocentrism, which may be only less extensive but no less emphatic. In a poignant scene Jackson as black Crusoe initially tries to rechristen the physical and metaphysical landscape of the Caribbean, away from English, with authentic African names (114–17). He fails woefully and finally gives up that African romanticism and makes his peace with English, meaning with history: "Table. Chair. Cup. Man. Jesus. I accept. All you win. Long time" (117). So, both Eurocentric and Afrocentric nostalgias are deconstructed in the play, but the outlines of a space of history as myth and invention refuses to emerge.

Neither Harry nor Jackson, master or servant, is ultimately able to go beyond the unequal history that unites them, though Jackson is more than willing to. The white Harry does return to play Crusoe, or master, his more natural role, and his own is a privatist, vapidly romantic, Eurocentric Crusoe consumed by a self-imposed sense of isolation in a supposedly hostile Caribbean environment without "the voice of one consoling creature" and "the look of kind eyes" (167). Jackson too could not, finally, overlook whatever Harry's parrot—inherited with the Guest House—means by its intermittent shouts of "Heinegger." The sound evokes certain memories painful enough to make Jackson toss the bird into the sea. "Him choke from prejudice," he says (151). In the lives of these characters, the hold of what Walcott denounces as "history as time" simply refuses to yield; both found its power relations inescapable and a battle they cannot not fight. And because they have not prepared a way of dealing with that history other than the conceptual proposition of soaring over it and not reopening old wounds—the "substantives" of that history—they run into a blind alley.

The lesson from the play, then, which we would not find (or find so clearly) in Walcott's poetry or critical writings, is that there is no such thing as a historical vision that is free and unhinged from the risks and partisanships of social existence in all their complex and a(nta)gonistic negotiations, including the often very vulgarly specific positions we have to take in such transactions. Liminality may be enabling against absolutisms, but it does not have to be ahistorical to be so; and attention to the substance of history need not automatically entail cultivating victimhood. History as myth may allow us to creatively read the archive of Eurocentrism, but it obviously may not enable us to grasp the broad social relations of which that archive is only a part. A liminal "nodal point" becomes most enabling only when it is fashioned out of critical engagement with the substantive issues of history.

### Notes

1. I am using the word "romantic" to represent a composite of attitudes such as idealism, utopianism, penchant for easy and value-laden polarizations such as in the old allegories of good over evil, and ambivalent expositions. Also, I am drawing on Walcott's opposition of "romance" to "fact" in "The Art of Poetry," an interview with Edward Hirsch: "I'm fifty-five now and all my life I've tried to fight and write and jeer and encourage the idea that the state owes its artists a lot. When I was young it looked like a romance: now that I am older and I pay taxes, it is a fact" (*Critical,* 77). I have benefited from Northrop Frye, *The Secular Scripture: A Study of the Structure of Romance,* and Fredric Jameson, *The Political Unconscious: Narrative as a Socially Symbolic Act.*

2. In the earlier essay, "Twilight," Walcott deployed mimicry negatively to denigrate the Carnival as "meaningless as the art of the actor confined to mimicry" (34).

3. In spite of the phrase and word—or precisely because they were passing gestures—"imperialistic defoliation" and "genocide" (56), Walcott remains primarily unconcerned with the larger ethicopolitical issues subtending the agonistic history he interprets so tendentiously.

4. On this score, mimicry could be seen, depending on one's ideological

viewpoint, as either *bolder*—because it rejects the easy claim of difference and opts instead to contest the terrain of the hegemonic—or *more timid*—because even while reforming the hegemonic, it affirms that hegemony as the only possible direction instead of asserting its own difference—than relativism.

5. This is the point cogently made by Robert Young when he writes that, for Bhabha, mimicry "at once enables power and produces loss of agency . . . [it] becomes a kind of agency without a subject, a form of representation which produces effects, a sameness which slips into otherness, but which has nothing to do with any 'other' " (*White*, 147–48).

## Works Cited

Bhabha, Homi. "Of Mimicry and Man: The Ambivalence of Colonial Discourse" (1984). In *The Location of Culture*, 85–92. London: Routledge, 1994.

———. "Signs Taken for Wonders: Questions of Ambivalence and Authority under a Tree outside Delhi, May 1817." 1985. In *The Location of Culture*, 102–22. London: Routledge, 1994.

Brathwaite, Edward Kamau. *The Arrivants: A New World Trilogy*. London: Oxford Univ. Press, 1973.

———. "Jazz and the West Indian Novel." *Bim* 44 (January–June 1967). Cited in Marina Maxwell, "Towards a Revolution in the Arts," Savacou, September 1970, 19–20.

———. "The Love Axe (1): Developing a Caribbean Aesthetic 1962–1974." In *Reading Black: Essays in the Criticism of African, Caribbean, and Black American Literature*, ed. Houston A. Baker, 20–36. ASRC Monograph Series 4. Ithaca: Cornell University, 1976.

Coombs, Orde, ed. *Is Massa Day Dead? Black Moods in the Caribbean*. New York: Anchor, 1974.

Defoe, Daniel. *Robinson Crusoe*. 1719. Ed. Michael Shinagel. New York: W. W. Norton, 1994.

Duff, David. *Romance and Revolution: Shelley and the Politics of a Genre*. Cambridge: Cambridge Univ. Press, 1994.

Frye, Northrop. *The Secular Scripture: A Study of the Structure of Romance*. Cambridge: Harvard Univ. Press, 1976.

Harris, Wilson. "Interior of the Novel: Amerindian/European/African Relations." In *Explorations: A Selection of Talks and Articles, 1966–1981*. Mundelstrup, Denmark: Dangaroo Press, 1981.

———. The Making of Tradition." In *Explorations: A Selection of Talks and Articles, 1966–1981*. Mundelstrup, Denmark: Dangaroo Press, 1981.

———. *The Womb of Space: The Cross-Cultural Imagination*. Westport CT: Greenwood Press, 1983.

Jameson, Fredric. *The Political Unconscious: Narrative as a Socially Symbolic Act*. Ithaca: Cornell Univ. Press, 1981.

Jeyifo, Biodun. "On Eurocentric Critical Theory: Some Paradigms from the

Texts and Sub-texts of Post-colonial Writing. In *Critical Perspectives on Derek Walcott,* ed. Robert D. Hamner, 376–87. Washington DC: Three Continents Press, 1993.

Mohanty, Satya P. "The Epistemic Status of Cultural Identity: On *Beloved* and the Postcolonial Condition," *Cultural Critique* 24 (spring 1993): 41–80.

Nettleford, Rex. *Identity, Race and Protest in Jamaica.* New York: William Morrow, 1972.

Palmer, C. A. "Identity, Race, and Black Power in Independent Jamaica." In *The Modern Caribbean,* ed. Franklin A. Knight and Colin A. Palmer, 111–28. Chapel Hill: Univ. of North Carolina Press, 1989.

Pantin, Raoul. *Black Power Day: The 1970 February Revolution.* Santa Cruz, Trinidad: Hatuey Productions, 1990.

Rodney, Walter. *The Groundings with My Brothers.* London: Bogle-L'Ouverture, 1969.

Rohlehr, Gordon. *"My Strangled City" and Other Essays.* Port-of-Spain: Longman Trinidad, 1992.

———. *Pathfinder: Black Awakening in "The Arrivants" of Edward Kamau Brathwaite.* Port-of-Spain: College Press, 1981.

Said, Edward. *The World, the Text, and the Critic.* Cambridge: Harvard Univ. Press, 1983.

Walcott, Derek. "The Antilles: Fragments of Epic Memory," Nobel Lecture, *New Republic,* 28 December 1992, 28.

———."The Art of Poetry." Interview with Edward Hirsch. In *Critical Perspectives on Derek Walcott,* ed. Robert D. Hamner, 65–83. Washington DC: Three Continents Press, 1993.

———. "The Caribbean: Culture or Mimicry." 1974. In *Critical Perspectives on Derek Walcott,* ed. Robert D. Hamner, 51–57. Washington DC: Three Continents Press, 1993.

———. "Crusoe's Journal." In *Collected Poems: 1948–1984,* New York: Noonday Press, 1986.

———. "The Muse of History." In *Is Massa Day Dead? Black Moods in the Caribbean,* ed. Orde Coombs, 1–27. New York: Anchor, 1974.

———. "National Theatre Is the Answer." *Trinidad Guardian,* 12 August 1964, 4.

———. *"Remembrance" and "Pantomime": Two Plays.* New York: Farrar, Straus and Giroux, 1980.

———. "What the Twilight Says: An Overture." In *"Dream on Monkey Mountain" and Other Plays,* 3–40. New York: Farrar, Straus and Giroux, 1970.

Young, Robert. *White Mythologies: Writing History and the West.* New York: Routledge, 1990.

# Contributors

**Mike Alleyne** is a visiting assistant professor in the Humanities Department at Florida A & M University.

**Catherine Den Tandt** is an assistant professor of Modern Languages and Comparative Studies at the University of Alberta.

**Belinda Edmondson** is an associate professor of English and African/African-American Studies at Rutgers University, Newark.

**Stefano Harney** is an assistant professor in the Department of Social Sciences at Pace University.

**Kevin Meehan** is an assistant professor of English at the University of Central Florida.

**Supriya Nair** is an associate professor of English at Tulane University.

**Tejumola Olaniyan** is an associate professor of English at the University of Virginia.

**Richard Price** is Dittman Professor of American Studies and Professor of Anthropology at the College of William and Mary.

**Sally Price** is Dittman Professor of American Studies and Professor of Anthropology at the College of William and Mary.

**Shalini Puri** is an assistant professor of English at the University of Pittsburgh.

**Faith Smith** is an assistant professor of English and American Literature and African and Afro-American Studies at Brandeis University.

# Names and Titles Index

Italicized page numbers refer to illustrations.

# New World Studies

New World Studies publishes interdisciplinary research that seeks to redefine the cultural map of the Americas and to propose particularly stimulating points of departure for an emerging field. Encompassing the Caribbean as well as continental North, Central, and South America, the series books examine cultural processes within the hemisphere, taking into account the economic, demographic, and historical phenomena that shape them. Given the increasing diversity and richness of the linguistic and cultural traditions in the Americas, the need for research that privileges neither the English-speaking United States nor Spanish-speaking Latin America has never been greater. The series is designed to bring the best of this new research into an identifiable forum and to channel its results to the rapidly evolving audience for cultural studies.

# New World Studies

Vera M. Kutzinski
*Sugar's Secrets: Race and the Erotics of Cuban
Nationalism*

Richard D. E. Burton and Fred Reno, editors
*French and West Indian: Martinique, Guadeloupe,
and French Guiana Today*

A. James Arnold, editor
*Monsters, Tricksters, and Sacred Cows*

J. Michael Dash
*The Other America: Caribbean Literature
in a New World Context*

Isabel Alvarez Borland
*Cuban-American Literature of Exile:
From Person to Persona*

Belinda J. Edmondson, editor
*Caribbean Romances: The Politics of
Regional Representation*

Steven V. Hunsaker
*Autobiography and National Identity
in the Americas*